Contents

INTRODUCTION   vii

Part I: The Proposed Genetically Related Analogues   1
  1 Determining Analogous and Genetically Related Material   3
  2 The Making of Heroes and Monsters   17
  3 The Hero's Fight against the Monsters   37
  4 A Sword by Any Other Name   54
  5 Hell and High Water   67

Part II: To Cement a Relationship   79
  6 The English Hypothesis   81
  7 Panzer's 'Bear's Son' Thesis   88
  8 The Common Origin Theory   96
  9 The Big Bang Theory   108

Part III: The Genetically Related *Beowulf* **Analogues in** *Grettis saga*
  in View of Icelandic Sources   117
  10 A Saga Author Shops Around: The Eclectic Composition of the Glámr and
      Sandhaugar Episodes   119
  11 Conclusion   130

NOTES   135
BIBLIOGRAPHY   161
INDEX   171

Introduction

For over a century most scholars in the fields of Anglo-Saxon and Old Norse have been convinced that *Grettis saga* and *Beowulf* are related, although the two works are on the whole very different, separated by several centuries in time and composed in different countries in different languages. This belief in a mutual relationship of some kind has rested on the perception that certain passages in both texts are so similar that the resemblance between them ruled out any possibility of accidental likeness. And there are indeed striking similarities, at least at first glance: Grettir and Beowulf both cleanse haunted houses by fighting supernatural opponents; they both wreck buildings in the process of doing so; and a monster loses an arm before succumbing in the struggle.[1]

The assumption of kinship between *Beowulf* and *Grettis saga* has understandably inspired scholars to make further and more daring comparisons between the saga and the poem. Each text has already been used extensively to interpret or clarify its counterpart, and many critics believe that the question of a genetic relationship between the analogues in *Beowulf* and *Grettis saga* has been resolved once and for all. As early as 1881, C.S. Smith declared that 'in the unbiased mind, no real doubt can arise of the parallelism between these two legends,'[2] and ninety years later Larry D. Benson concluded that the resemblances were 'so many, so obvious, and so detailed' that he could not be bothered to 'belabor them.'[3] Unfortunately, the issue in question is not quite this crystal-clear, and the supposed resemblances between the two works raise a number of problems that do indeed deserve a bit of belabouring.

The various problems that I perceive in the analogy-making process itself will be dealt with in subsequent chapters, but before going into detail, I would like to offer a few reasons for being sceptical about the so-called parallel texts that scholars have accepted as evidence of a genetic relationship in this case. In the first place, the human mind is 'a pattern-producing machine [that] sees shapes in random constellations,'[4] as T.A. Shippey – commenting on the endless stream of allegorical readings of *Beowulf* – observed some years ago, and texts that appear to resemble each other can turn out to be very false friends. Take, for example, the following Japanese analogue to *Beowulf* that was offered by F. York Powell in 1901:

There was in the tenth century, in Japan, a great nobleman, Yorimitsu of the famous Minamoto family, who had four champions famous for wisdom, courage, strength, and skill; one of these, Kintoki, is the Japanese Orson or Perceval, brought up by the Lady of the Mountain away from mankind, with bears for his playfellows. Another is the Watanabe-no-Tsuna, the Japanese Béowulf.

He was sent upon an errand on a wild and stormy night by his lord, Yorimitsu, and as he came back, by a certain deserted, haunted temple, a demon (at first trying to deceive him by falsely appearing as a forlorn maiden) suddenly seized him up and attempted to carry him off. With his master's renowned blade *Hinge-kiri*, which he was wearing that night, Watanabe freed himself, cutting off at a sweep the demon's arm that had grappled him by the helmet. This arm with its huge claws he bore off as a trophy, and, locking it up in a stone chest, congratulated himself on his exploit, which would, he believed, free the temple from the evil beings that made its neighbourhood dreadful and dangerous. Next day, however, the old lady who had fostered him, an aged kinswoman to whom he owed reverence, was ushered before him and he was prayed to show his trophy to her. He could not refuse so slight a favour; but as soon as the chest was opened the old lady turned to a horrid demon, caught up the grisly arm and dashed off through the roof, half wrecking the room as she left, before Watanabe was able to do anything to hinder her or recapture his enemy's arm. In the end, however, the demons are disposed of.[5]

In some respects, this story presents a closer analogy to *Beowulf* than *Grettis saga*, but any resemblance here is certainly nothing but a coincidence. In other words, because this analogue cannot be genetically related to *Beowulf*, it is merely an amusing literary curiosity, and if, by the same token, the analogues in *Grettis saga* that we shall soon be examining cannot be shown to be genetically related to *Beowulf*, they too can only be regarded as literary curiosities.

Secondly, there is the matter of loose ends. Beowulf and Grettir have never been altogether comfortable as bedfellows, partly because of the uncertainty over what material concerning the two was genuinely analogous, and partly because the proposed genetically related analogues differ sharply on a number of points. As we shall later see, the criteria that scholars have tried to use as their basis for accepting or rejecting any proposed genetically related analogue have always been quite subjective, and a century of scholarship aimed at smoothing away problems and deepening the reader's understanding of the relationship between the two texts has in reality done just the opposite. It has produced enough reasonable evidence to question many of the basic arguments that have been used to link *Beowulf* to *Grettis saga*.

A third reason for being sceptical is the context of some of the proposed genetically related analogues in *Grettis saga*. Take, for instance, the Sandhaugar episode (chapters 63–7), which is normally seen as the best parallel to Beowulf's fight with Grendel and his dam. The literary fate of these two supposedly genetically related episodes is amazingly different. In *Beowulf* the story of this epic struggle occupies centre stage in the entire first half of the poem and is the vehicle that elevates Beowulf to his heroic stature. In *Grettis saga* the Sandhaugar episode is no more than a small and insignificant digression and perhaps, as Wolf von Unwerth has argued,[6] an episode which is mainly made up of items borrowed from other Icelandic sagas or even earlier episodes in *Grettis saga* itself.

Finally, there is the matter of how to explain a kinship between *Beowulf* and *Grettis saga*. This is the most difficult problem that 'the faithful' have had to tackle, and it is here that the weakness of the whole argument becomes most apparent. Four different hypotheses have been proposed, and none of them is very convincing.

These are some of the doubts that brought this study about, and I now leave it to my readers – and their unbiased minds, of course – to assess the evidence for themselves.

MAGNÚS FJALLDAL

PART I
THE PROPOSED GENETICALLY
RELATED ANALOGUES

1

Determining Analogous and Genetically Related Material

This chapter presents a survey of the five episodes in *Grettis saga* that have been proposed as genetically related analogues[1] to *Beowulf*, as well as a look at the methods and the arguments of the scholars who originally suggested them. Criticisms concerning the validity of individual analogues – when such criticisms are to be found – are limited to those that were offered in the scholarly debate that took place at the time. In short, my aim in the following pages is primarily to sum up the academic work that established these five episodes as analogues to *Beowulf*, and in doing so, insisted that they were related to the poem.

1: The Sandhaugar Episode[2]

Grettir learns that a farm called Sandhaugar is haunted. The owner of the farm had disappeared one night while his wife attended a Christmas service, and the following year one of the farm workers vanished at Christmas as well. On the next Christmas eve Grettir comes to the farm to rid it of the hauntings. First, however, he carries the lady of the farm, Steinvǫr, and her daughter across an icy river, Eyjardalsá, so they can attend the Christmas service. Grettir then waits fully clothed and with a light burning for the troll to attack in the night. A troll woman carrying a trencher and a knife appears in the hall. They wrestle inside the farmhouse, and great damage is done to the building. The troll-woman drags Grettir out of the hall and all the way to the brink of a gorge. Grettir then succeeds in freeing one arm, reaches for his short-sword, and cuts off the troll-woman's arm. She falls into the gorge and disappears. The narrator then explains that according to local legend she did not fall into the gulf but was at sunrise turned into a stone image which can still be seen at the edge of the cliff.

Grettir is curious to discover the fate of the two missing men. He goes to the gorge with a single companion, lets down a rope, which his helpmate is to guard, and dives into the chasm and underneath a waterfall which is there. Behind the waterfall he finds a cave which he enters. Inside the cave he discovers a huge giant sitting by a fire. The giant attacks him with a weapon with a wooden handle (a *heptisax*). Grettir cuts the weapon off its handle and kills the giant as he tries to reach for a sword that is hanging on the wall of the cave. Grettir's companion sees blood stains on the river, concludes that Grettir is dead, and deserts the rope. Grettir searches the cave and finds the bones of the two men who had disappeared as well as treasure. No mention is made of the troll-woman. Grettir then climbs up the rope unaided and leaves the bones of the men at a local church with a rune staff on which he has carved two stanzas that relate his adventure in the cave.

Since Guðbrandur Vigfússon first compared this episode with events in *Beowulf* in his edition of *Sturlunga Saga ... and Other Works* more than a century ago and claimed that it proved a genetic relationship between the saga and the epic, it has become one of the best known and most frequently cited analogues to the Old English poem. There is a good reason for its primary status: in the first place it relates the only self-contained story within *Grettis saga* that invites a full-fledged comparison with a section of *Beowulf*, and secondly, all other attempts to see further analogies in the saga either depend on the Sandhaugar episode or relate to it in one way or another.

Although Vigfússon claimed a general resemblance between *Beowulf* and *Grettis saga* by arguing that 'Gretti's fight with Glam, and afterwards with the troll-wife and the monster below the water-fall, [was] the Icelandic version of the Gothic hero's struggle with Grendel and his witch-mother,'[3] he did not attach much importance to specific similarities between the two stories, except for one: 'Where everything else is transformed,' he wrote, 'one word remains as a memorial of [the story's] origin, viz. in the English epic *hæft-méce* and in the Icelandic Saga *hefti-sax*, both occurring in the same place of the legend, and both *hapax legomena* in their respective literatures.'[4] How Vigfússon came to see *hæftmece* and *heptisax*,[5] terms for different weapons that only share the same prefix, as 'one word,' he never explained, nor has it ever been clear precisely how their respective uniqueness should link the two texts. In light of this, it is somewhat strange that Vigfússon should put so much emphasis on the importance of this pair, unless he mistakenly thought that *heptisax* was a special term for Grettir's weapon, and that both heroes thus had swords described by words that sounded somewhat similar and that were not to be found anywhere else. *Corpus Poeticum Boreale*, published five years after *Sturlunga saga* and edited jointly by Vigfússon and York Powell, sums up the Sandhaugar episode in a way that might hint at this: 'Having dived below the force [waterfall], [Grettir] gets into a cave, where he finds a giant, whom he slays with a thrust of the famous short sword (hefti-sax, Beowolf's hefti-mæci).'[6] But whether the analogy between *Beowulf* and *Grettis saga* might have come about through Vigfússon's faulty memory is immaterial; the keystone of his argument – the *heptisax-hæftmece* parallel – was universally accepted and gradually became a myth in its own right.

Vigfússon's comparison implied that the general outline of the two stories was roughly similar; however, the analogy that actually proved them to be related, as far as he was concerned, really hinged on the *heptisax-hæftmece* pair, because in *Grettis saga* everything else had been transformed. This argument was short-lived. As other medieval scholars took notice of Vigfússon's discovery, everything in the two texts that could possibly be seen as similar was eventually accepted as evidence of their relationship, and the possibility of an accidental likeness between the poem and the saga was categorically rejected.[7] The following list contains the points of resemblance that critics proceeded to find in the Sandhaugar episode after Vigfússon had first presented his discovery:

- The hero learns there is a haunted place and comes from afar to seek adventure.
- He is strong and a good swimmer and performs a feat of strength that involves swimming prior to the battle (Beowulf's contest with Breca; Grettir's carrying Steinvǫr, the lady of the haunted farm, and her daughter across a swollen river).
- He fights a battle with a pair of cannibalistic monsters – one male, the other female – in two successive fights.
- The first battle takes place in a human dwelling at night. The hero wrestles with a monstrous creature and great damage is done to the building in the process.
- Like Beowulf in the battle with Grendel's dam, Grettir is tightly clutched by the troll-woman. Here, 'striking similarity in the phraseology' has also been claimed.[8]
- The monster loses an arm in the battle but escapes.
- The hero battles with a second monster that lives in a cave under water (under a waterfall). The hero has to dive to the bottom before reaching the cave.
- A fire burns in the cave, and a sword hangs on the wall.
- The hero's helper(s) see(s) blood on the water and depart(s) thinking that he is dead.
- The second monster is killed, but both in *Grettis saga* and in *Beowulf* there is a weapon – the *hæftmece* or *heptisax* – that fails.

- There is treasure in the monster's cave.
- After the second battle, an object with runes carved on it (the ancient sword in *Beowulf*, the rune staff in *Grettis saga*) is presented.
- The hero is rewarded by the host of the haunted place.

Which of these points different scholars have chosen to emphasize has of course varied, and the same item has not always been considered analogous for the same reason. Klaeber[9] and Halldórsson,[10] for example, see the icy river that Grettir crosses as a challenge to test his strength, whereas Malone[11] thinks its unseasonable rising recalls the mystery and terror of the marshes in *Beowulf*. But the different reasons that scholars may have had are not important in this context; what matters is that all these items have been brought forward as evidence, not just to show that the two texts are similar, but that they are genetically related.

Differences between the Sandhaugar episode and *Beowulf* were also noted in the course of the discussion that Vigfússon's discovery generated. As early as 1880, James Garnett observed that in spite of striking general resemblances, the differences were 'so numerous and so material' that accidental likeness could not be ruled out.[12] His criticism, however, did not go beyond this single comment and appears to have had no impact. The same may be said of the objections of the few other scholars who were either sceptical or refused to see the Sandhaugar episode as analogous to *Beowulf*, in the sense of proving that the saga and the poem were related.[13] Klaeber, Chambers, and other influential critics found the differences to be neither numerous nor material; and the ones they did find they waved away with the magic wand of textual corruption. Chambers, for instance, addresses the issue as to why Grettir first fights against a female monster and then a male one (in *Beowulf* the order is reversed) as follows:

In this the *Grettis saga* probably represents a corrupt tradition: for, that the female should remain at home whilst the male searches for his prey, is a rule which holds good for devils as well as for men. The change was presumably made in order to avoid the difficulty – which the Beowulf poet seems also to have realized – that after the male has been slain, the rout of the female is felt to be a deed of less note – something of an anticlimax.[14]

The only other difference that Chambers appears to notice is that the sword on the wall in the monster's cave has somehow changed hands. In *Beowulf* the hero uses it to attack the monster, whereas the giant reaches for it in his attack on the hero in the saga. Klaeber blames these and other changes in *Grettis saga* on what he calls 'an obscuration of the original folk-tale elements,' which explains why the female monster 'is not stated explicitly to be the giant's mother' in the saga and also why their 'natural roles' have been reversed.[15] This form of literary decay is, furthermore, responsible for making the motivation for the hero's visit to the cave in *Grettis saga* 'mere curiosity,' omitting all mention of the wounded she-demon in the second adventure, and 'completely blurring the motive of the wonderful sword which is hanging in the cave.' Among early commentators on the Sandhaugar episode as a genetically related analogue to *Beowulf*, only Stedman was concerned about the thorny problem of differences in landscape and setting:

However different the mere of the Grendels be from the force of the trolls, however they themselves differ in nature from the Grendel-kin, it seems to me that this is to be ascribed to the racial differences of thought, of imagination, of fear of the supernatural between the peoples by whom the stories were fostered and among whom they grew up.[16]

A simpler answer would later be found by moving Grendel and his dam into a waterfall and giving them a family tree that traced their ancestry to Scandinavian waterfall trolls, as we shall see in a subsequent chapter.

2: Glámr[17]

The reader first meets Glámr as a big and surly Swede who is employed by the farmer of Þórhallsstaðir to look after his sheep. He is warned that the place is haunted but pays no heed to the warning. At Christmas Glámr is killed in a fight with some kind of a monstrous creature. He is buried but does not lie still in his grave and begins to haunt the farm and its neighbourhood. Eventually, Grettir goes to the farm to meet the horrid living dead that Glámr has now become. Grettir waits for his arrival in the night under the cover of a cloak but fully dressed and with a light burning in the hall. Glámr enters the hall, grabs at the cloak, and a tug of war ensues until Grettir and the fiend tear it apart. Glámr and Grettir then wrestle and break up everything in their way during the struggle. Glámr manages to pull Grettir out of the house, but Grettir throws himself at him, and Glámr falls in the process. Grettir decapitates Glámr with his sword and places the head at the thigh of the fiend, but before that comes to pass, Glámr has spoken a curse: Grettir's deeds will turn against him, he will become a lonely outlaw, the eyes of Glámr will always follow him, and he will be afraid of the dark. As a result, Grettir will crave company, which in turn will lead to his death.

Those who accept the Glámr episode as a genetically related analogue have always considered him and/or his role in *Grettis saga* to be comparable to that of Grendel in *Beowulf*. This is by no means surprising, as even a cursory look at the poem and the saga is enough to show that Grendel and Glámr have special positions among the supernatural opponents of Beowulf and Grettir. To begin with, they both have names; in fact, Grendel is the only monster in *Beowulf* to be given one (cf. the nameless troll-woman and the giant at Sandhaugar). Like Grendel, Glámr has a considerable background – more detailed than any of Grettir's other opponents in the saga. They may both possess magic powers,[18] there is something sinister about their eyes, and they haunt human dwellings. Vigfússon and York Powell considered the story of Glámr to be even more important than the Sandhaugar episode, because they believed that the cursing of the Icelandic hero by the monster supplied vital clues to explain the fate of Beowulf, such as his childlessness and his unhappy end:

Here the haunting, the broken hall, the wrestling, the farmer's attitude, his gifts are all identical in poem and tale; the riven coverlet is paralleled by the torn limb of the fiend; only the curse is a fresh feature, and this may be a trait of the original legend which our poem has not preserved. It is almost needed as a thread to bind the whole life of Beowolf together.[19]

But although the Glámr episode had, in addition to all these features, the advantage over the Sandhaugar episode of being a central event in *Grettis saga*, there were still two knotty problems. Grettir's fight with Glámr could only be partly analogous to Beowulf's adventure, inasmuch as it was only a single fight against one Grendel-like adversary, and since Grettir's wrestling with the troll-woman at Sandhaugar was also supposed to be a parallel to the fight with Grendel, how could there be two analogues in the saga, considerably different from each other, recounting the same event as in the poem? Vigfússon and York Powell suggested that the Sandhaugar episode included 'a certain repetition of the Grendel story,'[20] but further than that they did not get. Much later, Nora K. Chadwick tried to solve this dilemma by making Glámr and the giant in the cave at Sandhaugar into the same monster, which she equated with Grendel. According to this argument the troll-woman at Sandhaugar is analogous to his mother, and as Grendel is finally disposed of after his mother's death, so is the Glámr-giant monster.[21] This solution, however, is not obtained without a sacrifice or two. Whatever differences there are between a ghost, a troll, and a giant are obviously immaterial in Nora Chadwick's argument, and so is the fact that in *Grettis saga* a distinction is normally made between the Glámr and Sandhaugar episodes. Chadwick's ideas concerning Glámr will be discussed in more detail in chapter 2, but we must now return to a time when critics still considered him to be a motherless ghost.

In the case of Glámr, as opposed to the Sandhaugar episode, a genuine tug of war between believers and non-believers was soon under way. The Glámr story was dismissed as a genetically related analogue by Gering on the grounds that there was no equation between a torn cover and an arm, that indoor wrestling matches with consequent damage to the building and the gifts that Grettir receives were commonplaces in the sagas, and, last but not least, that Glámr and the water monsters in *Beowulf* were very different creatures.[22] A number of scholars, including R.C. Boer, Sophus Bugge, W.W. Lawrence, Guðni Jónsson, and Joan Turville-Petre, have since concurred, although they do not necessarily agree with Gering's reasoning.[23] R.W. Chambers seems to have hesitated. He included the Glámr section as a genetically related *Beowulf* analogue in the first edition of his study of the poem (1921), presumably because of its 'great, if possibly accidental likeness to the Grendel story,' and then completely dismissed it in an article published a few years later with the comment that although many details were the same, there was but one struggle, the foe was disposed of, and there was no hint of any sequel.[24]

But various critics came to Vigfússon's defence by insisting that the Glámr section was truly analogous, and some even produced fresh evidence to bolster the original argument. C.S. Smith, although he did not like the idea that a rent cloak could substitute for Grendel's arm, addressed the problem of the two different saga versions by maintaining that Grettir's fight in the Sandhaugar episode was but a poor copy of the Glámr section – in other words the saga author was just repeating himself – and thus Glámr should be given priority status as a *Beowulf* analogue.[25] Douglas Stedman recognized additional similarities between Grendel and Glámr, such as: their mutual loathing of the sound of music,[26] the size and the ugliness of the monsters' heads, the horror in the eyes of both of them as they glare into the hall, and the fact that the hero in each case fights with his bare hands (as opposed to the troll-woman in the Sandhaugar episode, who is armed with a long knife and disposed of with Grettir's short-sword).[27] Fernand Mossé emphasized the gigantic size of the monsters and the fact that the hero lies down as he waits for them.[28] Vigfússon's supporters, however, remained divided on the question as to whether Glámr *per se* was related to Grendel or whether the two were merely attached to the same legend.[29]

And so the feud over the status of the Glámr story as an analogue that proves something or nothing about *Grettis saga* being related to *Beowulf* has continued. Klaeber, who in his edition of *Beowulf* tried the diplomatic approach by suggesting that the episode was 'of less significance' than Sandhaugar but 'worthy of mention as a parallel to the Grendel fight,'[30] has been noticeably short of followers.

3: Kárr the Old[31]

Grettir, while outlawed from Iceland, stays as a guest of a farmer who lives on an island in Norway. He sees a mysterious fire and is told that the farmer's father, Kárr the Old, a revenant who occupies a gravemound and has driven all his son's competitors for land away, lives there with his treasure. Grettir, accompanied by a single companion, breaks into the gravemound, lowers himself into it by using a rope, and puts the ghost to permanent rest. The noise from their struggle makes his companion, who has been left to guard the rope,[32] think that Grettir is dead, and he deserts his post. Grettir, however, gets out of the gravemound unaided and brings the treasure back to his host. Later, Grettir saves the farm from an attack by a group of berserks and is rewarded with a splendid short-sword (*sax*) from the grave-mound treasure.

Klaeber, in his edition of *Beowulf*, recognized that parts of this story resemble the Sandhaugar and Glámr episodes:[33] the fight with Kárr shares certain traits of both the wrestling match with Glámr and the encounter with the troll-woman at Sandhaugar, and, in the case of the latter adventure, a watchman who leaves a rope and presumes the hero to be dead as well. Klaeber did not consider the story of Grettir's encounter with Kárr the Old to be an analogue to *Beowulf*, in the sense of being genetically related to the poem, however, and neither did anyone else until A.R. Taylor argued for its admission into the canon in a short but seminal article published in 1952.[34] Taylor departed radically in his approach from the conventional method which had been used in respect to Sandhaugar and Glámr; i.e., the consideration of each episode as a whole and the use of the similarity of its narrative ingredients and sequence of events to make a case for it as a *Beowulf* analogue. Instead, he simply took it for granted that the authors of *Grettis saga* and *Beowulf* had both known and used the same legend and proceeded to assume that the saga author had been so interested in this old legend that he had decided to implant and re-implant bits and pieces of it into various parts of his work. Taylor readily admitted that the connection between the Kárr episode and the attack on the monsters' lair in *Beowulf* was slight and consisted mainly of the desertion of the hero by his companion and the removal of a sword from a chamber, but given his basic premise that did not really matter because the nature of the quest for analogous materials had changed. Taylor's argument clearly implied that the burden of proof for claiming new genetically related analogues was considerably lighter now that the relationship between *Grettis saga* and *Beowulf* could be dealt with as an established fact. This novel approach threw the critical discussion of the subject into an entirely different dimension and set an example which several later scholars have found immensely appealing.

R.W. McConchie, who thirty years later set out on the same mission as Taylor, is not, however, one of his disciples. McConchie seems to have been unaware of Taylor's article, and his approach is conventional in the sense that he tries to claim the whole episode as a genetically related analogue to the Grendel fight without relying on Taylor's *a priori* assumption of kinship between *Beowulf* and *Grettis saga*:

> There are several obvious points of similarity between Beowulf's struggle with Grendel's mother and Grettir's fight with Kárr. Both take place as a result of a series of violent hauntings. The heroes are both possessed of extraordinary powers and skill. Despite this their companions do not believe that they can succeed. The place of combat is reached by solitary descent, leaving companions, or a companion behind. These desert the hero, believing him to be dead. There is a hand-to-hand combat between the hero and the monster in which the hero comes close to defeat. In both instances there is a decapitation – in *Beowulf* it is Grendel, not Grendel's mother, who is beheaded. There is a splendid sword found in the place of combat, and the hero recovers some kind of treasure. Fire, or light, appears in each version.[35]

Nevertheless, McConchie also admits that there are 'many points of significant difference between the two versions.'

4: The Slaying of the Bear[36]

Grettir stays as a guest with a farmer named Þorkell in Hálogaland in Norway. A kinsman of Þorkell's, Bjǫrn, is also staying there. Bjǫrn is a vain, quarrelsome man who often drives Þorkell's guests away with his taunts. Predictably, he and Grettir do not get along well together. In the winter, a ferocious bear begins to ravage the area, including the farm of Grettir's host, preying on men and cattle at night. People blame this calamity on Bjǫrn and his companions because of their habit of loud merrymaking every night. The bear lives in a cave in a cliff that overlooks the sea and can only be reached by a single narrow track. Bjǫrn boasts that he will kill the beast but does not succeed in his attempt and is derided for his failure. At Christmas a group of men, including both Bjǫrn and Grettir, try to attack the bear but are forced to turn back. As he is making his way home Grettir, egged on by Bjǫrn, returns to the lair of the animal. He cuts off its paw, and then wrestles with the bear. Grettir and the bear both tumble down the cliff, but Grettir lands on top of the animal and kills it. He brings the bear's paw back as a trophy, and his feud with Bjǫrn becomes even more embittered than it had been.

It was A.R. Taylor, in the same article that made a case for Kárr the Old, who first proposed that this section of the saga should be considered as a genetically related analogue to *Beowulf*. Previously, Klaeber had noted Beowulfian touches in the way the saga describes the bear's den as being 'in a cliff by the sea where there was a cave under an overhanging rock, with a narrow path leading to the entrance,'[37] but Klaeber took the issue no further. Lawrence, who briefly considered the episode in his book on *Beowulf* in 1928, rejected it as a genetically related analogue: 'A fight with a brown bear recalls a bit the contests with Grendel,' he writes, but then discards the bear (and Glámr) as 'obvious reminiscences of the Bear's Son tale.'[38]

Taylor, on the other hand, pointed to the night attacks of the bear, to the cutting off of the paw and its use as evidence, to Grettir's remarkable short-sword, to his wrestling match with the animal, and last but not least, to the character and actions of Bjǫrn, which Taylor believed to mirror those of Unferð, the enigmatic courtier who insults Beowulf before he embarks on his mission against Grendel. To Taylor it seemed clear that 'the same basic legend' was present in Grettir's encounter with the bear as in the other parallels to *Beowulf*.[39] As he had done before in the case of Kárr the Old, Taylor carefully limited his comparison to certain details rather than insisting that the episode as a whole bore a close resemblance to Beowulf's fight with Grendel.

A. Margaret Arent, who was the next scholar to make a case for Grettir's fight with the bear as a *Beowulf* analogue, took a very different approach: 'No one, to my knowledge,' she declared, 'has taken into account the fact that both Grendel and dragon motifs appear in a recombined form in the Halogaland bear episode.' Arent's case for this discovery relies mainly on the following points:

- 'The bear in *Grettis saga* is roused by noise and gaiety like Grendel in his attack on Heorot.'
- 'Grendel holds such sway over Heorot and the misty moors that men may not venture forth (*Beowulf*, lines 161–3); the bear comes forth to stalk man and beast, particularly plaguing Thorkel's farm; the dragon lays waste the whole region with fire (*Beowulf*, lines 2333–5). (Similarly, Kár spirits away all the farmers on the island, Glám ravages cattle and men, the troll woman at Sandhaugar causes two men to vanish.)'
- 'The bear, like Grendel, the dragon and all the other ghosts and trolls, haunts at night.'
- 'Hand-to-hand grappling takes place when the bear and Grettir topple down over the precipice and when Beowulf struggles with the mere-wife in the cave (*Beowulf*, lines 1539–46). (Similarly, Kár falls over on his back, as does Glám with Grettir.)'
- 'Boastfully, like Beowulf in the fights against Grendel and the dragon –

although Beowulf in his eagerness disclaims all boasting (lines 2527–8), illustrative of the poet's innovation in handling his theme – Grettir wants to demonstrate his prowess and courage single-handed against the bear.'

- 'That the bear wards off all spear thrusts with his teeth and is hard to get at recalls an invulnerability to weapons and the bite of iron continually referred to in respect to Grendel, Grendel's dam and the dragon.'
- 'Grettir also follows well-known tradition by striking the bear to the heart ... The dragon, too, succumbs only when pierced in his most vulnerable spot.'
- 'Grendel, the Sandhaugar ogress, and the bear are all mutilated in a similar manner.'
- The bear's cave lair near the sea, with a narrow path, difficult of access, and with rocky cliffs plunging into the sea (*Grettis saga*, chapter 21, 74), recalls the dragon's lair (*Beowulf*, lines 2241–3).[40]

There has been no critical reaction to the different methods that Taylor, McConchie and Arent employ to obtain their results, and on the whole their findings have been met with approval. Subsequent commentators on *Grettis saga*, for instance Óskar Halldórsson,[41] Richard Harris[42] and Peter Jorgensen,[43] have all accepted Grettir's encounter with the bear along with the story of Kárr the Old as valid genetically related analogues to Beowulf's struggles with Grendel and his dam.

5: The Death of Grettir in Drangey[44]

Grettir takes refuge in Drangey, a fortress-like island in the North of Iceland, accompanied by his brother Illugi and a slave named Glaumr. The island is owned by a group of farmers who use it for their sheep over the summer. Grettir refuses to leave the island or give up the sheep and thereby incurs the wrath of the farmers. The job of ridding them of Grettir eventually falls to one Þorbjǫrn ǫngull. Þorbjǫrn first tries to plead with Grettir but meets with no success. He then sends an assassin to kill him, but the attempt on Grettir's life fails. Þorbjǫrn now seeks advice from his old nurse, Þuríðr, who is a known sorceress, and together they make a trip to the island. Þorbjǫrn pretends to offer peace in return for Grettir's departure, but Grettir declines the offer. Þuríðr then curses him, and Grettir retaliates by breaking her thighbone with a stone that he throws at her. Some time later the old witch carves runes on a piece of wood, sprinkles it with blood and magic, and sets it adrift. The log finds its way to Drangey where Grettir twice refuses to use it as firewood, but on a third occasion the slave brings it to their hut, and Grettir injures his leg as he attempts to split the log with his axe. Grettir's injury seems to heal at first but then takes a turn for the worse, and it becomes clear that the wound is fatal. Þuríðr now advises Þorbjǫrn to gather troops and set sail for Drangey. He does so and reaches the island successfully despite seemingly impossible weather conditions. The slave Glaumr, whose job it is to pull up the ladder which is the only means of reaching the hut occupied by Grettir, Illugi, and himself and who is also to stand guard that day, does neither, as he is overcome by sleep. Þorbjǫrn reaches the hut, kills Grettir on his deathbed and has Illugi executed. After Grettir's death Þorbjǫrn tries to remove his short-sword from his grip, but cannot wrench it loose and has to cut Grettir's hand off to release it. Þorbjǫrn then smites the short-sword against Grettir's head and nicks the weapon in the process. Finally, he decapitates Grettir and takes his head and sword with him as a trophies. Grettir's death is eventually avenged by his half-brother, Þorsteinn drómundr, who follows Þorbjǫrn ǫngull to Constantinople and kills him there.

In 1973, Richard Harris claimed that the story of Grettir's death contained a fifth genetically related analogue to *Beowulf*, as it resembled the poem – particularly the episode depicting the fight at Grendel's mere – in at least eleven of its details. Harris summed up his findings, insofar as they relate to this episode and *Beowulf*, in the following chart:

Grettir's Death	Beowulf
1/ Grettir occupies Drangey.	Grendel haunts Heorot.
2/ Grettir has a hut on Drangey; nearness to the sea.	Grendel has a waterfall cave, possibly near the sea.
3/ Þorbjörn arrives at Drangey toward the end of the day.	Beowulf takes most of day to reach bottom of mere.
4/ Þorbjörn climbs a ladder to reach Grettir's hut.	Beowulf plunges into mere.
5/ Glaumr sleeps, betrays Grettir.	Danes desert mere at sight of blood.
6/ Grettir previously disabled.	Beowulf wounds Grendel mortally in Heorot – dead in cave.
7/ Grettir loses his hand posthumously.	Beowulf tears off Grendel's arm.
8/ Grettir is beheaded in his hut by Þorbjörn.	Grendel is beheaded in cave by Beowulf.
9/ The beheading is done with Grettir's own sword, Kársnautr.	Sword found in cave.
10/ Sword is damaged by the blow.	Blade melts in blood of Grendel and mother.
11/ Head and sword are kept as trophies.	Head and sword hilt are kept as trophies.[45]

On the basis of this comparison of elements relating to the deaths of Grettir and Grendel and with complete faith in the four previously established analogues in *Grettis saga*, Harris concludes that 'the saga's author knew more of the material, in some form or other, upon which Grendel's story is based, than could be assumed without an awareness that Grettir's death does indeed offer another parallel to the narrative in *Beowulf*.'[46] Within the Drangey episode of *Grettis saga*, in which – up to now – the reader's sympathy has generally been considered to be on the side of the hunted outlaw, we have, in other words, a hidden story, cunningly embedded, in which the hero changes sides with the monster. It is not clear, however, from Harris's remarks, whether he is referring to a fuller story about Grendel as 'a victim' than the one that we have in *Beowulf*, or to a full-fledged story about Grendel (in his struggle against Beowulf?) told from the monster's point of view.

Aside from the eleven details that Harris offers as evidence, his argument involves a double role reversal: Grettir is made to take Grendel's place as a monster, and Þorbjǫrn ǫngull dressed up to be the hero who kills it. To explain the first of these two, Harris points to Arent's argument that the names Grettir and Grendel are related etymologically, that Grettir is spoken of as a troll and has troll-like qualities, that an attempt is made to kill Grettir with his own sword in chapter 55 of the saga, as if he was a giant ogre who could not be killed with any other weapon, and that Grettir's head and sword are kept as trophies; to N.K. Chadwick's idea that in *Grettis saga* Grendel has been transformed into a hero, and that a story originally told from the monster's point of view has left traces on him; and finally to James Carney's thesis that the curse of Cain carried by Grendel as his descendant was transferred to Grettir by an author who otherwise removed Cain from his material.[47] Harris believes that Þorbjǫrn's surly nature and the brutalities he commits as a young man give him, like Grettir, a hero's background as far as his youth is concerned. 'But what sort of hero does Þorbjörn actually become?' asks Harris. 'His exploit is accomplished with the help of a foster mother's magic. His only thanks for the act of cleansing is banishment. His glory as the slayer of Grettir, when he boasts of it in Constantinople, is short-lived. Grettir, on the other hand, is recognized as a hero and cleanser of the land for doing away with various harmful creatures.'[48]

The only criticism of Harris's ideas and of his treatment of the source materials has, so far, come from Anatoly Liberman, who in 1986 surveyed critically the various theories that seek to relate *Grettis saga* and *Beowulf*.[49] Liberman rejects the notion that a close identity of the hero's and the monster's nature has ever been proven to exist in Old English poetry or in the Icelandic sagas:

It is easy to admit that a monster will yield only to its equal in strength, ferocity, and, if necessary, magic powers. That in a mortal fight both opponents acquire awesome proportions can also be granted. Finally, there is nothing surprising in the constant dehumanization of Grettir (what else could be expected?) ... From the point of view of the audience, role reversal is unthinkable: a word of compassion for Grendel the exile does not diminish the distance between him and Beowulf the *aglæca*, and in the saga our sympathy is always with Grettir, whether he preys on the local farmers' sheep or not. It is only this sympathy that matters, unless we are prepared to substitute a motif index for the reader's/listener's reaction.[50]

Other critics have been more receptive. Peter Jorgensen[51] and Stephen Mitchell[52] have both noted Harris's discovery of a new analogue with approval, and Óskar Halldórsson lists his essay among those sources that he believes to be the most important in the study of the saga's relationship to *Beowulf*.[53]

These five analogues that have now been presented are all supposed to reflect material in *Grettis saga* that corresponds to Beowulf's fight with Grendel and his dam, or parts of that story, but as we have seen, the types of arguments that have been used in support of these five candidates are quite different. Most importantly, they vary in their approach to the text of the saga and the poem, and on the question as to what constitutes sufficient evidence to claim a genetically related analogue. In the first place, there are arguments that rely on specific points in the two texts in comparing the nature and deeds of heroes and monsters, the role of various objects and settings that surround them, and the sequence of events. For the most part, these concern the Sandhaugar and Glámr episodes. We have also seen arguments that take lesser or greater liberties with both texts, which obviously must be done if Grettir's fight with a gravemound ghost and a bear, and Þorbjǫrn ǫngull's struggle against Grettir as a monster are to be considered genetically related *Beowulf* analogues. It should also be noted that the last three genetically related analogues that critics claim to have found in *Grettis saga* hinge very heavily on the presumed existence of the first, or the first two. But let us now proceed to take a closer look at the heroes and monsters to see how well they actually compare.

2

The Making of Heroes and Monsters

The purpose of this and of the next three chapters is to examine the basic ingredients of the five genetically related analogues that critics claim to have found in *Grettis saga* against the relevant sections of *Beowulf*. Although a great deal of literature has accumulated around these five texts, comparisons have never been very detailed or thorough, even in the case of the most widely accepted analogues, namely, the Sandhaugar and Glámr episodes. Critical discussion has. in most cases revolved around a few fragments of a given analogue, usually to reach the quick conclusion that they presented ample evidence to relate the two works. Differences have, for the most part, been ignored. In this respect, later scholars have too often followed the example of Guðbrandur Vigfússon and F. York Powell, who only touched upon a few examples from the Sandhaugar and Glámr episodes and then pronounced their conviction that in the first text events described in *Beowulf* were repeated 'with little alteration' and that correspondence of incident was 'so perfect' in the second.[1]

Beowulf and Grettir as Heroes

The lives of Beowulf and Grettir are to a large extent dictated by the fact that as king and outlaw they inhabit opposite ends of the social spectrum. Before Guðbrandur Vigfússon lumped them together as monster killers no one had seen anything to compare in Beowulf and Grettir,[2] but soon after Vigfússon had published his findings critics began to peel away their differences to find a core of attributes that the two heroes might have in common. Four points seemed obvious: Beowulf and Grettir are sluggish youths; they possess great physical strength; they swim long distances; and, most importantly, they volunteer to overcome evil supernatural beings. But is this sufficient evidence to argue that as a character Grettir is partly fashioned with Beowulf in mind, or that the two share a common ancestor in their heroic exploits? Some critics have not found these apparent similarities enough to outweigh the differences. Guðni Jónsson, for instance, regards Grettir, in his land-cleansing efforts, merely as a new player in an old role,[3] but other critics have insisted that the two heroes are basically cut from the same cloth.[4] Textual comparison is always a treacherous business, and in this case it is more treacherous than usual because of the different techniques that the authors of the poem and the saga employ to present their main characters. *Grettis saga* is cast as the story of Grettir's life in the sense that it relates, in considerable detail, his origin, his career, and his death as an outlaw. *Beowulf*, on the other hand, is not a biographical poem, whether or not a king by that name ever existed. Only certain critical moments in Beowulf's life are ever described. Other information about him as a character is sketchy and incidental.

This lack of concrete information in the Old English poem has often forced critics who wish to claim a special affinity between the two heroes into a position of having to fall back on rather superficial comparisons and speculative arguments as evidence. We have, for example, already come across the observation that both Beowulf and Grettir come from afar to do their deeds and prefer to fight alone.[5] It has also been pointed out that each is a lonely man, who only has one friend in the final struggle, and who ends his life unhappily.[6] These factors do indeed apply to Beowulf and Grettir, albeit in different ways; but they are equally applicable to any number of heroes from Gilgamesh to Tin Tin. Guðbrandur Vigfússon and F. York Powell believed that, like Grettir, Beowulf had been cursed (by Grendel), and suggested that the curse had been 'a trait of the original legend which our poem has not preserved.'[7] They saw the curse as a missing link which explained Beowulf's childlessness and his sad fate as a ruler. But in the poem Grendel is silent on this and other matters, except for one mighty howl, and efforts of this kind have not produced any firm ground for comparing the two heroes beyond the four points mentioned at the beginning of this chapter.

The first of these concerns the question as to whether a background as an inglorious or a sluggish youth can be claimed as a common trait for both Beowulf and Grettir. The idea was first proposed by Friedrich Panzer, who believed that both Beowulf and Grettir were derived independently from the folktale figure of the Bear's Son, a creature who is often unmanageable or lazy in his youth.[8] The issue, however, is a great deal more complex than Panzer makes it appear. *Grettis saga* devotes a whole chapter (14) to Grettir's youth. We learn that he is not a precocious youngster, and the saga emphasizes this fact by specifically mentioning that Grettir is ten when he begins to show signs of any real growth. When his father asks him to pull his weight on the farm, Grettir promptly explains that he is not suited for such labour. Making the boy do domestic chores only results in a series of memorable, but nasty, pranks. Grettir obviously finds farm work demeaning and has presumably at the age of ten already decided on a career that involves more heroic exploits. In this sense, Grettir's youth may be disappointing or sluggish from a diligent farmer's point of view, but it is not necessarily inglorious for a hero to be. The question as to whether Grettir spent his youth as an ash-lad by the fire is addressed by the narrator of the saga and answered in the negative.[9]

We know that Beowulf is, on his mother's side, related to the royal family of the Geatas, but otherwise the story of his youth and upbringing is very unclear in the poem. The hero's undistinguished boyhood is alluded to only once (lines 2183b–9), where it is stated that he was long despised by the Geatas, who found him slack and lacking in courage and rewarded him accordingly until a change came about. But there are also passages in *Beowulf* that seem to contradict this statement. At the age of seven the boy is at the court of his grandfather, King Hreðel, enjoying treasures and feasts and being treated like one of Hreðel's own sons (lines 2428–31). Furthermore, when Beowulf, presumably still a very young man, arrives at the court of King Hroðgar to fight against Grendel, he does so with impressive credentials. According to the poem he has already performed many illustrious deeds (lines 408b–9a) and is an accomplished destroyer of sea monsters and giants (lines 418–24a and 549–76).[10]

Some scholars, especially those who believe that the poem seeks to depict a model prince, have found it impossible to reconcile these different pieces of information concerning Beowulf's youth and have therefore dismissed the reference to his inglorious early years as incompatible.[11] Others have sought to create a picture of Beowulf's youth that could accommodate his accomplishments as well as a period when something is seriously amiss.[12] There is, in other words, no clear-cut evidence to establish Beowulf as a youngster without promise of becoming a hero, and even if such a case could be made the comparison with Grettir as a boy would still be highly questionable because Grettir rebels against mundane tasks that he considers unworthy of a hero's attention.

Ever since Guðbrandur Vigfússon claimed that *Grettis saga* and *Beowulf* derived from the same legend, the great physical strength of the two monster killers has been considered one of the most obvious traits that they have in common. Ironically, this factor separates them no less than it unites them. The author of *Grettis saga* measures the strength of his hero on various occasions: he bails water like eight seamen (chapter 17); carries an ox single-handedly (chapter 50); and successfully wrestles against two men, each twice as strong as an ordinary person (chapter 72). These and other feats of strength that Grettir performs allow the saga author to conclude that he was indeed the strongest man in Iceland in his time (chapter 93). But strong though Grettir is, his physical prowess is always kept close to the borders of the humanly possible; what he might have become had Glámr's curse not stunted his growth by half we can only guess.

Beowulf, on the other hand, has no constraints of 'realistic' presentation imposed upon his strength. He is the strongest man alive (lines 789–90), with the strength of thirty men in his hand-grip (lines 379b–81a). These references would not necessarily indicate a strength of mythological proportions were they not coupled with descriptions of Beowulf's feats of swimming, which include five days in the sea in full armour (line 545a)[13] and a five hundred mile swim home after Hygelac's disastrous raid on Frisia (lines 2359b–72). Scholars have quibbled over various details in these descriptions, but there is no question that the author of *Beowulf* endows his hero with superhuman qualities of strength and endurance.[14] By comparison, Grettir's achievements in fresh or salt water are understandably paltry, as they are kept within the range of what a strong swimmer can actually do.[15]

The superhuman qualities of Beowulf make it very unlikely that the author of *Grettis saga* merely borrowed the physical attributes of his hero from the poem, but could the two hearken back to a legendary forefather – a strong swimmer who killed monsters? Larry D. Benson has argued along these lines in a well-known article entitled 'The Originality of Beowulf,' in which he maintains that whereas wrestling is a common accomplishment among Germanic heroes, great feats of swimming are more unusual. The idea of combining the two leads him to conclude that 'the fact that both Grettir and Beowulf demonstrate skill at swimming and wrestling raises the possibility that both works are based on some longer work that included the Grendel episode and had other similarities to the central fable in Beowulf.'[16] Benson's observation – i.e., that Germanic heroes who are both strong and can swim are few and far between – is incorrect insofar as it ignores the evidence of the later mythic-heroic *fornaldarsǫgur*, some of which are known to have influenced *Grettis saga*. *Örvar-Odds saga, Hálfdanar saga Brönufóstra, Egils saga einhenda*, and *Þorsteins saga Víkings-sonar* all include swimming heroes, so in this respect Grettir and Beowulf are not as exceptional as Benson would like to think. If, in the original story, it mattered that the hero had to swim to reach a second monster, his journey is not easily reconstructed by comparing the poem and the saga. Beowulf, in full armour, sinks to the bottom of the mere where he is immediately attacked by Grendel's dam and her ilk, whereas Grettir dives beneath a waterfall and uneventfully scales the rock behind it to reach the giant's cave. The real swimming feats of both heroes are reserved for other occasions.

The mythical strength of Beowulf and the human limitations of Grettir do not point to a common ancestor; on the contrary, they indicate different concepts of what comprises heroic prowess. The attitudes of the poem and the saga towards supernatural beings also reveal a wholly different definition of what forces the hero must combat. In *Beowulf*, not only Grendel, his mother, and the dragon, but all mystical creatures, are evil. They are all enemies of man and God alike, and Beowulf fights them and overpowers them by virtue of superior strength (and divine assistance) until his final battle with the dragon. In *Grettis saga*, supernatural beings more or less mirror the world of people in the story: some are hostile, like Kárr, Glámr, and the Sandhaugar trolls, and Grettir destroys them in much the same way as he does his human enemies; others are friendly towards him, like the half-troll Þórir and the mysterious Hallmundr.[17] Furthermore, the saga author always assumes that supernatural creatures are stronger than Grettir. This is abundantly clear in his wrestling bouts with Kárr, Glámr, Hallmundr, and the troll-woman. Grettir's victories against hostile supernatural creatures are won with the aid of good luck or cunning or both; either they trip over something in the course of the struggle and fall flat on their backs, like Kárr and Glámr, or they fail to avoid a wrestling trick, like the troll-woman at Sandhaugar.

Grendel and His Mother

In their comparisons of Beowulf and Grettir, Guðbrandur Vigfússon and F. York Powell paid little attention to differences in the heroes' supernatural opponents, although the nature of such creatures obviously mattered to the saga author and, even more so, to the *Beowulf* poet. Vigfússon and Powell regarded Grendel and his dam, Glámr, the troll-wife, and the giant at Sandhaugar primarily as hostile otherworldly creatures – 'fiends' and 'monsters' – not the same thing, perhaps, but easily interchangeable in the two different versions of the legend.[18] This trend has continued, and it is still common practice among critics to lump the supernatural adversaries of Beowulf and Grettir together on the facile assumption that they are all more or less the same, functionally speaking.[19] A structural approach is in itself neither better nor worse than any other, but the problem begins when the same critics start extracting sundry details in the description of the monsters, such as the cannibalism of the Grendels and the Sandhaugar trolls or the evil eyes of Grendel and Glámr, and then proceed to serve them up as evidence to support the idea that the poem and the saga are related.

The shortcuts that have been taken by various comparatists have not stemmed from a lack of critical efforts to determine the origin and nature of Grendel and his mother. The earliest views, however, which favoured rather abstract interpretations of them, did little to support Vigfússon's theory. The

Grendels were most commonly thought to originate in nature myths and Beowulf's victory against them was seen in the context of the prevailing of spring against the forces of winter. Alternatively, they were taken to be symptoms of diseases like malaria or hallucinations by the Danes, brought on by too much drink and lack of proper ventilation. But gradually Grendel and his mother took on more concrete shapes, and scholars began to trace their ancestry to the male–female rulers of the underworld of Persian and Greek mythology.[20] These developments opened the possibility of finding a more immediate forefather of the Grendels, preferably with descendants in *Grettis saga* as well.

In 1912, W.W. Lawrence published an article that offered new and persuasive evidence to link *Beowulf* and *Grettis saga*.[21] Lawrence was convinced that from the bewildering and seemingly contradictory description of the Grendels' abode in different parts of the poem it was possible to glimpse a reference to a waterfall in two places.[22] The waterfall linked the description of the landscape in *Beowulf* to Sandhaugar and led Lawrence to conclude that the original story, a *Märchen* of the Bear's Son type, had been set in Scandinavia and involved waterfall trolls as the hero's adversaries. From such stock the author of *Beowulf* had eventually fashioned Grendel and his mother.[23] Lawrence found further support for his ideas on the habitat of trolls in Icelandic materials such as the *Story of Grímur Helguson* and *Orms þáttr*, and in the presence of water sprites in Norwegian folklore. 'A waterfall among high rocks, in which a supernatural being is believed to dwell, is a common and characteristic feature of Scandinavian mountain scenery,' Lawrence declared.[24] It now seemed as though Vigfússon's hunch about a Scandinavian homeland from which the legend had derived had been correct after all.

Although there are glaring weaknesses in his argument, Lawrence's ideas concerning the origin of Grendel and his mother have had a lasting influence on *Beowulf* studies.[25] To begin with his thesis hinges on the notion that there is indeed a waterfall with a cave behind it to be found in the poem; an assumption that has come under stinging criticism from Kemp Malone, as we shall see in chapter 5. Furthermore, there is nothing in the poem's complex and ambiguous description of Grendel and his dam – other than their enormous size – to support the idea that waterfall trolls were the raw material from which the *Beowulf* poet formed his monsters. But the weakest link in Lawrence's theory is probably the fact that Scandinavian trolls do not as a rule live in waterfalls. They are roaming creatures who traditionally choose to live in mountains or hills.[26]

Grendel and his mother are no ordinary trolls; that much is certain from the poem. They may be huge, misshapen, diabolical, and beastly cannibals, but they are much more 'aristocratic' and have more human attributes than monsters in Scandinavian lore usually do. In *Beowulf* one of the first things we discover about the Grendels is their, criminally speaking, respectable background as descendants of Cain and inheritors of his curse. Like the Danes, they also keep their own court, in the sense that they occupy an underwater hall (*niðsele*) guarded by a band of water-monsters. Furthermore, we learn that for a number of years Grendel literally ruled over the Danes (*rixode*), until Beowulf put an end to his reign. The touch of magic that makes the Grendels immune to normal weapons also sets them apart from ordinary monsters in the poem, and as a tangible sign of family pride, mother and son possess an heirloom, a sword whose hilt records the history of their race. Other human touches are added as Grendel is on several occasions referred to as a man (*rinc, wer, healðegn*), and his misery as an outlaw equated with ordinary human feelings of loss and rejection (*wonsæli, dreamum bedæled*). His mother is similarly presented as a woman (*ides*), and in avenging her son she fulfils her duty as any self-respecting Germanic mother would.

Another factor that separates the Grendels from ordinary trolls in Scandinavian literature is the mystery in which the author of *Beowulf* shrouds them. His audience is never allowed to satisfy their curiosity by having a good look at them, or to discover a simple answer as to what kind of creatures they are. We have to imagine them to be unlike any known monsters, and their strangeness is emphasized by the frequent variation among terms that highlight their threefold nature: human, bestial, and diabolical. In the description of Grendel's mother the *Beowulf* poet goes still further by teasing his audience with contradictory statements about her. She is supposed to be weaker than a male warrior (lines 1282b–7) but, as Beowulf discovers, she is a far more dangerous opponent than Grendel.[27] With the proposed Sandhaugar analogue in mind, however, it is even more important that the poem refers to her with a masculine pronoun on four different occasions (lines 1260a, 1392b, 1394b and 1497b). Is this done to suggest that her sex is unimportant, as Lawrence and Goldsmith have argued,[28] or do we have to think of her separately as a mother and a monster, as Wrenn seems to think?[29] Whatever the answer is, these androgynous qualities make her more analogous to certain modern pop stars than to the troll-woman at Sandhaugar.

Grendel's name is of no help in determining family traits; it only adds to the mystery. Lawrence's theory that the word *grendel* may have been a generic term for a water monster in Old English[30] is pure guesswork, and there is no evidence to suggest that the poem's Anglo-Saxon audience had any more clues as to what the name actually means than modern scholars, who have proposed no less than five different etymologies to account for it:

1 / Old English *grindan* = 'to grind' (Old Norse *grand* = 'evil').
2 / Old English *grindel* = 'bar,' 'bolt.'

3 / Old Norse *grindill* = a poetic term for 'storm.'
4 / Latin *grandis* = 'full-grown,' 'great,' 'large.'
5 / Old English *grund* = bottom, cf. Old Norse *grandi* = sand, bottom ground of a body of water.[31]

Not everything about Grendel is as enigmatic as his name and nature, however. The facts that can be gleaned from different parts of the poem about his physical attributes and behavior as a man-eating monster are briefly as follows:

- Grendel is an (in)famous rover[32] of the fens and the moors that lie outside the borders of human habitation (lines 103–4).
- He is huge. Four men struggle to carry his head back to Heorot after Beowulf's final victory (lines 1637b–9).
- His fingers have nails that seem like steel-tipped spurs (lines 985–7b).
- An ugly, flame-like light emanates from his eyes (lines 726b–7).
- Unlike his mother, he does not care to fight with weapons (lines 433–4), and they do not wound him (lines 794–805b), except for his mother's magic sword (lines 1588b–90), if that is indeed the sword with which Beowulf decapitates him.
- Poisoned or corrosive blood runs through his veins (lines 1615b–17).
- Grendel is a ferocious cannibal who behaves much like an ordinary predator. For twelve years (line 147) he persecutes the Danes with frequent attacks at night (lines 1577b–9) to feast on them.
- Grendel's feeding habits have both predatory and human characteristics. He snatches as many as thirty Danes at a time, eats fifteen on the spot in one go, and carries another fifteen away with him for a later meal (lines 1581b–4a). He tears his victims apart, drinks the blood from their veins, and eats their bodies in huge mouthfuls, leaving nothing behind (740–5a).
- Grendel has a huge pouch or glove made of dragon skins (lines 2085b–8) in which he presumably carries victims that he intends to eat later.
- Grendel has no career as a 'living corpse,' (cf. Glámr and Kárr) either before or after Beowulf cuts his head off.

Glámr

Glámr is an uncommon name in Old Norse. Although the origin and meaning of the name are somewhat uncertain, it does not appear to be related etymologically to that of Grendel in any way. Glámr comes from Germanic **glé*, 'to shine with a dim or a faint light' (cf. Modern English 'gloom'), and later derivations of the word are usually associated with light or whiteness of some kind.[33]

Scholars are agreed that as a name, or a nickname, Glámr originally denotes someone who stares or looks foolish, but this association has attracted far less attention than the occurrence of his name as a poetic term for a giant and for the moon in Snorri's *Edda*. This latter connection has led some critics to believe that it might be indicative of his nature in the saga. Thus R.C. Boer associated Glámr with a moon myth and saw him (or rather his ghost) as the personification of the moonlight in winter.[34] Others, particularly Wolf von Unwerth, have stressed the giant-like size and nature of Glámr as a ghost.[35] But Glámr also occurs as an ordinary name in *Sturlunga* (*Íslendinga saga*), so it is by no means certain that the author of *Grettis saga* intended his audience to interpret it in a particular way, except to associate it with *glámsýni* (illusions), as he himself suggests.

It is not clear either what kind of creature Glámr is supposed to have been before he became one of the living dead. Boer and von Unwerth regard him as a demon or a magician who only feigns a human form and has evil intentions, whether he is living or dead.[36] No one, however, had seen any connection between the pre-ghostly Glámr and Grendel until James Carney found a way to unite them. In *Beowulf* (line 107) we are told of Grendel's descent from the exiled Cain, who becomes the progenitor of monsters and giants in medieval lore, and Grendel thus owes his monstrous form to inherited guilt. Carney maintains that this account in the poem has been transformed in the story of Glámr into his 'personal guilt,' because of his failure as a 'normal human being' to observe Christian rites, for which he is punished by becoming 'not a mere ghost, but a physical monster':

just as Hrothgar's palace was changed into an Icelandic farmhouse, so too the tale was brought up to date in medieval Iceland by discarding the idea of Cain's guilt for an analogical idea – failure to practice religious observance – that had some relevance in contemporary Iceland ... Grettir slew the monster Glam who became a monster because he, in his own person, had refused to attend Mass and had eaten meat on a fast-day.[37]

This is pretty far-fetched stuff, and Carney has to make a few shortcuts through the facts of the matter on his way to his conclusion. In the first place, Glámr hardly qualifies either as a 'normal human being' or as a 'monster,' the term under which Carney conveniently lumps Glámr and Grendel together. Secondly, he has no convincing means of explaining why the idea of monsters springing from Cain should have been replaced by a more relevant notion in medieval Iceland. There is indeed a hint of divine retribution in the tale of how Glámr meets his end, but there is no suggestion in *Grettis saga* that his existence as a ghost is a form of punishment or due to anything other than his own evil nature.[38] As opposed to Grendel, Glámr seems to enjoy his supernatural state; the punishment is reserved for Þórhallr's farm and the rest of the community.

Although Glámr as a ghost haunts farms and kills people, he is in most respects entirely different from Grendel. Glámr has no taste for human flesh, he can speak, he is as vulnerable to weapons as anyone else in the saga, and no mother or a female partner avenges his second and permanent death at the hands of Grettir. Icelandic ghosts are as a rule 'more material than the ghosts of English tradition,'[39] as E. V. Gordon so aptly put it, and Glámr is no exception, so a physical presence after death does not *per se* make him a monster on par with Grendel, as some critics like to think. Glámr's ghostly exploits: riding housetops, making a whole region desolate, driving people mad, breaking the bones of and killing animals and people, are all well known ghost story motifs from Icelandic texts, many of which the author of *Grettis saga* has been shown to have been familiar with.[40] It is also possible, as Hermann Pálsson has suggested,[41] that the account of Glámr's nature and powers is sprinkled with ideas that can be traced to medieval commentaries on the subject of ghosts and demons. But the main traits that Glámr and Grendel share – haunting places and killing people – are far too common among ghosts and monsters to establish any particular link between the two. Of the contact points between Glámr and Grendel that have been suggested, only three are specific enough to indicate that they might hearken back to a common origin or be directly related in some other manner: their great size, their evil eyes, and the matter of cursing or being cursed.

Grettis saga makes it quite clear that Glámr's size varies. As he enters the farmhouse where Grettir awaits him (chapter 35), he towers up to the ceiling, but a moment later the two wrestle in a manner that would be impossible if Glámr was the giant that he had just appeared to be. Hermann Pálsson has explained this with a reference to the illusionary powers that *Antoníus saga* ascribes to demons,[42] and the note which the saga author inserts into his text to relate the word *glámsýni* to the story of Glámr supports Pálsson's reading. Grettir's vision of Glámr as a giant is only a fleeting illusion, whereas Grendel's gigantic size is an integral part of his ancestry from Cain.

It is only as Glámr is about to meet his death that his evil eyes and his stare begin to play a part in the story, whereas the ugly flame-like light from Grendel's eyes presumably scared the Danes all along. The idea that evil persons who possess magic powers can do harm by looking at someone at the moment of their death was, however, already well established in Icelandic literature before *Grettis saga* was composed[43] and has nothing whatsoever to do with Grendel.

Finally, there is the matter of the curse. James Carney includes Grettir in the second part of his Cain hypothesis and presents the following argument:

Part of the curse of Cain was that he was to be a '*vagus et profugus in terra.*' When the
monster Glam is dying he curses Grettir and part of his curse is: 'Thou shalt be outlawed
and doomed ever to dwell alone, away from men.' This suggests that Cain figured in the
author's source material; when Cain was eliminated the terms in which he was cursed
were retained; but he is made, in the person of Glam, to utter the curse of which, in the
source material, he was the recipient.[44]

Carney's theory is based on his conviction that the author of *Grettis saga* had
direct access to a manuscript of *Beowulf*, something which is very unlikely, as
we shall see in chapter 6. But the most amazing part of Carney's speculation is
that, having just explained how the author of *Grettis saga* felt compelled to substitute Grendel's ancestral guilt for Glámr's personal guilt in order to emphasize
the importance of observing Christian customs in Iceland, the same author
decided to cast the ghost of that stubborn heathen Glámr in the role of God
almighty to banish and curse Grettir, as Cain was banished and cursed.

Whether Glámr's role in the 'old legend' is the same as Grendel's we have
yet to examine, but nothing about the origin, nature, or behaviour of Glámr
seems to point to any special affinity with Grendel. The differences between
them far outweigh any superficial traits that they might seem to share, and statements to the effect that 'after his death [Glámr] distinctly resembles Grendel'[45]
are not based on much more than wishful thinking.

The Troll-Woman and the Giant of the Sandhaugar Episode

Some scholars think that the Old Norse terms *trǫll* ('trolls') and *jǫtnar*
('giants') may have indicated a degree of difference between the two at a very
early stage, i.e., that giants were considered to be remote, prehistoric figures in
comparison to trolls. In late sagas (especially *fornaldarsǫgur*) and in folktales,
trolls and giants have merged and for the most part share the same characteristics.[46] In this literature, trolls and giants are huge, supernatural beings who live
in the mountains far to the north and are as a rule hostile towards people. This
is, of course, not without exceptions, as we see in *Grettis saga* itself.

Unlike the battle against Glámr, whose curse follows Grettir to the end of his
days, the Sandhaugar episode is self-contained and independent; much like a
chapter in a picaresque novel. Late in the saga (chapter 64), the reader is
informed that at a farm called Sandhaugar in Bárðardalur people are spooked
by the presence of trolls. For two years in a row a man has been kidnapped
from the farm at Christmas, a season that also inspired Glámr to do evil deeds;
however, unlike Glámr, whose persecutions extended throughout the dark
months of winter, these creatures only strike once a year. During the first

attack, when the farmer was snatched away, there were other people present in the hall of the farmhouse, which clearly shows that these evil beings are only interested in taking a single person. The farmer disappeared without a trace, and no one saw anything, although a great deal of noise was heard by his bed. Then, in one sentence, the saga author makes a year go by and has nothing to say about anyone's reaction to the man's disappearance. It is only after the second attack, when traces of blood are found by the front door of the hall, that people conclude that some evil beings must be responsible for the kidnapping of the two men. Unlike with Grendel and his mother or Glámr, nothing is known about these trolls; they are (and remain) nameless, and no one knows where they come from. This is how matters stand when Grettir – who after his tangle with Glámr is the last person the reader expects to turn up in a haunted place – appears on the scene.

The above-mentioned account looks like a summary of a story, but in fact it is not; there is no more information in the saga concerning the famous hauntings at Sandhaugar prior to Grettir's fight with the trolls. What little we have is a disappointingly short and incomplete story, especially if we keep in mind that Vigfússon believed his 'old legend' to have been percolating in people's imaginations for hundreds of years. And it is not just that the saga version is short. As it stands, this first part of the Sandhaugar episode, i.e., the counterpart to the national disaster that Grendel brought on the Danes, leaves some awkward questions unanswered. There is no explanation as to why these evil beings only strike at Christmas,[47] why they kidnap people but only take one person at a time, or what they actually do with their victims. The fact that when the troll-woman attacks Grettir she is armed with a long knife and carries a *trog*,[48] and the discovery of the bones of the two missing men in the giant's cave, would seem to indicate that the Sandhaugar trolls are cannibals like Grendel. But if that is indeed the case, it does not say much for their monstrous appetite that they strike only once a year and take one person at a time. Grettir's discovery of the bones in the cave also shows that their eating habits must be a good deal more sophisticated than those of Grendel's. If, on the other hand, we are not meant to think of the Sandhaugar trolls as cannibals, there is no explanation as to why they kidnap people. These uncertainties, which affect the very nucleus of the story, do not give the impression of a legend polished by centuries of oral transmission. The hints which the author drops are inconsistent, as if he has not fully formulated the story that he wants to tell. The blood by the front door would, for example, seem to suggest that someone was attacked and perhaps eaten on the spot, and the troll-woman's long knife and *trog* could create the same impression. But the bones in the cave point in the opposite direction, i.e., towards people being abducted live and in one piece and killed there.

Grettir's involvement does not add a great deal of knowledge about the Sandhaugar trolls, as the reader is never given any information beyond what little Grettir actually sees. They remain without a background, there is no attempt to develop them as characters, and there is nothing about them to suggest that they enter the story with the identifying marks of a long tradition. The troll-woman is big and is armed with a long knife (*skálm*), as troll-women in Icelandic lore commonly are.[49] The *trog* she carries is, however, a more interesting and unusual prop. In his introduction to *Beowulf*, Klaeber states his belief that the *trog* and Grendel's *glof* ('glove,' 'pouch'?) point to a connection between the two stories, as both articles serve the identical purpose of holding food,[50] but this comparison is somewhat misleading. Grendel obviously uses his glove to store and carry his victims, whereas the troll-woman's *trog* might be used as a cutting tray or a container in which to store food, but as a substitute for Grendel's 'rucksack' it will not do. The giant's entry into the story adds very little to what we know (or rather what we do not know); he is huge, black, and ugly, as giants in folklore are expected to be,[51] and like the troll-woman, but unlike Grendel, he uses weapons.

Critics who wish to equate the Sandhaugar pair with Grendel and his mother have usually chosen to ignore the fact that *Grettis saga* suggests no relationship of any kind between the giant and the troll-woman, although in recent years some scholars have seen a ray of hope in one of the kennings that Grettir uses to refer to the giant in a stanza (no. 61) that he composes about the battle against him in the cave. The epithet in question is *mellu vinr*, which literally means 'the troll-woman's friend.' The two main editors of *Grettis saga*, R.C. Boer and Guðni Jónsson, take this kenning to mean 'a giant' and read nothing else into it. It is therefore somewhat surprising to encounter the giant as the 'she-troll's ugly husband' in the translation of this stanza in *Beowulf and Its Analogues*.[52] Unfortunately, the translator does not explain how and when this match has come about. Another attempt to establish a relationship has been undertaken by Peter Jorgensen, who maintains that *mellu vinr* might be taken to mean 'a lover,' but the kennings for lovers that he points to as a basis for his reading are too far removed from *mellu vinr* to prove his point.[53]

The only thing that the Sandhaugar trolls really have in common with Grendel and his dam is the fact that they are male and female, and even that evidence comes with certain caveats. It must be kept in mind that, unlike in *Beowulf*, their sex is of no importance, and that in the saga they appear in the wrong order. Critics who have the imagination to see Grendel and his mother 'in all their monstrosity and superhuman powers' in the giant and the troll-woman of Sandhaugar[54] are only testifying to the might of Glámr's eyes.

Kárr the Old

Nothing but the art of finding the lowest common denominator through a play on words can make Kárr the Old resemble Grendel or his mother. Kárr is a ghost (one of the living dead) who lives in a gravemound on Háramarsey. According to the saga he has managed to increase the wealth and power of his son, Þorfinnr, by scaring other farmers off the island and making Þorfinnr the sole owner of all property there. Only those who enjoy Þorfinnr's favour are unmolested by Kárr's hauntings.[55] R.W. McConchie, who, as we have already seen, maintains that the story of Kárr the Old is a genetically related and neglected *Beowulf* analogue, readily admits that Kárr is quite unlike Grendel, and that the whole episode is relatively unimportant in the context of the saga. Instead he chooses to emphasize the similarity of events and how the two heroes react to them. McConchie suggests that the first of 'several points of similarity between Beowulf's struggle with Grendel's mother and Grettir's fight with Kárr' is the fact that both 'take place as a result of a series of violent haunt- ings.'[56] It is, of course, a matter of literary sensibility whether we see fit to equate a national disaster, like Grendel's reign of terror, and Kárr's spooking a few farmers away (he does not kill anyone) under the neat semantic umbrella of 'a series violent hauntings.' However, it is simply not true that Grettir tangles with Kárr as a result of his hauntings, as McConchie maintains. *Grettis saga* makes it quite clear that the hero's motive has nothing to do with cleansing the island of an evil being; Kárr has achieved his goal anyway, and there is nothing to be gained by his destruction except treasure. Like all others who break into gravemounds in the sagas, Grettir does so for precisely this reason.[57]

The Bear

A.R. Taylor and A. Margaret Arent, the first scholars to maintain that the bear episode was analogous and genetically related to *Beowulf*, saw nothing in the description of the brown bear that Grettir fights except a brown bear. Their readers were thus spared a detailed comparison of the nature and characteristics of the beast and Grendel. But is there no way of equating the two? Recently, Arthur A. Wachsler has attempted to do so and presents his case as follows:

According to Norse Lore, a man was said to possess a soul called a '*fylgja*' which could leave the body and reappear in the form of an animal. Indeed, the *fylgja* often shared the personality of its human partner. 'The animal *fylgja* often had some corresponding aspect to that of the character of its owner – bulls and bears attended great chiefs, foxes people of crafty nature.' Along with the bull, then, the bear, according to Norse tradition, was the spirit form of a great leader.

The supernatural and manlike qualities of the bear are attested also in the Norse belief in lycanthropy. Men who had the gift of shape-shifting frequently changed into animals, often appearing as bears as well as wolves ...

Besides the Scandinavians, other northern races held the bear in special esteem. The Lapps, Finns, Ostiaks and Voguls regarded the bear as the most holy of wild animals and held feasts in its honor. They considered the animal to be more intelligent and stronger than a man. One northern race, the Votiaks, believed that the bear could understand human speech. In addition, these people believed that the bear, if provoked enough, could return from the dead to punish its enemies. The awe in which the Votiaks held the bear was based no doubt on its ghostly nature, on its ability to return from the dead ...

The evidence in ancient northern lore suggests that the bear, along with more obvious examples, was considered to be a revenant, one of the *draugar* or animated dead. For that reason, the bear can be considered no less formidable and worthy an opponent than Glamr, the female troll at Sandhaugr and Kar the Old to all of whom the animal is related.[58]

Wachsler's method puts the cart squarely before the horse. Even if we accept all his findings at face value, it is still not easy to see how they lead to the desired conclusion. If there is a connection to be made between Scandinavian beliefs in *fylgjur*, or shape-shifting – which, as it happens, only affect living persons – and the Votiaks' belief that the bear could return from the dead, it certainly does not turn the brown bear in *Grettis saga* into a *draugr* on par with Glámr and Kárr, as Wachsler would like us to think. None of this has anything to do with the bear in *Grettis saga*, unless we are meant to think of the animal as someone's *fylgja*, a chief who has taken on the shape of a bear, or the ghost of the beast rather than an ordinary brown bear of flesh and blood.

Various other points that concern the bear episode, in addition to Grettir's fight against the beast and the descriptions of its lair, have been thought to show contact with *Beowulf*. There is, first of all, Taylor's contention that the character and actions of Bjǫrn, the obnoxious relative of Þorkell, mirror those of Unferð. Taylor based his comparison on their 'discourtesy towards guests and strangers,' which he found so strongly emphasized in the saga writer's portrait of Bjǫrn that he believed it to have been a 'characteristic of the prototype of the two men.'[59] However this comparison is not as simple as it looks. It is quite true that Unferð challenges Beowulf's credentials in the poem (lines 499–528), but it is by no means certain that he does so out of discourtesy or hostility. As

V/

Hroðgar's þyle ('spokesman'?), it may well be that he is merely carrying out his duties.[60] Later in the poem, Unferð appears as Beowulf's friend and lends him Hrunting – the famous hæftmece – to use against Grendel's mother. Although Bjǫrn and Unferð may both be jealous men, there are too many other factors that separate them in the poem and the saga to suggest that they go back to a common ancestor. In the first place, Bjǫrn has no official position at Þorkell's farm, and he has no skeletons in his closet like Unferð (who is guilty of fratricide). Secondly, Unferð makes no attempt to tangle with Grendel, whereas Bjǫrn tries to kill the bear. Finally, it must be kept in mind that Bjǫrn is eventually killed by Grettir. As Geoffrey Hughes has rightly observed, there is no character in Germanic literature with whom Unferð can be readily compared, and Bjǫrn is no better than previous candidates.[61]

Wachsler, however, thinks that he can detect echoes from 'the original stories' in the way in which Bjǫrn and his companions arouse the 'primal monster':

It is not unreasonable to suppose that Bjorn and his company drank to excess and celebrated by playing instruments, singing loudly and generally behaving as drunk men do. They 'lifted their voices' (*reysta*) causing a din (*háreysti*). And there is nothing to suggest the Danes in Heorot were any less boisterous than their Icelandic [*sic*] counterparts. They expressed their joy by celebrating loudly (drēam). During their noisy celebration, both groups, apparently, provoked their neighbors who in great anger retaliated by attacking their inconsiderate tormentors. In keeping with his Christian background, the *Beowulf* poet places Grendel in league with the kin of Cain. In contrast, the author of the saga, with his monstrous bear, remains squarely in the pagan world, and he is probably closer to the original stories. In each case, however, it is loud noises or the sounds of celebration which arouse a primal monster and cause it to attack those who have disturbed its peace.[62]

This may look convincing, but most of the analogous material that Wachsler claims to find in *Grettis saga* either is not there or is made to appear in a greatly emended form. In the saga Bjǫrn and his cronies are said to have loitered outside and to have made loud noises (74), but there is no mention of singing or drinking or other forms of celebration; nor are such activities normally practised outdoors in Scandinavia during the winter. It is a also a mere play on words to argue that both Grendel and the bear are 'roused' by noises, which cause them to attack, or to compare them as 'primal monsters.' Grendel is attracted – and presumably tormented – by the happy noises of celebration that he hears coming from Heorot every day; the brown bear is awoken from its hibernation and behaves as a hungry bear might be expected to do: it attacks sheep – anyone's sheep. Þorkell suffers more damage than other farmers simply because he is the wealthiest of the lot, as *Grettis saga* duly explains. To find in the brown bear episode of the saga essentially the same story line as in *Beowulf* can obviously be done, but only if we are prepared to emend both texts in the manner that Procrustes employed to make his visitors fit his infamous bed.

Grettir as a Monster

The hypothesis that Grettir has an alter ego as a monster was first suggested by Nora Chadwick in 1959, and has since become increasingly fashionable among *Beowulf* scholars. Chadwick's transformation of Grettir seems to have come about as a result of her failure to fit him into a theory that would make *Beowulf* and *Grettis saga* (along with several other texts in Old Norse) ritualistic repetitions of an ancient story, which supposedly involved 'a hereditary feud between a heroic member of a ruling Scandinavian dynasty and a closely knit group of supernatural foes [a *draugr*, an evil supernatural woman and a dragon], located to the east of the Baltic.'[63] Chadwick finds two of these foes in *Grettis saga*, but no trace of landscapes east of the Baltic or a dragon. As luck would have it, *Bjarnar saga Hítdælakappa* contains these missing elements, and that leads Chadwick to the following extraordinary conclusion:

It is strongly to be suspected that Grettir's adventures against monsters nowhere else associated with Iceland, but consistently located east of the Baltic in 'Bjarmaland,' have been derived by the author from traditions proper to Björn Hítdælakappi's Russian sojourn with King Cnut.[64]

What Chadwick omits to explain is why, if these traditions are indeed associated with Bjǫrn, they are not included in his saga? And where does this leave poor Grettir? Given a family tree with half-trolls and warlocks on its distant branches and with no immediate prospects of qualifying as 'a heroic member of a ruling Scandinavian dynasty,' his fate at Chadwick's hands is rather predictable. As she meditates on Grettir's name – which she believes to be unusual and sinister – his metamorphosis from a hero to a monster is a matter of smooth speculation:

Is it possible that the name itself carries with it a troll connotation? What is its origin? Can it be a Norse form derived from *grandi-*, and is the corresponding Anglo-Saxon form *Grend-il*? Is it possible that in origin Grendel and Grettir are identical, and that in the Norse story the monster has been transformed into the hero – that a story, originally told from the monster's point of view, has left traces on this strange and capricious, pitiful yet very sinister, outlaw?[65]

Nora Chadwick's ideas have been firmly opposed by Anatoly Liberman, who, as we have already seen, also rejects the notion that there could have been an Old English text in which Grendel's story was related from the monster's point of view. But is it possible that the names Grettir and Grendel are related through grandi-[66] or grenja ('to bellow'), as Margaret Arent has proposed?[67] Grettir's name is normally traced to grantian (i.e., related to words meaning 'to snarl' or 'to growl'), but it has also been argued that the name might not be of Norse origin and hence that it is uncertain what it means.[68] Liberman, who has discussed the possible etymologies of the names Grettir and Grendel in detail, sees no possibility of tracing their origin to the same root. His argument may be summarized as follows:

1 / Although the etymology of Grendel is debatable, the root grend is probably the umlauted form of *grand.

2 / Another Germanic root, gran-, is related to the root grant-, as in *grantjan, from which we have the verbs grenja and gretta, and eventually Grettir as a name.

3 / The relevant question is thus whether the roots *grand- and *grant- can be related, which they cannot be unless we can find a way of explaining the last consonant in each word: i.e., the d in *grand- and the t in *grant-. This was indeed attempted during the last century by Sophus Bugge, but his hypothesis was demolished by historical linguists a long time ago. In short, the bottom line is that *grand- and *grant- have to be taken to be two separate and unrelated etyma and, given that conclusion, there is no possibility of tracing the names of Grettir and Grendel to the same root.[69]

Arent and Chadwick have also used chthonic connotations, which they claim to be present in the names of Grettir and Grendel, as evidence to link them. It goes without saying, however, that in the final analysis the argument stands or falls on etymological evidence, and any speculation about common connotations, chthonic or otherwise, which critics may feel that they share, is simply irrelevant.[70] It may well be that Nora Chadwick's ideas represent 'the most daring questioning to date,' as Richard Harris has stated,[71] but there is not a shred of reasonable evidence to support her hypothesis concerning Grettir's monstrous origin.

As we saw in chapter 1, the fifth analogue that Harris claimed to have found in Grettis saga represents an attempt to develop Chadwick's ideas much further than she herself was prepared to do. Harris looks for textual evidence and finds that 'the death of Grettir resembles in at least eleven details the first part of Beowulf, particularly the fight at Grendel's Mere.'[72] Harris's evidence inevitably consists of sundry events and details that are extracted from the two texts. Apart from this, his approach to the two texts does not appear to follow any particular method, except to connect them at any cost.[73] Sometimes the order of these elements, as they originally appear in *Grettis saga* and *Beowulf*, seems to matter – and is kept; in other instances it must be re-shuffled to make a comparison.[74] But this is not the only liberty that Harris takes in the presentation of his evidence. There is also a tendency to 'emend' some of it in the process. Take points 2 and 3, for example:

Grettir has a hut on Drangey; nearness to the sea. Þorbjörn arrives at Drangey toward the end of the day.	Grendel has a waterfall cave, possibly near the sea. Beowulf takes most of day to reach bottom of mere.

Grendel has no waterfall cave like the giant at Sandhaugar; he has an underwater hall, and according to the poem it takes Beowulf *hwil dæges* (line 1495) – 'a good part of the day,' not most of it – to reach the bottom of the mere.

In the course of Harris's discussion these seemingly unrelated items are stitched together with literary exegesis of the kind that Isidore of Seville practised to perfection in the seventh century. Take point 4, for example:

Þorbjörn climbs a ladder to reach Grettir's hut.	Beowulf plunges into mere.

For the reader who is slow to see a connection between Þorbjǫrn's climbing a ladder to reach Grettir's hut, and Beowulf's plunging into the mere, Harris offers the following explication:

Þorbjörn climbs a ladder to reach Grettir's hut. Panzer's description of the Bear's Son Tale includes the motif of the hero climbing to a world, the Demon Kingdom, above or below the earth to confront the monster. Presumably an ascent would be involved where the opening in the earth, by which access is gained to the other world, is on a mountain or the top of a hill. The monster is reached only by descent elsewhere in *Beowulf* and *Grettis saga*. The necessity of climbing in the opposite direction doesn't seem to me to rule out the possibility of this being an element parallel to the climbing in the other episodes. The ladder would simply be a modification of the rope used by Grettir in the Háramarsey and Sandhaugar adventures.[75]

In *Grettis saga*, it is perfectly true that Grettir plays many and sometimes contradictory roles,[76] and in conclusion, I want to emphasize that I do not reject

Nora K. Chadwick's role reversal theory because I find it shocking that Grettir could be cast as a monster; I reject it because there is no reasonable evidence to support that particular role reversal for Grettir, and Harris's attempt to develop the original theory further changes nothing in that respect. In essence, Harris's fifth analogue shows Grettir to be a sheep-eating outlaw whose death, scene by scene, does not mirror that of Grendel, unless we are prepared to suspend common sense altogether in reviewing the evidence. However, Harris's argument is neither better nor worse than others that we have examined in this chapter from the hands of critics who would like to equate Beowulf and Grettir as heroes or their various adversaries as monsters. Undoubtedly, these arguments are inspired by academic climates that place a great value on critical imagination in literary analysis, but some issues – like the questions we have examined in this chapter – simply cannot be resolved on the basis of what critics would like to imagine. Having considered the ingredients that make up the heroes and the monsters in *Beowulf* and *Grettis saga*, I do not think there is convincing evidence to suggest a relationship between the two. As 'heroes' Grettir and Beowulf have little in common, and as 'monsters' their supernatural adversaries have even less.

3

The Hero's Fight against the Monsters

The five episodes in *Grettis saga* which have been claimed to be analogous and genetically related to *Beowulf* all contain battle scenes, and in all five the battle between the hero and his adversary is the climax of that episode. If there was indeed an old legend about a hero who overcame two monsters – a story that served as a common source for the authors of both *Beowulf* and *Grettis saga* – there is no reason why the form of the struggle, or parts of it, might not have survived intact, even if the original protagonists were no longer the same. An argument along these lines has been proposed by Guðni Jónsson, who in his edition of *Grettis saga* describes Grettir in his fight with the Sandhaugar trolls as a new player in an old role.[1] There is common agreement among critics who see a connection between *Beowulf* and *Grettis saga* that the 'old role' in both works included two fights against different monsters, and with that pattern in mind we can begin to look at the first fight in the poem and the saga.

Beowulf's Fight against Grendel

During the nineteenth century *Beowulf* scholars, German for the most part, tended to view the hero's battles with Grendel and his dam allegorically and therefore paid little attention to the actual details of the two battle scenes. But ever since Guðbrandur Vigfússon claimed that there was a genetic relationship between Beowulf's struggle with Grendel and the Sandhaugar and Glámr episodes, critics have analysed these combat scenes on the assumption that both authors were attempting to describe the battle in realistic terms. In the case of Beowulf's encounter with Grendel, there are some questions that remain unanswered, but the main outline of what takes place is fairly clear:

1 / Beowulf waits for Grendel to attack Heorot.
2 / When Grendel enters the hall in the night, Beowulf is awake and awaits him. He watches Grendel devour one of his retainers but does nothing to stop him.
3 / Grendel then reaches for Beowulf, who is lying down, with his hand. Beowulf seizes it – with one hand, apparently – and holds it firmly in his grip. Grendel struggles to get out of Beowulf's hand-grip, and in the course of their struggle Heorot is damaged.
4 / Beowulf's retainers hack at Grendel with their swords but to no avail.
5 / Beowulf tears Grendel's arm off, and the monster flees, leaving a trail of blood.
6 / Grendel's arm is kept as a trophy, and he is presumed to be mortally wounded.

There is some very strange stuff in this description. Take, for instance, the question as to why the hero, while waiting for Grendel, lies calmly on his bed while one of his men (Hondscioh) is eaten by the monster. The motif of waiting does indeed occur in the Sandhaugar and Glámr episodes of *Grettis saga*, and it also occurs in *Þorsteins þáttr uxafóts* and in *Þórodds þáttr Snorrasonar*, but the part of the scene that has the hero watch the monster eat one of his followers as a preamble to battle has no counterpart in Icelandic literature. Fr. Klaeber believes that the attack on Hondscioh was inserted into the original story by the author of *Beowulf*, but the only evidence that such an interpolation actually took place is Klaeber's faith in the above-mentioned episodes from *Grettis saga* as proof that there was indeed a literary ancestor.[2] But even if we accept that *Grettis saga* preserves the original story by making the hero fight the monster unaided, there are still some very important differences between the first fight in *Beowulf* and any of the genetically related analogues that critics claim to have found in *Grettis saga*. For the most part, these differences concern the actual form that the fight takes, the manner in which victory is achieved, and the aftermath of the battle.

Let us first consider the manner of fighting. In *Beowulf* the hero 'wrestles' with Grendel, and in *Grettis saga* the hero also 'wrestles' with a troll-woman and with Glámr, but these fights in the saga and the poem have little in common, although the same word is often used to apply to both in English.[3] In *Beowulf* it is not certain whether the fight begins with the hero sitting up, leaning on his own arm and then proceeding to fight the monster's hand, or whether he grasps Grendel's hand straightaway,[4] but what happens during the rest of the struggle is something like this: As soon as Beowulf has locked the monster's hand in the grip of his own hand, Grendel seeks to pull himself free with the well-known result that his entire arm is torn off. In other words, it is the hero's (one) hand that fights the monster's hand, and the poem offers no suggestion that Beowulf uses his free hand or his feet in the ensuing struggle with Grendel.[5]

This unusual method of fighting is the essential feature of the whole battle scene at Heorot, and it dictates what the hero must do in order to succeed, namely, tear the monster's arm off. It leaves Beowulf and Hroðgar's court in possession of Grendel's arm as a trophy, which in turn leads to his mother's visit to collect it and to Beowulf's subsequent battle with her at the mere. Thus everything in this account hangs together, and everything comes down to the fate of Grendel's hand or arm as an instrument of fighting and an instrument of his own fate and the fate of Hroðgar's court, as has been amply demonstrated by a number of studies.[6] Critics who view this battle scene simply as one in which 'a monster loses an arm' and readily equate it with Grettir's fight at Sandhaugar are obviously prepared to ignore the logic behind this chain of events. As we shall soon see, the fact that Grettir cuts the troll-woman's arm off is only a means of disposing of her; it has no integral relationship with their battle or later developments in the saga.

Grettir's Fight with the Troll-Woman at Sandhaugar[7]

As we saw in chapter 1, various critics have sought to account for some of the most obvious differences between this episode and Beowulf's fight with Grendel. Efforts of this kind have explained why Grettir fights with the female before the male, noted the saga author's omission to relate the two trolls and lamented his failure to motivate Grettir's visit to the giant's cave by anything other than mere curiosity. The two different versions that the saga offers of the troll-woman's fate,[8] both without much similarity to that of Grendel, seem also to have been discussed and settled to the satisfaction of most scholars.[9] Our concern at the moment, however, is not with these so-called textual corruptions of the poem and the saga, but rather with Grettir's fight with the troll-woman. What happens between them may be summarized as follows:

1 / She enters the farm house carrying a long knife and a *trog* and goes straight to Grettir's bed to attack him. He jumps up to meet the attack.
2 / The troll-woman pulls him out of the farm house, and having done great damage to it, they find themselves outside wearing the frame for the front door around their shoulders.
3 / Grettir feels exhausted but realizes that if he cannot do better than this, she will succeed in tossing him into the ravine.
4 / The troll-woman has so far held Grettir tightly to herself, making it impossible for him to use either of his hands, as he can only clasp his arms around her waist.

5 / As they reach the edge of the chasm, Grettir gives the ogress a swing, frees his right hand, grabs his short-sword, and cuts off her right arm. Whichever version of the saga we choose to follow, this leads to her death and disappearance from the story.

Aside from the manner of fighting as compared to the Grendel fight, three other differences may be noted. In the first place, the troll-woman's arm plays no special role, either in the fight itself, or as a trophy, or in Grettir's later encounter with the giant. Secondly, she is portrayed as being stronger than the hero. We see this from the fact that she is on the offensive until the final moment of the fight, and that she, rather than Grendel, decides how the battle is fought. As Martin Puhvel has observed, the troll-woman, like Grendel, is struggling to get out of the building, but for an entirely different reason: she is not trying to escape; she wants to throw Grettir into the ravine;[10] and it is luck rather than strength which brings Grettir victory. From a different point view, we need only examine what prospects of victory the authors of the poem and the saga assign to their respective heroes to confirm this. In Beowulf's fight against Grendel there is no element of suspense; the poet drops hints to his audience from the first moment of the battle, and then at regular intervals while it lasts, to indicate that his hero will prove victorious.[11] By contrast, the author of *Grettis saga* invites the reader to expect that Grettir may lose: the troll-woman is stronger than Grettir, stronger than any being that Grettir has ever fought, and he can see that he is about to be defeated, etc.[12]

The third point of difference concerns the hero's use or non-use of weapons – the fact that Beowulf fights Grendel barehanded, whereas Grettir uses his sword against the troll-woman. The usual way to account for this is to point out that Grendel is gifted with magic powers that make swords useless against him, whereas the troll-woman has no such powers or protection. Another possibility has been suggested by Larry Benson in his article 'The Originality of *Beowulf.*' Benson argues that in the first fight of the common original, the hero has to grapple with a monster who tries to drag him from a hall. Consequently, the hero must be a proficient at wrestling. Beowulf, according to Benson, evidently does 'not have previous experience as a wrestler, since he makes quite a point of facing Grendel without his usual weapons (a point that Grettir, who has already demonstrated his skill at wrestling, need not make).'[13]

This theory may well work for Beowulf as a hero but for Grettir it will not do. The fight against the troll-woman demonstrates to Grettir (and to the reader) that, for all his prowess at wrestling, there are beings out there who are stronger than he and who must be defeated with the aid of a good weapon. The supposed common original hardly made much of that point in respect to the hero. Furthermore, Benson's argument ignores a very simple pattern of poetic justice which the author of the saga follows in Grettir's dealings with Glámr and the Sandhaugar trolls:

- Glámr likes to break the backs of men and beasts. He meets his own death lying on his back with Grettir on top.
- The troll-woman arrives armed with meat-processing instruments and presumably intends to go to work on Grettir. He carves her arm off.
- The giant reaches for a sword to use against Grettir, who promptly kills him with a sword.[14]

Here the comparison with *Beowulf* does not contribute much to our understanding of *Grettis saga*.

Grettir's Fight with Glámr

Grettir's fight with Glámr may be divided into the following stages in the saga:

1 / Glámr enters the farm house, his head towering up to the rafters, and notices that something is lying on a bench covered by a cloak. He pulls at the cloak so hard that Grettir, who is hiding underneath it, is pulled up from the bench. Between them, they rip the cloak apart.
2 / Grettir leaps under Glámr's arms, grasps him around the waist, and clasps him as hard as he can, but Glámr grips Grettir's arms so tightly that he is forced to break away.
3 / Glámr now seeks to drag Grettir out of the hall, but it is clear to Grettir that it will be worse to deal with the fiend once they are outside, so he resists all he can. As they struggle, they break everything in their way.
4 / Glámr pulls Grettir to the vestibule of the hall, and Grettir realizes that he cannot resist any longer. He puts his feet against a half-sunken boulder and throws all his weight against Glámr, who is pulling in the same direction. Glámr falls out of the door and lands on his back with Grettir on top.
5 / Glámr meserizes Grettir with his eyes and utters his curse. Grettir comes to, cuts Glámr's head off, and places it against his buttocks.[15]

Some critics have been reluctant to accept this account as a *bona fide* genetically related analogue to *Beowulf*. R.W. Chambers, for example, eventually rejected it on the grounds that *Grettis saga* offered no sequel to Grettir's fight with Glámr.[16] In his edition of the saga, Guðni Jónsson makes no attempt to relate this fight to Beowulf's tangle with Grendel, but unlike Chambers he does not do so for structural reasons. Jónsson seems to think that there is a kernel of truth to the Glámr episode; that it somehow relates to an event that actually took place in Grettir's life.[17] Others have objected because they have failed to find much in Grettir's fight with Glámr that compares with the Grendel fight in *Beowulf*. As we have just seen, Grettir fights alone, the only tug of war is over a cloak (the actual wrestling part is entirely different from Beowulf's fight with Grendel), Grettir is weaker than Glámr, and uses a trick to beat him.[18]

These two fights in the poem and the saga may also be compared according to their relevance *per se* to each work, and in terms of how victorious each hero actually is. The Glámr fight in *Grettis saga* is indisputably the climax of the story and a turning point in Grettir's life, but it is hardly an event of national importance. Furthermore, it is a Pyrrhic victory. Grettir defeats the demon but loses to the forces of darkness, which will haunt him for the rest of his life as a consequence of Glámr's curse. In *Beowulf*, the hero's victory over Grendel is a career move and no climax, although it affects the fate of an entire nation; and it is an absolute victory, although it leads to the hero's discovery of another evil being that also must be defeated.

Some *Beowulf* scholars have been much less fastidious than Chambers with regard to the absence of a sequel in the Glámr episode. They accept that the 'old legend' probably contained an account of two fights against monsters, and that each story – or even fragments of each of them – might have survived independently. Armed with this conviction, these critics have looked at the Glámr fight and found what they wanted to find. A century ago John Earle concluded that the circumstances of Grettir's encounter with Glámr were 'full of parallels' with the Grendel fight,[19] and some later commentators have found themselves in agreement with him.[20] In the literature on the subject, the number of parallels that I have been able to find is rather smaller than Earle's pronouncement would lead one to think – five to be exact – and there is much to be imagined and explained before they fit the circumstances of Beowulf's battle with Grendel:

1 / We are asked to accept that the tug of war over the cloak is a distant echo of the tearing off of Grendel's arm.
2 / The destruction of the farmhouse during the battle is to be read as equivalent to the damage of Heorot.
3 / Grettir's moment of weakness when he is sitting on top of Glámr is a parallel to Beowulf's brief 'lapse' in the battle with Grendel's mother.
4 / The ugly, flame-like light that shines from Grendel's eyes (lines 726b–7) is the same as the evil stare of the ghost.
5 / Glámr's curse relates to Grendel's descent from Cain and to the curse of Cain.

"whippletree"

The matter of the curse was discussed in chapter 2 in connection with Glámr's nature, but the other four items merit further attention. As early as the 1920s, Heinz Dehmer showed that the tug of war over the cloak in *Grettis saga* matches a similar scene in *Hávarðar saga Ísfirðings* and is quite common in later Icelandic folktales.[21] Dehmer believes that in the Glámr episode Grettir hides underneath the cloak as a means of protection against the evil powers of the demon, whereas the tug of war part is a traditional first test of strength (Old Norse *skinnleikr*, which literally means 'a game involving a hide') in a fight between two parties. If Dehmer is right, it is very hard to imagine that these two uses of the cloak in the saga have much to do with Grendel's arm. In his study, Dehmer also looked for examples of damage to houses as a result of fights in the Icelandic sagas and found the motif to be fairly commonplace. It occurs in sagas that describe a ghost fight, a fight against a bear, and ordinary fights between men of flesh and blood.[22] There is, in other words, no reason to think that this aspect of the fight relates *Beowulf* to *Grettis saga* any more than to other Icelandic stories in which the same motif occurs.

Grettir's inability to draw his sword and kill Glámr has been linked to *Beowulf* from two very different angles. Peter Jorgensen maintains that there is a connection between *Beowulf* and *Grettis saga* through what he calls 'the useless sword motif,' which supposedly originated in a legend where the sword is the gift of a king whose court is plagued by an ogre. Hrunting, the sword that fails Beowulf against Grendel's mother, goes back to this 'original version,' according to Jorgensen, and 'another remnant of the useless weapon, realized as the sword which can't be drawn, may occur in Grettir's battle with Glámr.'[23] The validity of Jorgensen's 'useless sword' theory is beyond the scope of this discussion, but as it relates to *Grettis saga*, suffice it to say that Grettir's shortsword is drawn and turns out to be a very useful weapon indeed against Glámr. Furthermore, the saga attributes the hero's faintness to a combination of his exhaustion after the struggle and the effect on him of Glámr's evil stare,[24] so in his speculation Jorgensen is simply asking us to brush the text aside.

Commenting on the same moment of suspense in the hero's fight with Glámr, Martin Puhvel wonders aloud whether 'Grettir's fateful faintness from the gaze of Glám's baleful eyes may recall Beowulf's startling weakness in his grapple with Grendel's Mother.' 'Is this coincidence,' Puhvel asks, 'or an instance of a confused, muddled connection?'[25] The parallel that Puhvel proposes is a new one, but the methodology on which it rests is not. It has indeed been argued before that 'the old legend' exploded into tiny fragments which scattered all over Icelandic literature, and the various ideas that this thesis has spawned stand or fall on the basis of the approach itself. What we are really dealing with in respect to Puhvel's 'muddled connection' is a theory concerning the transmission of literary motifs from one country to another, and that aspect of the question of affinity between the poem and the saga is not our concern at the moment but will be in a later chapter.[26]

Finally, there is the issue of the frightening eyes of Glámr and Grendel. Margaret Goldsmith, who accepts the Glámr episode as 'the closest analogue we have to the scene of the wrestling in Heorot,' explains the relationship between the two in this way:

> it is a fair inference that the adversary's gleaming eyes were a traditional feature of the story, which each author has fitted to the surroundings, the eyes of the *draugr* reflecting the moonlight, the eyes of the giant glinting red in the glow of the fire so that they seem to emit flame. We have no means of knowing at what stage in the transmission of the story the detail of the frightening eyes appeared; it is quite conceivable that it had become a commonplace of horrifying tales.[27]

Of course the eyes of Grendel and Glámr are frightening, but that is hardly surprising since everything else about these creatures is frightening as well. The important issue is how and why their eyes are frightening and whether the answers to these questions suggest a common ancestor. Goldsmith's idea that the common denominator in both stories is the reflection of light – moonlight in the case of Glámr, a fire burning in the hall in the case of Grendel – has no support in either text. *Grettis saga* does not tell us that Grettir became frightened because he could see the moon reflected in Glámr's eyes; on the contrary, it suggests that he was struck with fear because the moonlight enabled him to perceive the evil stare of the ghost. (Here Goldsmith seems to forget the role that Glámr's eyes are made to play, in the sense that they are his ultimate weapon in the fight against Grettir.) As for the theory that 'the glow of the fire' made Grendel's eyes 'seem to emit flame,' we first have to imagine that there is in fact a fire burning in Heorot on the night of his attack, because the text of the poem does not mention it. I do not see much point in rationalizing the ugly light which shines from Grendel's eyes in this fashion, unless one wants to rationalize everything else about him as a monster. The flame-like light is more likely to be a reminder of his hellish origin,[28] and at the same time a useful prop, because it lights up the field of battle in Hroðgar's presumably darkened palace.

The basic question thus remains unanswered: how and why would the eyes of the monster have been frightening in the original story? In the descriptions of Glámr and Grendel I cannot see anything that gives us much of a clue in reconstructing this aspect in the monstrous make-up of their supposed common ancestor.

Other First Fight Analogues in *Grettis saga*

Two other fight descriptions in *Grettis saga* have been claimed to be partly related to Beowulf's battle with Grendel. These involve Grettir as a hero in the scene where he kills the brown bear and as a monster in the Drangey episode, when he is killed by Þorbjǫrn ǫngull. In Grettir's fight with the brown bear the following items have been offered as evidence of its relationship to Beowulf's contest with Grendel:

- The bear wards off spear thrusts and is hard to get at, and these two features compare with Grendel's invulnerability to weapons.
- Grettir's wrestling match with the animal is reminiscent of Beowulf's battle with Grendel.
- The cutting off of the paw and use of it as evidence or a trophy parallels what is done with Grendel's arm in Heorot.
- The hero is deserted by his companions both in the bear episode and at the mere.[29]

In the Drangey analogue, two items from Richard Harris's list are said to correspond to battle descriptions in *Beowulf:*

6 / Grettir previously disabled.	Beowulf wounds Grendel mortally in Heorot – dead in cave.
7 / Grettir loses his hand posthumously.	Beowulf tears off Grendel's arm.

It complicates any discussion of these points that they have been submitted by four critics who view the issue of what constitutes analogous and genetically related material in *Grettis saga* from somewhat different premises. Thus Arnold Taylor and Richard Harris, who also allow for role reversals, think it permissible to search for matching if unconnected details, A. Margaret Arent sees Grendel and the dragon appearing in the brown bear in a recombined form, and Arthur Wachsler stresses similarity in what he calls 'essential plot and major themes.' But it is not by what tricks of literary imagination these observations have come about that really matters; what these scholars have in common is that they have all set out to seek further evidence for a relationship which they already believe to have been established beyond any shadow of a doubt.

In the comparison concerning the brown bear there is little new. Two of the points of comparison are variations of similar items from the Sandhaugar and Glámr fights, and the other two (the bear's invulnerability and the desertion of Grettir by his companions) are simply not in accordance with the text of the saga. In Harris's case the point has already been made that his findings cannot be isolated from the method that he uses to obtain them, and for the purpose of this discussion his comparisons are much too general. Grettir's leg wound is thus equated with Grendel's loss of his arm, and in the next item Grettir's cut-off hand becomes a variation of his previous wound.

Beowulf's Fight with Grendel's Mother

I have already discussed the various links which the second monster fight has with the first one in the poem, and it is worth emphasizing that in the two fights in *Grettis saga* that have been considered as possible genetically related analogues, no elements of continuity are present. This is not, of course, to say that the second fight in *Beowulf* proceeds predictably in all respects in comparison to the first. It comes as a surprise, for instance, that Beowulf should arm himself at the mere, although he knows that Grendel has proved invulnerable to (ordinary?) weapons, and, contrary to all expectation, Grendel's mother turns out to be a far more dangerous opponent than her son. Finally, it is to be noted that whereas the first battle is rather simple and unexciting in its format, the second contains a number of different stages in which the fortunes of the combatants are reversed:

1 / Beowulf dives into the mere. Grendel's mother grabs him, tries to stab him with her (steel-tipped?) fingers and drags him to the bottom.

2 / The monster carries Beowulf, who cannot wield his weapons, into her underwater hall. Sea monsters attack him in the process.

3 / Inside the hall Beowulf is suddenly free. (The poem does not tell us how this comes about, but it is as though Grendel's mother carries him to her water-free den and then releases her grip on him.) Beowulf can now draw Hrunting, and he strikes at her head. The famous sword will not penetrate, and Beowulf throws it away.

4 / Beowulf then seizes Grendel's mother by the hair and pulls her to the floor.

5 / She clutches at him, and Beowulf falls.

6 / The ogre sets upon Beowulf and tries to stab him with a knife.[30] Beowulf's coat of mail and God protect him.

7 / Beowulf somehow gets up again.[31] He sees a sword belonging to Grendel's mother, grabs it and swings at her neck with it, and (we assume) cuts her head off.

8 / Beowulf notices Grendel's dead body and cuts his head off as well.[32] The blade of the giant sword begins to melt.

9 / The mere becomes stained with blood. The Danes leave, but Beowulf's

retainers keep to their station, although they do not expect to see their lord again.

10 / Beowulf sees many treasures in the cave but returns to the surface with only Grendel's head and the hilt of the giant sword.[33]

In a recent article, Ward Parks has compared the behaviour of Grendel and his mother in their respective battles and finds it strangely different. He sees Grendel's reaction in his fight with Beowulf as characteristic 'of a predator suddenly meeting up against more than he has reckoned on,' as opposed to the second fight, which 'proceeds much as a battle of champions ... a single combat on fairly equal terms,' marked by the internal symmetry of the action.[34] Critics who have tried to reconcile the second fight with Grettir's battle against the giant at Sandhaugar would probably be reluctant to subscribe to Parks's analysis of it. Both R.W. Chambers and Fr. Klaeber were unhappy about the inglorious manner in which Beowulf enters the underwater hall, and both sought to explain it away. Chambers put it down to inconsistencies in the poem:

We may note the further inconsistency that Beowulf is seized by Grendel's mother in the water and carried powerless to her den: when he reaches the den, the words used seem to imply that he perceives Grendel's mother and attacks her, as if he had entered free.[35]

But Chambers does not specify what vocabulary he has in mind, and there is nothing in lines 1512b–20 that readily supports his idea. He is merely looking at the poem through the spectacles of the Sandhaugar analogue, and Klaeber's proposed solution is an even better example of where too much faith in a genetically related analogue can lead us:

In the *Grettissaga* the hero straightaway enters the cave to fight the monster; in the *Samsonssaga* the hero is seized by the troll-woman in the water and dragged by her to the bottom. This dual conception, possibly, is responsible for the lack of clearness in *Beowulf.*[36]

Klaeber does not care to elaborate on this cryptic explanation, which may be interpreted in two different ways: (a) the old legend had a hero who was both seized by the monster and also entered his or her cave freely. Later Icelandic authors had the good fortune to inherit this schizophrenic account in separate parts, which surface in the two different sagas, whereas the poor *Beowulf* poet was stuck with a contradictory description of the hero's entry into battle and could only respond to the tyranny of the original story by obfuscating this part of it as best he could. Or (b) *Grettis saga* inherited its version of events from one 'old legend' (descended from the original story) and *Samssons saga* from another, in which case there was a confused ur-story that influenced *Beowulf,* or the author knew two conflicting versions of the 'old legend' and tried to combine them for some reason.

Critics who lament inconsistencies or lack of clearness in this part of *Beowulf* are hardly going to find much consolation in this theory of Klaeber's.

Grettir's Fight with Kárr the Old

R.W. McConchie, who believes that Kárr the Old has been grossly neglected in the discussion of analogous and genetically related material in *Grettis saga,* maintains that the following aspects of Grettir's fight with the gravemound ghost in Norway are comparable with Beowulf's struggle against Grendel's mother:

1 / Despite the extraordinary powers and skill of the hero, his companions do not believe that he can succeed.
2 / The place of combat is reached by a solitary descent, leaving a companion or companions behind.
3 / There is a hand to hand combat between the hero and the monster in which the hero comes close to defeat.
4 / In both instances there is a decapitation.
5 / The hero is deserted by his companions, who believe that he is dead.
6 / There is a splendid sword found in the place of combat, and the hero recovers some kind of treasure.[37]

This list of items is obviously not an actual comparison of two events. It is simply an abstract which may be said to fit a very broad summary of two different stories. As soon as we go beyond generalities, misrepresentations, and plays on words, the so-called analogous and genetically related material evaporates into thin air. There is, for instance, not a word of doubt uttered by Beowulf's followers before he sets out to fight Grendel's mother; Grettir's lowering himself into a gravemound and Beowulf's jumping into the mere become their 'solitary descent'; Grettir is, as it happens, never 'close to defeat' in his battle with Kárr; it is not Grendel's mother who is decapitated after the battle; Beowulf is not deserted by his retainers, and the giant sword does not become his special weapon, in contrast with the splendid short-sword that Grettir recovers. Add to this list the fact that Grettir enters the gravemound to look for treasure and that no land-cleansing comparable to the killing of the monsters in *Beowulf* takes place, and what is there left to compare?

Neither McConchie nor Taylor before him seem to have realized that the Kárr episode in *Grettis saga* follows a very traditional pattern of describing an entry into a gravemound:

- A ghost in a burial place is also found in *Andra saga, Harðar saga*, and *Hrómundar saga*.
- Descent by means of a rope into a cave or a gravemound of a ghost or a dragon takes place in *Játmundar saga, Andra saga, Gull-Þóris saga, Harðar saga*, and *Hrómundar saga*.
- Odour or preternatural stench is described in *Andra saga, Gests þáttur, Harðar saga, Hrómundar saga*, and *Orkneyinga saga*.
- The fight with the dragon or the ghost is delayed in *Gull-Þóris saga, Gests þáttur, Harðar saga*, and *Hrómundar saga*.
- A light is there in *Gull-Þóris saga* and *Harðar saga*.
- A sword is discovered in *Andra saga, Gull-Þóris saga, Harðar saga*, and *Hrómundar saga*.
- The hero is abandoned in *Játmundar saga* and *Harðar saga*.[38]

This episode is not simply traditional; it also resembles the second half of Grettir's Sandhaugar adventure in containing a descent, a rope, and a watchman who is frightened off. It has been argued that the story of Kárr the Old is merely a copy of the Sandhaugar episode in which the din from the gravemound substitutes for the blood on the water of a proper Beowulfian tale,[39] but given the traditional nature of gravemound entries, it is more likely that the relationship between the two is precisely the reverse.

Grettir's Fight with the Giant at Sandhaugar

Even before Kárr the Old, the brown bear, and the Drangey analogues were entered into the debate over the relationship between *Beowulf* and *Grettis saga*, there was always some confusion as to what to compare to what. Those critics who accepted the Glámr fight as genetically related and comparable to Beowulf's struggle against Grendel faced a bit of a dilemma in dealing with Grettir's two fights at Sandhaugar. Most chose to regard the Glámr and the troll-woman fights as variants of the first fight in *Beowulf,* but some wanted to include both the troll-woman and the giant in the comparison with Beowulf's fight with Grendel's dam.[40] A third solution has been proposed by Nora K. Chadwick, who equates Grendel and Glámr, and also Grendel's mother and the troll-woman, who is Glámr's mother in Chadwick's theory. Accordingly, Grettir's killing of the giant in the cave is 'the quietus of the *draugr* Glámr, and, as in *Beowulf*, the final episode.'[41]

Before we look at the actual contest between Grettir and the giant, it will be interesting to compare the nature of the hero's mission at Sandhaugar to that of Beowulf in Heorot. The poem tells us very clearly that Beowulf makes his journey from Geatland to Denmark for the express purpose of cleansing Hroðgar's land of a single monster.[42] A second monster is discovered, and dealt with, only because of circumstances that arise in the wake of the killing of the first. It has been argued that *Grettis saga* matches the poem on this point, i.e., that Grettir knows nothing of a second monster when he sets out to explore the cave behind the waterfall.[43] This is not so. In his introduction to the Sandhaugar episode the saga author informs his readers that the region was known to be haunted by trolls, and this information is given before anyone is reported to have disappeared from the farm.[44] Since it is public knowledge that there is more than one troll about, we must assume that Grettir knows this as well and is not surprised by the discovery of a second troll, although his reason for wanting to explore the cave is not to look for one. Grettir's unwillingness to dive into the waterfall with a rope tied around him, and the fact that he carries his sword with him, also suggest that he expects to have to fight with someone in the course of his exploration.

The actual battle between Grettir and the giant is an extremely simple and straightforward affair:

1 / A rope is let down into the ravine for Grettir to make his way back, and Steinn, the priest, is instructed to look after it.
2 / Grettir dives underneath the waterfall and scales the cliff behind it until he reaches a cave.
3 / Grettir enters the cave and sees a giant sitting on a chair by a fire. The giant grabs his *heptisax*[45] and strikes a blow at Grettir.
4 / Grettir meets the blow with his short-sword and cuts the handle of the giant's weapon apart.
5 / The giant reaches for a sword that is hanging on the wall in the cave, but before he can reach it, Grettir cuts his chest and belly open with a blow and continues striking at the giant until he is dead.
6 / The priest sees blood on the water and runs off. Grettir climbs up the rope unaided with the bones of the missing men and treasure from the cave.
7 / Grettir leaves the bones and a rune staff, on which two verses that describe his adventure are carved, on the porch of the local church.

Those who have compared this battle description to Beowulf's adventure at the mere have been forced to note two obvious differences.[46] In the first place, there is Grettir's motivation: he is convinced that the missing men have been taken into the ravine, but the priest Steinn has his doubts. The only reason Grettir undertakes his mission is to prove the priest wrong. That this is one of the many 'latter [sic] alterations in the tale,' as W.W. Lawrence argues in making his comparison,[47] is pure speculation. Secondly, there is the complete lack of proper introduction of the giant as Grettir's adversary, and, perhaps not surprisingly, the embarrassingly short and simple account of the actual battle: the giant goes to attack the hero; the hero is faster and kills him; end of story. In addition, the saga relates this unexciting battle scene in a strangely casual manner; in fact, it reads much like a short newspaper article. There is little drama in the account, and the reader is never in doubt about the outcome of the fight. In short, it goes without saying that it takes no small amount of imagination to equate this part of the Sandhaugar episode with Grendel's mother and her fight with Beowulf at the mere.

The manner in which the giant meets his death is also of some interest. Like Grendel's dam, he is killed with a sword. But to argue, as one analogue enthusiast has done, that the two are stabbed to death 'in more or less the same way' is stretching the truth a bit too far.[48] Then there is the matter of the giant's weapon, the *heptisax*. It would undeniably strengthen the analogy with Hrunting, Beowulf's *hæftmece*, if it were Grettir and not the giant who wielded the weapon. In an effort to get past this obstacle, Peter A. Jorgensen has proposed an emendation of the stanza in which the giant's weapon is named by combining readings from the three extant vellum manuscripts of *Grettis saga*. His emendation would change the traditional reading of the lines in question from 'I cut the shaft of his *heptisax*' to 'I caused the *heptisax* to chop the hard edges from the shaft.'[49] This editorial 'improvement' of the saga text has not, however, met with everyone's approval. Anatoly Liberman, in particular, has been critical of Jorgensen's methods:

He views the extant variants of the verses as attempts to change the meaning of a text that was no longer understood. It is likely, says he, 'that scribes intentionally made changes in the verses, for the word heptisax had obviously become archaic by the saga-writing period, making it almost impossible for a familiar, beloved Icelandic hero to brandish a mysterious weapon no one had even seen or heard of' (1973.58–59). The emendation is Jorgensen's, but the idea behind it belongs to York Powell (1900.413, Note 2); Powell also thought that 'the Beowulf sword incident ... was probably difficult to reconcile with what was known of Grettir and his weapons.' Neither the emendation nor the idea of an incongruous weapon is supported by weighty arguments. Emending three texts in order to obtain a satisfactory version is hardly a tenable procedure, and, as far as a difficult word is concerned, Icelanders would certainly have forgiven the saga-man a touch of antiquarian spirit.[50]

Let us now proceed from the question of weapons to look at Grettir's return from battle. Critics who view the Sandhaugar episode as a genetically related analogue to *Beowulf* have uniformly endorsed the idea that the blood on the water and the cowardly priest correspond to the bloodstained mere and the Danes who choose to leave in the poem. There is no question that blood and gore on the water, misinterpreted to signal the death of the hero, is a motif that *Grettis saga* shares with *Beowulf*, but does this have to indicate a special relationship between the two works? J. Michael Stitt points out that this motif has its roots in Indo-European dragonslayer tales (a passage of the *Ramayana* and the Vedic account of Indra's battle with Vrtra),[51] and there no reason to assume that its only occurrence in Northern Europe was limited to a common ancestor of *Beowulf* and *Grettis saga*.[52]

The matter of desertion is a great deal more complicated, as R.W. Chambers readily admits:

> it is true that the departure of the Danes homeward because they believe that Beowulf has met his death in the water below, bears only the remotest resemblance to the deliberate treachery which the companions in the folktale [i.e., the Bear's Son Tale] mete out to the hero. But when we compare the *Grettir*-story, we see there that a real breach of trust is involved, for there the priest Stein leaves the hero in the lurch, and abandons the rope by which he should have drawn Grettir up. This can hardly be an innovation on the part of the composer of the *Grettis saga*, for he is quite well disposed towards Stein, and has no motive for wantonly attributing treachery to him. The innovation presumably lies in the *Beowulf*-story, where Hrothgar and his court are depicted in such a friendly spirit that no disreputable act can be attributed to them, and consequently Hrothgar's departure home must not be allowed in any way to imperil or inconvenience the hero. A comparison of the *Beowulf*-story with the *Grettir*-story leads then to the conclusion that in the oldest version those who remained above when the hero plunged below *were* guilty of some measure of disloyalty in ceasing to watch for him. In other words we see that the further we track the *Beowulf*-story back, the more it comes to resemble the folk-tale.[53]

Chambers is right. There is no treachery involved in the Danes' leaving the mere, but nor is there in Steinn's leaving the rope in *Grettis saga*. He does not purposely 'betray' Grettir by any stretch of the imagination; he merely makes a mistake by wrongly assuming that the hero is dead. Grettir, who is not the sort of person to leave treachery against him unpunished, later reminds the priest that he was slack in his rope-watching duties. Steinn admits to his shortcomings, and with that the matter is over. In other words, the folktale desertion motif that Chambers would like to see in *Grettis saga* is not really there. Consequently, the idea that the *Beowulf* poet had to deviate from an original story,

which prescribed desertion at this point in the chain of events because of defer-
ence to Hroðgar and his court, is quite simply ridiculous. In his desire to find a
folktale origin for the poem, Chambers commits the intentional fallacy of pre-
suming to know both the original story and why the *Beowulf* author decided to
change it. Hroðgar and his court have known nothing but cowardice and humil-
iation for twelve years; would one more instance have made much difference?

Finally, we can compare how success in the second battle benefits the two
heroes and how they perceive it. To Beowulf, the victory over Grendel's mother
is, strangely enough, not the zenith of his career; the contest with Grendel is. In
preparing to meet the dragon, he wishes that he might fight it as he fought Grendel in the old days (line 2521). As Larry D. Benson has put it, he 'seems aware
that his entire life has been a falling off from that one moment of triumph.'[54]
Still, the aftermath of the second fight brings Beowulf all the recognition and
treasure that a hero can desire. By contrast, the Sandhaugar fights do not do
much for Grettir, except to grant him a temporary refuge. The killing of either the
troll-woman or the giant brings Grettir no glory that he has not already achieved.

At the beginning of this chapter we set out to examine whether the form of the
two monster battles, or even parts of their form, might have survived intact in
Grettis saga. In the course of this examination we have seen that there are
indeed certain specifics that some of the proposed genetically related analogues
share with *Beowulf*. Both texts include, for instance, male and female adversaries, an arm that is lost, a head that is cut off, blood on the water, companions
who leave, etc., as we have already seen in the individual analogues. But the
form that each of the two battles takes in *Beowulf* is not to be found in *Grettis
saga*, if by form we mean some kind of a pattern in a chain of events, or even
the details that make up a single link in such a chain.

Within the context of the saga, Grettir's battles against Kárr the Old, the
brown bear, Glámr, and others hang together as a series of tests – a form of initiation perhaps, as Mary Danielly has argued.[55] They create the impression of
some unfulfilled greatness in Grettir which vanishes after his battle with Glámr.
Whether or not we choose to ascribe his bad luck to the effects of the curse,
everything still turns to his misfortune. Even his stay at Sandhaugar is ultimately a sad story, in the sense that it gives Grettir a son who is seen to have the
strength and valour of his father, but who dies in his youth. Beowulf also has an
unusual career as a hero because of the strange absence of triumphs in his life
after his defeat of Grendel and his mother, but the curse that Guðbrandur Vigfússon believed Grendel to have put on him simply is not there in *Beowulf*, and
thus the poem and the saga must be reckoned to follow their separate ways in
terms of what fortunes the killing of monsters brings the hero.

4

A Sword by Any Other Name

When Guðbrandur Vigfússon proclaimed the Sandhaugar and Glámr episodes of *Grettis saga* to be analogous and genetically related to *Beowulf*, he offered the *heptisax-hæftmece* parallel as his best evidence. Vigfússon gave three reasons for the special importance of this pair: as far as he was concerned, the two were one and the same word, they occurred at the same place in the legend, and they were unique in their respective literatures.[1] Although the first two points are obvious exaggerations, the idea of equating the two words has gone unchallenged for more than a century, and such is the faith of the converted that it now seems acceptable to translate *hæftmece* as 'the sword with a long wooden hilt,' a gloss which clearly echoes the words that the author of *Grettis saga* uses to define the *heptisax* of the giant at Sandhaugar.[2] This translation effort is merely a single example; a great deal of scholarly work aimed at bringing *Grettis saga* into line with *Beowulf* also rests on the basis of Vigfússon's equation. But how secure is the kinship between *hæftmece* and *heptisax*, and do these two words actually provide a definite link between the poem and the saga?

Beowulf, as the poem tells us, borrows the famous sword Hrunting from Unferð, and Hrunting, in line 1457a (as Beowulf arms himself before his dive into the mere), is referred to as a *hæftmece*. The *heptisax*, on the other hand, belongs to and is used by the giant in the saga, so our starting point in this story of swords must be the mess which the author of *Grettis saga* makes of the old legend by failing to place either the giant's *heptisax* or the sword on the wall in the hands of the hero. Peter A. Jorgensen, as we saw in the previous chapter, has tried to correct the misplacement of the first weapon, and H.R. Ellis Davidson has made a similar attempt for the second:

It is not clear either from the verses or the prose account with what weapon he [i.e., Grettir] actually slew the giant, but the prose account refers to a sword hanging up in the cave which the giant tries to reach, and the introduction of this into the story is quite pointless unless it was used in some way.[3]

Davidson does not actually say that the giant is killed with his own sword, but she implies it. It is true that *Grettis saga* does not say with which sword the giant is killed, but the introduction of the giant sword is far from being pointless, even if he is not actually killed with it. In the cave scene, the saga shows Grettir holding his short-sword, which he has just used to cut apart the handle of the *heptisax* in a moment of great suspense, while the giant goes for another weapon which is within easy reach behind him. Davidson would like us to imagine that in this situation Grettir puts his own sword down, gets past the giant and behind him to collect the other sword, then traces his steps back to his original position so that he can face the giant – who has politely waited while all this took place – and cut his guts open. This kind of sophistry is hardly to the point, since we are dealing with a literary text and not a real estate contract. The sword on the wall does play its part in this story, but not the one that Davidson thinks that it should play.

The only weapon that the giant actually uses against Grettir has no name but is described with a word (*heptisax*) that would seem to identify it as a particular and recognizable type of weapon. But what does the term *heptisax* mean, and where does the word come from? Although the compound is only recorded in *Grettis saga*, there is nothing very strange or mysterious about it. In Old Norse the handle of a full-length sword was usually called a *meðalkafli* (i.e., 'the middle piece'), whereas the corresponding part of a short-sword (Old Norse *sax*) or a long knife (Old Norse *skálm*) was called either *hepti* or *mundriði*. Hjalmar Falk, who lists this vocabulary in his *Altnordische Waffenkunde*, gives an example of a sentence from a Norse text where both components of Vigfússon's mystery word are actually present: '*fell saxit or hepti*'; i.e., 'the blade of the short-sword was detached from its handle.'[4] It follows from this that neither of the two nouns that make up the compound is rare or obscure, nor is the meaning of the word which they combine to form. *Heptisax* must mean a short-sword with a plain handle, as opposed to the sword-type handle (*meðalkafli*) that Grettir's own *sax*, the *Kársnautr*, has.

Perhaps because it is so transparent, the meaning of the word *heptisax* has never interested the analogue makers very much; however, its single occurrence in Old Norse has always had its romantic appeal. On the basis of this limited circulation, and nothing else, it has been generally assumed from early on that the word *heptisax* must be of foreign stock, although the critical camp has always been sharply divided over where to seek its origin. Scholars who believe *Grettis saga* to have been directly or indirectly influenced by *Beowulf* have looked to Old English as a source, whereas those who favour the idea of a common source – preferably Scandinavian – for the saga and the poem, have promptly rejected any such ideas. R.C. Boer, who produced the first scholarly edition of *Grettis saga*, was inclined to think that *heptisax* was a literary borrowing from a now lost Anglo-Saxon poem because he found it hard to believe that an oral tradition could preserve a single unique term for centuries.[5] Other *Beowulf* scholars, such as Hermann Schneider[6] and Carl W. von Sydow,[7] were also convinced that the word had to hearken back to a literary source. By contrast, Joan Turville-Petre, who sees a common source for the poem and the saga, thinks that the *heptisax-hæftmece* is originally a technical term, specifically associated with cave-warfare, which each author interprets in his own way.[8]

In *Beowulf* the word *hæftmece* occurs as a sword term for Hrunting with no greater fanfare than other synonyms for swords in the poem. In *Grettis saga*, on the other hand, the author pauses to add a brief comment on the weapon of the giant:

when Grettir came to him, the giant leaped up and seized a pike, and hewed at the newcomer: for with the pike he could both cut and stab. It had a handle of wood: men at that time called a weapon made in such a way a *heptisax*.[9]

Much has been made of this brief comment. John Earle called attention to it in a translation of *Beowulf* that he made only a few years after Guðbrandur Vigfússon had advanced his theory on the relationship between the poem and *Grettis saga* : 'The author of the Saga ... treats the word [*heptisax*] as curious and strange, by the explanation which he offers of it. There must be some common source ...'[10] This statement has been repeated and elaborated on by various scholars since Earle's time.[11] It has even been hypothesized that the author of *Grettis saga* had problems understanding the stanza (no. 61) in which the hero describes his battle with the giant. According to this theory, the stanza was his only source, and he wanted to include it but felt compelled to explicate the meaning of *heptisax* – which he did not quite understand – in the prose account of Grettir's adventure.[12]

In this effort to provide the giant's *heptisax* with an ancient and mysterious origin, the first assumption that everyone seems to take for granted is that the slightest digression, in the form of an explanation or a comment that the author of *Grettis saga* makes, is a sign that something extraordinary is happening in the text. For the saga as a whole this is hardly the case, since its author is not averse to tagging explanatory notes and even longer digressions on to his narrative on sundry occasions, as may be seen from the following examples:

Then the king ordered his berserks to advance. They were called wolfskins and could not be injured by any iron weapons. (5)

Þorgeirr was in charge of the farm of the brothers at Reykjarfjǫrðr. He regularly went fishing, for then the fjords were full of fish. (26)

The ship which the merchants had built was very broad, and people called it the Wooden Sack, and from this epithet the inlet takes its name. (32–3)

Þorsteinn had had a church built on his farm. He had a bridge made which led away from the farm. It was built with great ingenuity. On the bridge, underneath the support beams, there were rings and chiming bells, so that if anyone walked across it, the rings shook so much that the din could be heard all the way to Skarfsstaðir, a couple of miles away. Þorsteinn, who was a very skilled blacksmith, put a great effort into this bridge. Grettir took great turns at hammering the iron, when he could be bothered to do it.[13] (173)

If the *heptisax* comment was a rare occurrence in an otherwise sparsely worded saga, there might be some merit to this argument, but *Grettis saga* is not that kind of text.

It is also very difficult to imagine that the two stanzas in which Grettir sums up his battle with the giant and mentions the *heptisax* go back to high antiquity, as Jorgensen has maintained. Since the nineteenth century, scholars have agreed that most, if not all, of the forty-seven stanzas which the saga attributes to Grettir were composed later than the eleventh century,[14] and Jorgensen does not *per se* dispute that conclusion. His argument, however, is perfectly circular, because the attempt to prove that these two verses are older than other stanzas in the saga rests on an *a priori* assumption that they contain genetically related parallels with the Grendel fight in *Beowulf*.[15]

Jorgensen further maintains that the saga author's description of the giant's *heptisax* is inconsistent both with the meaning of the word itself and with the reference to it as *fleinn*, in other words, as yet another sign of a misunderstood relic from the old legend:

It seems highly improbable that the word *heptisax* should occur only once in all of the extensive battle descriptions in Old Icelandic prose and, by chance, at precisely the same point in a narrative where the corresponding English text employs the cognate term. There is no reason, no special motivation for its occurrence at this point or, indeed, for its occurring at all. Furthermore, the Icelandic prose passage in which the word appears makes little sense. The reader is told that the giant came at Grettir with a *fleinn* and chopped at Grettir with it. But the Icelandic term *fleinn* is normally used to denote an arrow or javelin. Having once informed the reader that the giant attacked Grettir with a *fleinn* or javelin, the writer hastily adds that one could both thrust and chop with this instrument and that it was called a *heptisax*, which etymologically should be some sort of sword. The use of the weapon would bear this out, but we are also told that the handle was made of wood, which would further indicate a spear or javelin. Much more usual expressions in Old Icelandic for the weapon evidently intended in the prose text are *hǫggspjót, kesja, brynþvari,* and *atgeirr.*

The preservation of the word *heptisax* is more likely due to its presence as a necessary formal entity in a poetic line.[16]

The issue of a dichotomy between *fleinn* and *heptisax* has also been discussed by Joan Turville-Petre, who concludes that the author of *Grettis saga* is describing 'an impossible composite weapon.'[17]

The basic assumptions behind both these theories are that the word *fleinn* cannot mean the same as *heptisax* and that neither term fits the spear-sword type weapon in question.[18] Haakon Shetelig and Hjalmar Falk address both issues in their *Scandinavian Archaeology,* and fail to notice the drama that Jorgensen and Turville-Petre would like to see in the text:

A special type of *fleinn* is mentioned in *Grettis saga* (chap. 66) under the name *heptisax.* This weapon consisted of a sword-like blade fixed at the end of a wooden shaft, and differed from the other types of *fleinn* in not being a throwing spear, but was used as a *hǫggspjót,* for hewing and thrusting. It must have been similar to the *kesjufleinn,* or, more probably, identical with it; this was evidently a *kesja* ... with a longer blade than usual. It was doubtless by reason of the long narrow blade that the *heptisax* was classed by *Grettis saga* as a *fleinn.* The same sort of weapon was known in other Germanic lands, too: OE [Old English] *stæfsweord,* glossing 'dolo' and OHG [Old High German] *stapaswert,* 'framea,' must also have consisted of a sword-like blade on a wooden shaft.[19]

If Shetelig and Falk are correct in their analysis, we may safely assume that the author of *Grettis saga* was neither trying to gloss over his ignorance of that 'ancient' term *heptisax,* nor allowing his imagination to fashion an impossible weapon.

Like *heptisax,* the term *hæftmece* only occurs once; and Guðbrandur Vigfússon, and many others after him, firmly believed that this uniqueness somehow related the two and made them special. But just how special is *hæftmece* within the context of *Beowulf* as a whole? It is often conveniently forgotten that several terms and kennings for swords – other than Hrunting – also appear only in the poem and nowhere else in the Old English corpus,[20] although the old legends that gave us *beado-mece, eald-sweord, guð-sweord, hilde-mece, maðþum-*

sweord, sceaden-mæl, and *hilde-leoma* have obviously yet to be discovered. It is only the presumed relationship with the Norse term that has elevated *hæft-mece* to the special position that it enjoys among these peers.[21]

As a weapon, the *hæftmece* was very different from the *heptisax*; that much at least is undisputed. In Old English the *mece* was a long two-edged sword with a long handle. What precisely the *hæft* was meant to indicate is uncertain. The usual meaning of the word is 'fetter' or 'captive,' which would make it likely that the compound either denoted a sword whose blade was attached in some special way, or that it was fastened to its scabbard, or had a hilt with some kind of fastening, perhaps like the *fetelhilt*, the sword that Beowulf finds in the cave.

It further complicates the *hæftmece* issue that the sword in question, Hrunting, is not always called a *mece*: on one occasion the *Beowulf* poet also refers to it as a *hildebill* (line 1520b). According to Caroline Brady, both *bill* and *mece* are terms that denote long, slender two-edged swords with either sharply pointed or rounded tips, but although archaeologists are not in agreement as to what precisely the difference between the two is supposed to have been, the two words appear to refer to two distinct sword types in the poem. Brady points out that the *Beowulf* poet is, on the whole, 'remarkably consistent in maintaining a distinction between the two types,'[22] with this one notable exception. Even if we accept that calling Hrunting a *bill* is an isolated error on the part of the poet or a later copyist, however, it remains to be explained why the author of *Beowulf* uses the word *hæftmece* so extremely sparingly. As we have already seen, a variety of other terms are applied to Hrunting, and if *hæftmece* was a key word in the old legend on which he was basing his story, one would expect this term to play a more important role.

As a legacy of Guðbrandur Vigfússon's faith in the secrets that the *heptisax-hæftmece* parallel might unlock, Hrunting, the actual name of the sword, has received much less attention than the illustrious pair. But if Hrunting is the sword with which the hero kills the monster in some version of the old legend, then what is it doing in the hands of the coward and fratricide Unferð? The poem makes no attempt to explain this, and yet it is obvious that the sword must have qualities that make it special. Beowulf, who has brought his own excellent sword to Heorot and been given another by Hroðgar,[23] rejects both in favour of Hrunting as he prepares to fight with Grendel's mother, and we may thus assume that Beowulf perceives that Hrunting is superior to these other swords.

Names of swords sometimes give an indication of their appearance or special qualities, but unfortunately the etymology of Hrunting remains uncertain. The word has been connected with **hrut*, 'to resound' (cf. Old Norse *hrjóta*, 'to fall' or 'to snore') and with **hrunt* (cf. Modern English 'runt' and Hrotti, the name of Fáfnir's sword).[24] Kemp Malone, who has been one of the proponents of the latter etymology, believes that Hrunting originally got its name from an owner nicknamed Hrunta; a name which, like Hrotti, indicated the owner's great size and grimness. Malone also notes that Hrunting is probably related to Old English *hrung*, 'rung' or 'pole,' which ultimately derived from a Germanic base denoting a thick, stout segment of a tree or a branch.[25] Norman E. Eliason also takes Hrunting to be a nickname, although unlike Malone he thinks it stemmed from the shortness of the weapon rather than the characteristics of its original owner.[26] Haakon Shetelig and Hjalmar Falk, on the other hand, interpret Hrunt- as an extended form of the Old English base *hrung*; i.e., as a 'long piece of wood' or a 'rung.'[27] If the name Hrunting does indeed indicate that the sword had a wooden handle, it would seem to give us something to compare with the giant's *heptisax* in *Grettis saga*, although it does not explain what was special about the wooden handle in the original story. But even if we accept that Hrotti and Hrunting are cognates, it does not lend much strength to this argument that saga author knows the sword name Hrotti and uses it in two early stanzas, nos. 4 and 17, without the slightest hint that the word has any special significance either for Grettir's weapons or for Grettir himself.

Another method which has been tried in order to find out more about Hrunting is to assume that the author of *Beowulf* meant his audience to take the few references that are made to the sword literally. The clues that this gives us are:

hringmæl, (adj.)   = 'ring-marked'[28] (line 1521b)

wundenmæl, (n.)   = 'a sword with curved markings'[29] or a 'twisted pattern'[30] (line 1531a)

ecg wæs iren   = the edge – or the entire sword – was made of iron (line 1459a)

atertanum fah   = decorated with 'poison twigs'[31] or 'gleaming with tiny serpents'[32] or 'of gleaming or fiery hilt or pommel.'[33] (line 1459b)

The sundry details that may be deduced from this vocabulary do not form any coherent picture and obviously leave a good deal of room for speculation. Not surprisingly, two contradictory lines of interpretation have emerged. Thus, H.R. Ellis Davidson thinks that the poet is describing a sword with a pattern-welded blade, whereas W.P. Lehmann believes Hrunting to be a weapon which had an iron edge covering a wooden shaft.[34] It does not matter which of these readings we favour, for neither one sheds any light on the connection between the sword and the *heptisax* of the saga. The best link between Hrunting and the *heptisax* remains the same: they are both weapons that fail, albeit for very different reasons. To reconstruct a legend that could function as a common ancestor, it must furthermore be assumed that one of these weapons is in the wrong hands, and somehow both heroes must be found with a victorious sword with a special haft or hilt, a task which various *Beowulf* critics have been more than willing to perform.

One further possibility is to wrest the *hæftmece* from its association with the useless Hrunting and turn it into a reference to the sword with the wonderful hilt that actually kills Grendel's dam. This is precisely what R.W. Chambers does in his *Introduction to the Study of the Poem*:

Presumably, in the original story, as it existed before our *Beowulf* was composed, an important part was played by the sword with a wonderful hilt which the hero met in the cave. In *Beowulf* ten lines are devoted to describing the presentation of the hilt to Hrothgar, twelve lines to describing the hilt itself. The sword is characterized by its hilt ...

When we turn to the prose of the *Grettis saga*, we find that much is made of the 'hafted cutlass' (*hepti-sax*) which Grettir encounters in the hands of the giant in the cave. Further, that this was an important part of the story, as the compiler of the *Saga* knew it, is also indicated by the important part the *hepti-sax* is made to play in the verses, late as these doubtless are. Just as Beowulf brings back to Hrothgar the rune-inscribed hilt which is all that is left of the sword, so Grettir leaves with Stein a stave of wood upon which is inscribed in runes an account of the separation of the haft of the 'hafted cutlass' from its blade ...

In the original story – say of the sixth century – the sword was probably described in a number of words compounded with the element *haft* or *hilt*: one of these *haft*-compounds survives in the *Grettis saga*, whilst in *Beowulf* it also survives, but has got into a different context.[35]

Several other scholars have also favoured this avenue of approach towards establishing the old legend.[36] Of course, we must assume that both authors made a bit of a mess of the story in the process of retelling it, the *Beowulf* poet by putting a key word 'into a different context' – to use Chambers's polite phrase – and the composer of *Grettis saga* by failing to have the giant at Sandhaugar killed with his own *heptisax*. As Martin Puhvel has observed, it makes no sense that the role of the essential weapon – Chambers's *hæftmece* of the original legend – could be so greatly altered in both the poem and the saga,[37] even if we turn a blind eye to his method of emending both stories to reconstruct the original.

It is not easy to determine what kind of a weapon the cave sword is meant to be before its blade melts. The poem informs us that it was wrought by giants (line 1562b) and huge, but mostly refers to it with very ordinary synonyms for swords: *bil(l)* (line 1557b), *ealdsweord* (line 1558a), *fetelhilt* (line 1563a), *hringmæl* (line 1564b), *ecg* (line 1575b), *wigbil* (line 1607a), *brogden-mæl* (line 1616a), *hildebil* (line 1666b), and *wreopenhilt* (line 1698a). From this list of references, *hringmæl* and *brogden-mæl* would seem to indicate that the cave sword was damascened, and *fetelhilt* might refer to a hilt furnished with a ring or a chain.[38] As these sword references have no apparent connection with Grettir's second adventure at Sandhaugar, critics have preferred to look for one by comparing the story that is carved on the hilt of the cave sword to the rune-staff that Grettir leaves behind for the incredulous Steinn. However, it is far from clear what Hroðgar actually sees as he muses over the hilt in lines 1687–98. The poem tells us that it has something to do with the beginning of an ancient strife (*on þæm wæs or writen / fyrngewinnes*), and then seems to proceed to allude to the Genesis story about the deluge that destroyed the race of giants (*syðþan flod ofsloh / ... giganta cyn*). Given the genealogy of the Grendels, it seems feasible to take *syðþan* as an explanatory conjunction ('when'), and thereby link the ancient strife and the ultimate destruction, but *syðþan* may be an adverb ('afterwards'), in which case we have no means of knowing what the ancient strife was all about. A runic inscription on the hilt also tells Hroðgar for whom the sword was originally made.

But how does the hilt of the wondrous sword relate its story? In their editions of the poem, Fr. Klaeber and C.L. Wrenn assume that it did so through engraved designs,[39] but scholars who are more analogue-minded have favoured runes. The most ambitious attempt to link this scene in *Beowulf* to *Grettis saga* is to be found in H.R. Ellis Davidson's study, *The Sword in Anglo-Saxon England*:

Heptisax is the name given to the weapon of the giant whom Grettir meets under water, and Grettir, using his famous short sword, cuts the giant's weapon from its shaft. Later on Grettir leaves in the church a bag of bones he has brought up from the giant's cave and with it a piece of wood carved in runes, a *rúnakefli*, on which two verses are said to have been 'excellently carved.' Could this possibly be the wooden shaft of the Heptisax? The saga does not tell us what became of the giant's weapon after Grettir destroyed it, but the coincidence of the strange term, the separation of the giant's weapon from its hilt (as in *Beowulf*), and the reading of runes on it after the battle is over (again as in *Beowulf*) is certainly striking, all the more so because there is so much difference in the two accounts.[40]

Davidson furthermore rejects the idea that the reference which the poem makes to rushing waters and the destruction of giants has anything to do with Genesis, and finds it 'not impossible' that Beowulf recorded his struggle against the Grendels on the hilt before presenting it to Hroðgar. Another possibility that

Davidson suggests is 'that the hilt bore some prophetic inscription in runes, emphasizing the fact which we know from the poem, that it was the only weapon which could kill Grendel's mother and cut off Grendel's head.'[41] Vera I. Evison, who reviewed Davidson's book, flatly rejects this speculation. She points out that most armour in *Beowulf* appears to be of the sixth century, and that it is 'quite impossible that a sword of this period should have an inscription in runes long enough to tell a story,' as inscriptions from this age are extremely short, giving little more than a name.[42]

Departing from the more usual rune staff comparison, A.R. Taylor focuses his analogy on Grettir's own weapon, the *Kársnautr*:

Professor Chambers has tried to show that *Grettis saga* is clearer in its account of the weapons used. But it would seem more probable that the real purpose behind the *hepti-sax-hæftmece* has been obscured by both authors; possibly in the original story it was the sword which the hero found in the cave and used to slay his opponent. It is, however, certain that the weapons used to slay the monsters in both *Grettis saga* and *Beowulf* have one thing in common: they are both remarkable for their hilt. This common characteristic is almost certainly a reminiscence of the original legend. In *Beowulf* the sword blade melts away in Grendel's blood, and the hero can bring only the hilt to Hroðgar. The hilt is noteworthy, and the poet makes this clear by spending twenty-two lines on it. Grettir's short-sword is unique in Old Norse literature. It is the only *sax* with a regular sword hilt. Normally, the name given to the handle or grip of a *sax* is *hepti* or *mundriði*, but the handle of Grettir's *sax* is twice called a *meðalkafli*, a name usually reserved for the grip of a sword. It may perhaps be argued that the thirteenth-century Icelandic author of the *Grettis saga* made a slip when he gives this name to the hilt of Grettir's short-sword, but the uniqueness of the nomenclature argues rather that tradition had preserved this remarkable feature of the weapon.[43]

I have commented before on the both-authors-got-it-wrong approach, and suffice it to add that if this kind of methodology becomes acceptable in medieval studies, we shall see an astronomical growth of analogue-making efforts at the expense of common sense. In Taylor's case, however, not even this questionable approach can carry the argument. That Grettir's *sax* is unique in Old Norse in having a sword hilt is entirely correct, but I wonder if the author of *Grettis saga* realized how unique he was being in endowing the *sax* with a handle of this kind. What Taylor omits to mention is that there is nothing special about the hilt, except the saga author's placement of it on Grettir's *sax*. The hilt is casually mentioned twice in the saga, first when Grettir ties the weapon to his hand before going to meet the bear (76), and again when an unsuccessful attempt is made to wrest the *sax* is from the hero's grip after his death (261). In both instances it is as if the author assumes that he is referring to an ordinary type of a handle for a short-sword, and, as we saw, even Taylor has to admit that this might have come about through sheer ignorance. The unique *meðalkafli* of Grettir's *sax* plays no role in the saga over and above being a handle for his short-sword, and with that in mind, the comparison of a word that occurs twice in the saga to the twenty-two lines of musings over the hilt of the ancient cave sword in *Beowulf* becomes rather far-fetched.

It should be clear from the various critical efforts that I have just cited that it is no easy task to make Guðbrandur Vigfússon's theory of equating *heptisax* with *hæftmece* pan out. On the matter of weapons, *Grettis saga* and *Beowulf* – as we have them – simply cannot be made to fall into line. If a relationship between the actual weapons cannot be established in the texts without emending them both, we are bound to come back to the starting point of our enquiry, namely, the assumption of a special relationship between the two words.

Vigfússon never cared to elaborate on what precisely constituted their kinship,[44] so later critics have had to discover this for themselves, and they have done so in a variety of manners. Ideally, the kind of proof of a relationship that one would want would be etymological, one that would account for the two words as cognates descending from a Germanic etymon that could be reconstructed, but there is no such proof to be had. This, however, has not prevented some analogue-minded critics from describing *heptisax* and *hæftmece* as cognate terms.[45] It is true, of course, that *hæft* and *hepti* are cognate prefixes, but taken as a whole the two words are not otherwise related. Another linguistic avenue which has been tried is to find a 'semantic resemblance' between the two: *hæftmece* glossed as the 'hilted sword,' and *heptisax* as the 'hafted short-sword.'[46] This may appear to be a promising approach, but it is extremely misleading. As we have already seen, the prefix *hepti-* in the saga almost certainly means a 'plain handle,' and, as it happens, we have nothing with which to compare this reading because we do not know what precisely the first part of *hæft-mece* is supposed to mean. Under the umbrella of 'semantic resemblance' we can presumably also include statements that link the two words as 'counterparts' or take them to be 'of the same kind.'[47]

Other attempts, i.e., ones that are neither linguistic nor based on the texts, to account for a relationship between the pair are – and only can be – pure speculation. Most commonly, critics have turned their imagination towards ancient rituals and magic. Vera I. Evison has suggested that the meaning of the two words 'may be connected with something altogether unsuspected and be a lost memory of the ritual of exorcism.'[48] Anatoly Liberman believes that in the original story there was magic contained in the haft of the weapon, and that the terms *hæftmece* and *heptisax* originally 'belonged to a stock of ritual words.'[49] The latest and most ambitious hypothesis in this vein comes from Carlo A. Mastrelli, who argues that the elements *hæft-* and *hepti-* originally implied divine or demonic power. According to Mastrelli, the two words go back to a version of the Indo-Iranian myth about Indra's victory over the demon Valla and the snake Vrtra, in which a marvelous sword with its power contained in the handle was of central importance. In *Beowulf* the characteristics of this sword are divided among three weapons: the *hæftmece* Hrunting, the dagger with which Grendel's mother attacks Beowulf, and the magical giant sword. *Grettis saga* is also found to have corresponding weapons. With the transition from paganism to Christianity, the myth itself and the meaning of the key word gradually faded so that by the time that the poem and the saga were recorded, the magical associations of *hæftmece* and *heptisax* had been forgotten, and they had come to denote no more than a weapon with a handle.[50]

However, not all critics – not even scholars who are convinced that *Beowulf* and *Grettis saga* must be somehow related – have been equally impressed by the importance that Guðbrandur Vigfússon attached to his discovery of the unique pair. Henrik Schück, for example, voiced his criticism as early as 1909. Schück rightly observes that in Anglo-Saxon literature there is not a great deal of secular poetry that has survived and consequently finds it questionable to read too much into the single occurrence of *hæftmece* in *Beowulf*. According to Schück there is a similar danger in the saga, because although the compound is unique, both components of *heptisax* are common words. He also wonders about the incomplete correspondence between Vigfússon's pair; after all we should expect to find a **heptimækir* in *Grettis saga* or a **hæftseax* in *Beowulf*.[51] More recently, A. Margaret Arent has maintained that the occurrence of the two forms 'should not carry too much weight in establishing a dependency or common source for the motifs in *Beowulf* and *Grettis saga*.'[52]

It goes without saying that these objections have not been greeted with much enthusiasm, nor have they inspired other scholars to re-examine the elusive relationship that Vigfússon postulated. In the eyes of the faithful, the magic of the verbal talismans *hæftmece* and *heptisax* is both proven and sacrosanct. Perhaps the most fallacious idea in all the literature on this pair is the general assumption that it is their uniqueness in Old English and Old Icelandic that makes them so special. We are tacitly asked to believe that they could only be associated with one particular 'old legend' and could not have come about in any other manner. But it is only through the hindsight of good dictionaries in both languages that we know the two words to be unique, and critics – awestruck, as it would seem, by the presence of two words recorded only once –

often tend to forget that the authors of *Beowulf* and *Grettis saga* hardly shared this information with us. Given this scenario, the unbeliever feels like the child in Hans Christian Andersen's story 'The Emperor's New Clothes,' who saw that His Highness was naked even though the rest of the court kept admiring his fine new suit.

5

Hell and High Water

In this chapter we round up the examination of the proposed genetically related analogues by inspecting the dwellings in which the monsters of saga and poem live, and the landscape through which Beowulf and Grettir must travel to reach them. The logic behind this comparison is much the same as in chapter 3, namely, that similarities in respect to settings, or perhaps some details relating to their description, might have survived in the two stories that supposedly developed from the same original legend. Landscape and other settings are indeed one of the main areas of comparison where Guðbrandur Vigfússon's followers felt there was work to be done, and armed with the kind of methodology that I have just described, they have generated more books and articles on this one subject than on any other concerning the relationship between *Beowulf* and *Grettis saga*. In the early decades of this century Carl W. von Sydow tried to stem this tide by arguing that details of the landscape of an original legend were quickly stripped away in the process of transmission within an oral tradition.[1] But the triumvirate of Klaeber, Lawrence, and Chambers thought differently. To them it seemed entirely logical that even though this part of the poem described a battle between a hero of superhuman qualities against a pair of supernatural enemies the landscape of the monsters' abode should meet all rational criteria – and in the ensuing critical battle, their ideas won the day.

If we retrace the journey that Beowulf makes to the abode of the monsters, the first parallel to *Grettis saga* that has been proposed is the road he must take: the narrow footpath ('*enge anpaðas, uncuð gelad,*' line 1410). In his edition of *Beowulf*, Klaeber notes that Grettir must also follow a narrow path to reach the bear's cave lair, but stops short of suggesting that it might be an analogous feature.[2] Later critics, particularly A. Margaret Arent and Peter A. Jorgensen, have been less hesitant, and both have maintained that the narrow path was part of the original legend.[3] There are, however, a number of reasons that make this very unlikely. The most obvious one is the absence of a narrow footpath to take Grettir to his fights with otherworldly creatures, such as the giant at Sandhaugar or Glámr. Secondly, the narrow footpath in *Beowulf* is part and parcel of a description which seems to be aimed at giving an impression of the hero's entry into a hellish realm, as opposed to the *einstigi* in *Grettis saga*, which merely serves as a precariously narrow battle ground for the bear fight.

The next feature of landscape which has been claimed to have a counterpart in *Grettis saga* is the famous mountain stream (*fyrgenstream*, line 1359b) that goes down under the darkness of the hills and forms a flood under the earth, to which King Hroðgar alludes in his description of what is in store for Beowulf on the perilous journey that he must undertake to reach the abode of Grendel's mother. This allusion is somewhat mysterious, because the lines that actually describe Beowulf's trip to the mere (1399–1417a) make no mention of a mountain river. As early as 1881, C.S. Smith suggested that there was a parallel between the mountain stream of the poem and the waterfall of the Sandhaugar episode,[4] but it was not until later – after W.W. Lawrence had fully developed Smith's idea – that the 'waterfall theory' gained critical momentum in *Beowulf* studies. It must be borne in mind, however, that the waterfall is only a part of a larger landscaping effort which Lawrence had in mind. His general aim was to clear up and rationalize the surrealistic and conflicting images of natural scenery that *Beowulf* seems to offer, and he did this by assuming that *Grettis saga* preserves features of landscape that are closer to the hypothetical original legend than the English poem. Lawrence then proceeds to superimpose the Icelandic inland scenery of the waterfall in *Grettis saga* onto the salty surroundings of the mere, and here, as might be expected, he runs into the difficulty of reconciling the vocabulary of the poem with the landscape that he wants to see. His solution to this obstacle, however, is both sweet and simple: 'Anglo-Saxon poetry was not particular about the propriety of its synonyms ... Hence poetic elaborations were often used with considerable looseness.'[5] In other words, the *fyrgenstream* in *Beowulf* was not really a mountain stream, as the elements that make up the compound would seem to suggest, but a waterfall:

It will be observed, in the first place, that the general location of Grettir's contest under water is much like what we may believe to be the original scenery of Beowulf's second adventure. There are in the Scandinavian tale the same high cliffs, from which one looks down to the waters below, and the same waterfall breaking down over the rocks, and plunging into a turbulent whirlpool. These general and essential features of inland mountain scenery are the same. Certain details naturally vary; there is less suggestion of a river in the Anglo-Saxon, although a waterfall such as is there described could hardly exist without something like a river as tributary to it ... The place where the demon has dragged Beowulf is a cave behind the waterfall – *under firgen-stréam*, 2128, – where, as the poet tells us, she had previously taken the luckless Æschere. Beowulf dives to the bottom, just as Grettir did, in order to avoid the whirlpool and thus get up underneath the waterfall.[6]

Both R.W. Chambers and Fr. Klaeber warmly embraced this theory and did their share to promote it, Chambers by incorporating it into his highly influential study on *Beowulf*, and Klaeber by glossing the crucial word *fyrgenstream* as 'waterfall' in his edition of the poem.[7] Chambers's account of how Lawrence's theory brought the light of reason to his and W.P. Ker's understanding of the mere episode in *Beowulf* illustrates well what Margaret E. Goldsmith has called 'an ingrained preference for naturalism in literature':

To many of us this [i.e., the waterfall setting] now seems clear – but only with the *Grettis saga* before us, and even then only after reading Lawrence's excellent demonstration: I remember W.P. Ker saying, 'Strange, that none of us ever noticed that before.' The waterfall-setting in *Beowulf* is almost obliterated, visible only when searched for, like the original writing of some palimpsests. It is one of those things which, however obvious after they are pointed out, are not noticed till they *are* pointed out ...

In any case it is certain that in *Beowulf* there is no suggestion that the cave is just behind the waterfall. Beowulf plunges to the bottom, and in course of time finds himself in a cave free from the water. Nothing is said of his rising after his dive – the cave appears to be at the bottom of the mere: it is sheer un-reason. Of course such un-reason *does* occur elsewhere in *Beowulf*. But when we confront the *Beowulf* account with the Sandhaugar episode, the episode reveals itself as eminently reasonable. The hero, in order to get *under* the waterfall, *has* to dive to the bottom. 'Can it be done?' I remember asking W.P. Ker. 'Yes,' said Ker, 'I have done it.' (All depends, of course, upon the volume of the waterfall.)[8]

Although Lawrence's theory has convinced many *Beowulf* scholars, in addition to Klaeber and Chambers,[9] there have always been those who found it simply too good to be true. One of the first critics to voice his objections was W.S. Mackie, who bluntly rejected the idea of a waterfall in the poem as an interpolation from *Grettis saga*:

Lawrence translates *fyrgenstréam* by 'waterfall,' and suggests that *under næssa genipu* may refer to 'the fine spray thrown out by the fall in its descent, and blown about the windy nesses.' There is a waterfall in the *Grettissaga*; is there one in *Beowulf* also?

Fyrgenstréam, 'mountain stream'; *fyrgen* is translated 'mountain' because that is the meaning of the cognate Gothic *fairguni*, which translates Greek ὄρος. In Old English *fyrgen* never occurs as a simplex, but only as the first element in three compounds found only in poetry. Only one of these, *fyrgenstréam* itself, occurs outside of *Beowulf*; and then it seems always to mean 'the sea,' or, at most, 'the flowing sea,' 'the sea waves.' See, for example, *Andreas* 390, *Anchor Riddle* 2, *Cotton Gnomic Verses* 47. So it would seem that the original meaning of the archaic *fyrgen* had weakened to vanishing point, and that the word survived in poetic compounds principally for the sake of providing an *f* alliteration. *Fyrgenholt* in *Beowulf* 1393 probably means nothing more than 'forest,' and the *fyrgenbéamas* that lean over the grey rock (*Beowulf* 1414) are merely trees. Similarly *fyrgenstréam* is simply equivalent to *stréam*, 'stream,' 'running water,' or merely 'water.' 'The running water descends, a stream below the level of the earth' is most probably meant to describe a stream running into the mere through a gorge, but it is possible that what the poet has in mind is a whirlpool in the mere, or even the turbid mere itself. At any rate, notwithstanding *niþer gewíteð*, the translation of *fyrgenstréam* by 'waterfall' is very doubtful indeed.[10]

In addition to his criticism of Lawrence's interpretation of *fyrgenstream*, Mackie also called attention to the fact that the poem describes Beowulf's return from the abode of the monsters as a dive up through the water without any hint that he must dive under a waterfall.

Lawrence replied to Mackie's objections and tried to defend his translation, but he could neither refute Mackie's argument nor offer anything new. As before, Lawrence simply insisted that Anglo-Saxon poetry 'possessed a large choice of epithets for its own limited range of subjects, but few for those outside its range. Consequently, in the obligatory repetition, variation, and alliteration, terms not strictly applicable were often used.'[11]

A few years before Mackie's article appeared, Lawrence's waterfall theory had come under attack from Kemp Malone who, in a review of the second edition of Chambers's study of *Beowulf*, flatly rejected Lawrence's ideas and criticized Chambers for promoting them. Like Mackie, Malone did not believe that it would have occurred to anyone to interpret *fyrgenstream* as a waterfall, were it not for the supposedly analogous and genetically related Sandhaugar episode. In his review Malone argued that the first element of *fyrgenstream* should be read as an intensifier ('mountainous,' 'vast'), and that the word as a whole could only mean 'the great stream of the Ocean (the sea pure and simple).'[12] Years later, Malone came back to this subject in an article entitled 'Grendel and his Abode,' in which he thoroughly examined the variety of simplex nouns and compounds that appear in *Beowulf* for bodies of water, and concluded, as he had done previously, that *fyrgenstream* could only mean a 'stream that is a mountain (of intensity)' and that the word most likely referred to the ancient notion that a stream of gigantic size – the world river Oceanus – encircled the world.[13] These objections from Mackie and Malone to Lawrence's waterfall argument have, insofar as I know, never been refuted, and yet they seem to have had very little impact on analogue-minded scholars, who have simply ignored them.[14]

From the point of view of *Grettis saga* there is also a serious weakness in Lawrence's line of reasoning. If the Sandhaugar episode is supposed to clear up ambiguities and contradictions in the physical settings of the mere scene in *Beowulf*, then we must assume that the saga is crystal-clear in its description of the relevant details. Lawrence indeed made this claim in his original article on the subject of landscape in the poem, 'The Haunted Mere in *Beowulf*,' and later. repeated it in his *Beowulf and Epic Tradition*.[15] This opinion has since come to be generally accepted, apparently both by Lawrence's followers and his critics.[16] But just how accurate is this assessment of the waterfall scenery in the saga?

The waterfall described in the saga does not reflect any actual scenery in Bárðardalur, where Grettir's fight with the giant is said to have taken place. Lawrence assumed that this was further proof that *Grettis saga* had faithfully preserved the scenery of the ancient legend,[17] but of course that need not be the case. The saga author might just as easily have fashioned an imaginary landscape for Grettir's battle, and the ambiguities in his account of the waterfall and the cave would seem to suggest that this is indeed what he did. One such ambiguity – the question of the location of the cave in respect to the waterfall – was well known before Lawrence published his 'Haunted Mere in *Beowulf*.' When Grettir goes with the priest to explore the gorge, the passage in question can be read to mean that they see either a cave behind the waterfall or simply the precipitous sides of the ravine, and whatever they see is said to be ten fathoms away from something which the text does not clearly identify.[18] It says all that needs to be said about the supposed crystal clarity of this landscape that, for instance, Friedrich Panzer, R.C. Boer, and W.W. Lawrence all see in it a cave, specifically, the cave in which Grettir later has his fight with the giant, behind the waterfall, but cannot agree as to what the ten fathoms are meant to refer,[19] whereas R.W. Chambers does not believe that there is any cave, and even if there was one, he maintains, it would surely have to be yet another cave, different from the one in which the giant lives.[20]

Turning from the landscape of the Sandhaugar episode to the details of what takes place in the cave, the reader who wishes to seek consolation in the clarity of *Grettis saga* after the muddy waters of *Beowulf* is also likely to be disappointed. As we have already seen, the Sandhaugar episode as a whole is riddled with question marks and inconsistencies, and its final chapter is no exception. The prose account of chapter 66 of the saga informs us that Grettir dives under the waterfall and scales the cliff until he reaches a ledge from which he enters the cave. He walks into the cave, which is huge, and well inside the cave fights his battle with the giant. But this course of events is squarely contradicted by the two stanzas, nos. 60 and 61, which Grettir composes to inform the priest of his adventure. Stanza 60 describes Grettir's difficulty in battling against the strong current of a river which runs through the cave, and in stanza 61 the giant is said to have left his cave and come outside to meet him.[21] This is confusing, to say the least. Is the cave dry or does a river run through it; and if a river runs through it, is it supposed to be the same river as the one that forms the waterfall? In the prose account the reader is definitely intended to visualize Grettir in a dry place – after all there is a fire burning in the cave – but at the same time we are also told that the entrails of the giant fell into the river. Are we meant to imagine a virtual avalanche of blood and gore, which flows from the cave and into the river below, or is the saga author being inconsistent at this moment in the narrative by reaching for a a stage prop in the form of a stream, because a river is a handy means of carrying the gory message that signals the outcome of the battle to the timid priest? How we choose to resolve these textual difficulties is actually immaterial for the purpose of this discussion; it is their presence in the text that matters. The description of Grettir's journey to the giant's cave and what takes place once he is there is not a realistic narrative by any stretch of the imagination.

In presenting his waterfall argument Lawrence insisted that the scenery surrounding the mere was characterized by inconsistent features. According to his view, the poem's description of the haunted mere revealed no less than three different conceptions of its nature and location: (a) in a moor or fen, (b) in high and rocky land, and (c) in or near the sea.[22] These could not be reconciled to produce a single consistent picture of natural scenery, in his opinion, because they represented traces of older versions of the story, which had had different stage settings, and which had left their traces on his work when the *Beowulf* poet drew on them for his poem.[23] Furthermore, Lawrence argued that at the core of the poem, in particular in its description of the landscape of the mere, lay a Scandinavian original set in the mountainous country of the Scandinavian peninsula, which was preserved in *Grettis saga*.[24] In other words, the original conception of the scene in *Beowulf* was an inland body of water set in rocky heights, and any traces of the sea or fens were merely secondary stages introduced later in the evolution of the original story.[25]

There is no small amount of arrogance implicit in this analysis. If this is the process through which *Beowulf* came about, we are forced to assume that the author was a bungling realist, a poet who presumably tried to harmonize and digest a number of conflicting versions of his story and who failed miserably in attempting to do so. A less heavy-handed approach might be to accept the contradictions in the scenery of the mere and to allow for the possibility that the author of *Beowulf* set out to create a certain kind of mood rather than realistic scenery. This line of interpretation was in fact suggested by James R. Hulbert as early as 1929,[26] and has influenced some of the later criticisms of Lawrence's reading of the poem.[27] But the waterfall theory was soon criticized for more than being a heavy-handed interpretation. Serious doubts were raised with regard to two of the basic ingredients of Lawrence's theory: first, his claim that references to the sea in the description of the mere were late and unimportant additions to the original legend, and secondly his assumption that the general landscape of the poem could not be visualized as one consistent image.

With respect to Lawrence's dismissal of terms related to the sea in the mere scene, Mackie found numerous examples of words of that kind that Lawrence had overlooked, as well as flaws in the conclusions drawn from the vocabulary that he had examined. Mackie showed beyond any shadow of a doubt that, in the vocabulary of the poem, the mere becomes the sea as soon as the Geatas and the Danes have reached it, and he concluded that the mere must be considered to be a large landlocked arm of the sea, 'even though the resemblance of the scenery in *Beowulf* to that in the *Grettissaga* becomes thereby more distant than before.'[28] Malone, who later examined the entire vocabulary of words denoting bodies of water in *Beowulf,* came to the same conclusion. In the course of his discussion, Malone also had some harsh words for Klaeber, whom he accused of being completely inconsistent in his glossing of sea vocabulary in his edition of the poem in order to accommodate Lawrence's theory.[29]

In his article Malone also examines Lawrence's notion of the three inconsistent descriptions in *Beowulf* of the mere and its surroundings and completely rejects it. Malone's conclusion is that 'the poet gives us not a confused and distorted description of natural scenery but a consistent and carefully-wrought picture of a hell on earth.'[30] Malone shows that Grendel is on numerous occasions referred to by words and phrases that would appear to identify him as a member of a tribe of devils. Grendel is 'a devil in thought and deed,' although he is 'no fallen angel but a monster of human stock and the poet gives him an abode to fit, a hell on earth.'[31] But the strongest evidence for such a reading is undoubtedly, as Malone emphasized, the close resemblance between St. Paul's vision of hell in Blickling Homily XVI, and the passage in *Beowulf* that describes the landscape of the mere.[32] A relationship between the two texts was recognized long before Malone published his article, but there has never been any agreement among scholars as to whether the poem borrowed its description of hell from the homily or the homily from the poem, or whether they both drew from the same source, and this debate still continues.[33] It might be added that Malone's interpretation of the mere scene has not escaped criticism either, as some scholars do not think that the image of hell that he finds in it is hellish enough.[34] What matters for the purpose of this discussion, however, is that a key element in Lawrence's theory, namely, his notion of three conflicting pictures of landscape in the descriptions of the mere in *Beowulf*, has thus been shown to be wrong, and with that the idea of superimposing the landscape of *Grettis saga* upon the poem no longer has any foundation. The shift that has occurred in respect to the issue of landscape in the poem has recently been summed up by Charles D. Wright, who suggests that Lawrence was on the wrong track all along:

Although Lawrence and other earlier scholars believed that the famous analogue in the Icelandic *Grettissaga* preserved 'the original conception of the dwelling of the demons' in *Beowulf*, most recent scholarship concurs that the *Beowulf*-poet has adapted conventional features of hell for his description.[35]

Much of the context of Lawrence's thesis was, as we have seen, demolished decades ago, but strangely enough, some *Beowulf* scholars still cling to certain aspects of the saga's description of landscape as analogues to the poem. In a fairly recent edition of *Beowulf*, for example, we are told that the 'scenery [of Grendel's mere] generally follows the pattern of the waterfall and cave in chapter 66 of *Grettis saga*,'[36] and these two features of landscape still commonly crop up in comparisons between the poem and the saga.

Let us now turn to the caves of Grendel's dam and the giant at Sandhaugar. The first difference between the two that meets the eye is the matter of their respective locations. However we choose to interpret the landscape of the mere in *Beowulf*, at least it is clear that it is set in a howling wilderness, a place which both men and animals avoid at all costs. The giant at Sandhaugar, by contrast, has his cave in the midst of a human settlement, and Grettir's actual journey to the cave is as short as it is uneventful. If we follow the prose of the saga, there is no doubt that the cave is located behind and under a waterfall. In his edition of *Beowulf*, Klaeber, taking his cue from and partly quoting Lawrence, also places Grendel's mother in a corresponding location:

Grendel's dam, aroused by a stranger's appearance in the water, goes to the bottom of the lake (to which Bēowulf had plunged, like Grettir, 'in order to avoid the whirlpool and thus get up underneath the waterfall'), and drags him to her cave.[37]

But there is absolutely nothing in the text to indicate a cave under or behind a waterfall; Grendel's dam in all likelihood inhabits a cave at the bottom of or under the sea. This is what everything points to in the description of Beowulf's entry into the world of the monsters:

- Beowulf dives in, and a long time passes until he has descended far enough to see the floor of the sea, the *grundwong* (line 1496a).
- Unlike the giant at Sandhaugar, Grendel's mother goes to meet her visitor, and after she has grabbed Beowulf, they come to the sea bottom, *to botme* (line 1506b).
- Grendel's dam then carries Beowulf into her cave, and since nothing in the lines of this passage of the poem suggests that they move upwards after having reached the bottom, it seems easiest to suppose that Grendel's mother takes Beowulf into a submarine cave.

In his article entitled 'Grendel and his Abode,' Kemp Malone calls attention to an interesting speech that Beowulf makes just before he sets out on his mission to seek the haunt of Grendel's mother (lines 1392–4), in which he accurately predicts where he intends to look for her:

> Ic hit þe gehate,   no he on helm losaþ,
> ne on foldan fæþm,   ne on fyrgenholt,
> ne on gyfenes grund,   ga þær he wille!

'I promise you, she will never escape into a safe place, not (if she flees) to the bosom of the earth nor to the grove of gigantic trees nor to the bottom of the sea, go where she will.'

In the search that followed, Beowulf first reached the *fyrgenbeamas* 'giant trees' (1414), the *wynleasne wudu* 'joyless wood' (1416) that overshadowed the *mere*. He then dived into the *mere*. Hours later he got far enough down to see the *grundwong* 'bottom' (1496). There, as he said in his report to King Hygelac (made after his return to Geatland), he found the *grundhyrde* 'keeper of the deep' (2136), Grendel's mother. She carried him off to her *hof* in the bosom of the earth, where he killed her after a hard fight. In my opinion the three places of refuge that Beowulf mentioned in lines 1393–1394 foreshadow the three places that he later reached in the course of his search.[38]

It is common enough to see analogue-minded critics equate Beowulf and Grettir as two heroes who battle a 'monster who dwells under water,'[39] but such comparisons conveniently stretch the meaning of 'under water' to unite very different circumstances under the same umbrella.

If the 'old legend' contained a description of the monster's abode, that description cannot be said to have been evenly divided among the supposed literary offspring. Chapter 66 of *Grettis saga* informs the reader that the giant's cave was big, and makes no further attempt to describe his dwelling place. By contrast, the *Beowulf* poet shows considerable interest in the home of the Grendels. As might be expected in a habitation where the occupants are supernatural beings, the place has magic properties. The sea floor forms the roof of the cave and keeps it dry, we are told, even if the cave is 'open,' in the sense that it must have a doorway or some kind of an entrance. Sheer un-reason, as Chambers would say, but for a hero who has held his breath for the better part of the day, this incredible feature must be a welcome relief.

There is another aspect concerning the home of the Grendels that firmly separates it from the cave at Sandhaugar. As James L. Rosier notes in an article entitled 'The Uses of Association: Hands and Feasts in *Beowulf*,' the vocabulary that the poem uses to describe the cave of the monsters often has curiously royal overtones:

Grendel's abode at the bottom of the mere and the description of Beowulf when he descends to that abode are not dissimilar to Hrothgar's hall and the depiction of Grendel at Heorot. For example, the mere-dwelling is called *niðsele*, 'hostile hall,' and *hrofsele*, 'roofed hall.' Just as Grendel is ironically referred to as a 'hall-thane,' so Beowulf is here called a *gist* (1522) and the *selegyst* (1545).[40]

The band of water monsters that guard the hall of the Grendels and attack Beowulf in his effort to reach them also give the impression of a court with its band of retainers. In comparison to all this pomp, the Sandhaugar cave has nothing to offer except its great size, and it is entirely fitting that for all we know about the underwater abode of the Grendels, the poem never mentions whether it is large or small.

It has long been an established fact among analogue enthusiasts that the fires that burn inside the caves of the monsters provide yet another proof of the relationship between *Beowulf* and *Grettis saga*. The following statement exemplifies the casual equation between saga and poem that some critics are ready to make concerning this supposedly analogous point: 'The fire, in each work, is the focus of domestic life, showing that these underwater creatures use the same means of heating and cooking as human beings.'[41] This may sound convincing, but actually there is not so much as a grain of truth in the whole sentence. In the first place, contrary to popular belief, there is no fire in the monster's cave in *Beowulf*, there is only some kind of light, *fyrleoht* (line 1516b), translated by Klaeber as 'fire-light.' In the text another phrase, *blacne leoman* (1517a), 'a shining light,' follows as a variation on *fyrleoht*. As *fyrleoht* is a nonce word, it is difficult to be certain what exactly the compound is supposed to mean, but since in both phrases a particular type of light is being described, it seems most logical to take *fyr-* as a qualifying prefix meaning 'fiery.'[42] It further complicates this discussion that in the poem another light is described just as Beowulf has succeeded in cutting off the head of Grendel's mother:

> Lixte se leoma,   leoht inne stod,
> efne swa of hefene   hadre scineð
> rodores candel, (lines 1570a–2a)

i.e., 'the gleam shone, a light streamed within, even as the candle of the sky shines brightly from heaven.' Is this the same light as the *fyrleoht* in line 1516b, or is this yet another light? Klaeber takes them to be the same, and so does Mackie,[43] but not all critics have concurred with his view. Both Chambers and Lawrence wanted to keep the fire-in-the-cave analogy between the poem and the saga and insisted that the second light should be seen as a 'miraculous radiance sent to help the hero.'[44] However, the issue that matters in this context is the question of a fire or no fire in this passage of the poem, and on this point I agree with Mackie's 'one-and-the same light' interpretation:

the supernatural abode of the demons in *Beowulf* is illuminated not by the large, almost homely fire beside which sits the giant in the *Grettissaga*, but by a lurid supernatural light, bright as the sun in the skies.[45]

As we have seen so often before in our discussion, *Grettis saga* simply does not compare with *Beowulf* on this point unless Procrustean methods are applied to stretch the text of the poem.

After having killed the giant, Grettir kindles a light to examine the interior of the cave. As might be expected, this action has been compared to the 'second light' in Beowulf's battle with Grendel's mother. What is perhaps most striking about this comparison is the lack of sensitivity that parallel-hunting critics have shown for the nature of the texts that are being compared. In *Beowulf*, the essence of the second light that flashes in line 1570 is its strange and unexplained appearance and its mysterious nature. In the poem it comes about at a moment which is in between the main events of Beowulf's adventure in the cave: Grendel's mother has been killed, Grendel has yet to be decapitated, and the blade of the ancient sword has yet to melt. This light comes about despite the hero and not because he wills it. Lawrence's explanation of this light as a 'miraculous radiance sent to help the hero' is somewhat strange, because the great light appears after the battle with Grendel's mother, not before or during the struggle, and therefore appears too late to be of any help to the hero. It is, as so much else that happens in this supernatural region, totally inexplicable. By contrast, the description of Grettir's striking a light in the cave is motivated entirely by realism. The purpose of his journey is to search for the two people who had been abducted by the trolls, and after his brief encounter with the giant, this is precisely what he does, and what the reader expects him to do. The cave is big, more light than just the giant's fire is needed to explore it, and so Grettir strikes a light. As Martin Puhvel has remarked, 'lights illuminating dark or dim places need not necessarily have any connection,' and in this instance *Beowulf* and *Grettis saga* have none.[46]

In this chapter we have examined analogous and genetically related features that critics claim to have discovered in respect to landscape descriptions and other elements of settings in the two works. In respect to all such features – be they narrow footpaths, waterfalls, caves, or fires – there can only be one conclusion. What these so-called genetically related analogues have in common is that none of them can stand up to much scrutiny, and as a rule they are established by seriously distorting the text of the poem or the saga or both. Presumably, analogues are sought in *Beowulf* and *Grettis saga* so that a passage in one work may illuminate or clarify a corresponding section in the other. In this first section of the book, I have looked at all genetically related analogues that I know to have been proposed between the two works, and I have not found a single instance where this has actually been successfully achieved. The deeper one probes in examining these supposed genetically related analogues, and the harder that *Beowulf* and *Grettis saga* are pushed together, the more they tend go their separate ways, so that in the final analysis, no mental acrobatics can bridge the gap between them as different and unrelated texts. However, this is obviously not what analogue-minded critics have thought in the past, and ironically this last point brings us to the next section of this enquiry, which will deal with the question as to how critics have sought to explain the relationship between *Beowulf* and *Grettis saga*, and the different theories that have been proposed to account for their alleged kinship.

PART II
TO CEMENT A RELATIONSHIP

6

The English Hypothesis

It goes without saying that postulating a genetically related analogue to a literary work demands that some form of contact be established between the work in question and the source of the prospective analogue. In presenting his original discovery, Guðbrandur Vigfússon did not shirk from the duty of informing his readers how certain episodes in *Beowulf* and *Grettis saga* had come to be related:

[The Beowulf legend] gives the clue to Grettis Saga, which is otherwise obscure. The old legend shot forth from its ancient Scandinavian home into two branches, one to England, where it was turned into an epic, and one to Iceland, where it was domesticated and embodied in a popular Saga, tacked to the name of an outlaw and hero.[1]

Vigfússon never elaborated much on this brief pronouncement, although, he did remark in a later publication that he took his newly discovered analogues in *Grettis saga* 'to be an echo, not of the present diluted epic [i.e., *Beowulf*], but of the lays from which the epic was later made up.'[2]

Vigfússon's theory was, however, soon challenged by one of the leading medievalists of the Victorian era, Sophus Bugge. Bugge preferred to think that the analogues in *Grettis saga* originated from a saga composed in the North of England, which in turn had been based on an ancient song that was either identical to *Beowulf* as we now have it or closely related to it.[3] In an article entitled 'Beowulf-Grettir,' Liberman calls this type of approach 'the English hypothesis,' and defines it in general terms as a 'solution, according to which the episode in the *Grettla* [i.e., the Sandhaugar episode] owes its origin to a similar episode in *Beowulf*.'[4] The term 'English Hypothesis' actually denotes a number of different but related theories that can fall under Liberman's definition, and in this chapter I take the liberty of using both Liberman's name for this type of approach and his definition of it.

It weakened Bugge's claim for an English origin for *Grettis saga* that he seemed inadvertently to contradict himself in the article in which his hypothesis was first proposed. Critics who came to Vigfússon's defence therefore had an easy first round in defending his ideas,[5] although several early critics voiced their support of Bugge's thesis.[6] In the following debate R.C. Boer eventually emerged as the main advocate and defender of the English Hypothesis. Boer made his case first in an article on *Grettis saga* published in 1898, and then in his edition of the saga two years later. Boer argued for the English Hypothesis in its simplest form, namely, that the saga was directly or indirectly influenced by the poem. He rejected Vigfússon's idea that the Glámr episode was analogous and genetically related to *Beowulf,* and maintained that the saga author was merely copying that episode in Grettir's fight with the troll-woman at Sandhaugar. Grettir's fight with the giant in the cave Boer believed to be an interpolation from *Beowulf;* according to his view the interpolator had taken an indigenous story about a hero who fights against a troll-woman (cf. the local account of how the fight ends, in which she is petrified at daybreak) and combined it with an English version of the Beowulf legend. The *heptisax-hæftmece* analogy was, in Boer's opinion, too close to suggest any solution other than a direct influence from *Beowulf* on the saga.[7]

It shows how much room for different views there actually was among followers of the English Hypothesis that many scholars had ideas that were quite different from those of R.C. Boer as to how much and what kind of a relationship there was between the poem and the saga. Thus Axel Olrik foreshadowed the arguments of several later *Beowulf* scholars (for example, Peter A. Jorgensen, Richard L. Harris, and George Clark) by suggesting that the Beowulf legend had left its mark not only on *Grettis saga,* but also on other Icelandic *þættir* and *fornaldarsǫgur.*[8] Andreas Heusler, on the other hand, believed the Sandhaugar episode of *Grettis saga* to be an eleventh century reworking of the *Beowulf* poem,[9] and Carl W. von Sydow and Hermann Schneider thought that the Grendel part of the Beowulf legend had been brought to Iceland in the twelfth century by someone who had travelled to England, picked up the story, and retold it once he was back home.[10]

In the decades that followed Boer's edition of *Grettis saga,* more and more scholars began to detect *Beowulf* analogues which they believed to be of Irish origin, and they too were bound to favour the English Hypothesis and reject Vigfússon's old Scandinavian legend as a means of contact between *Beowulf* and *Grettis saga.* Richard L. Harris, who surveys the claims for Irish ancestry for Beowulf's fight against Grendel and his mother in an article entitled 'The Deaths of Grettir and Grendel: A New Parallel,' sums them up as follows:

The Irish school is ... made up of two groups, the former having been interested chiefly in oral sources, especially The Hand and Child Tale. In this tale, a hero waits in a room from which, over a period of time, children have previously disappeared one by one. As he waits, an arm comes down the chimney, its hand reaching out into the room. The hero seizes the arm and pulls it off the intruding monster. He then chases and kills it and returns the children.

The latter group is concerned also with possible literary and ecclesiastical sources, in such works as the early eighth century *Táin Bó Fráich*, the *Vita Columbae* of Adomnán, upon which the former story is itself partially dependent, and the *Sex Aetates Mundi*, from which the brood of Cain as it is described in *Beowulf* is supposed to come.[11]

No potential common source has been found for the Irish materials. Consequently, proponents of the Irish version of the English Hypothesis, who have proven to be highly analogue-minded critics, can only assume that *Beowulf* directly (or indirectly) influenced *Grettis saga* if their own discoveries of Irish analogues are supposed to hold. Among critics who belong to the Irish school, only Martin Puhvel has been able to imagine a hypothetical compromise with Guðbrandur Vigfússon:

It should ... [in] this discussion of the thorny problem of the origin of the Grendel story, be admitted that the possibility of some form of basic influence by Scandinavian folk-tale, so much theorized about, cannot be totally dismissed, even if there seems, to me, no need for any such assumption – the pieces of the jigsaw puzzle seem to fall reasonably well into place without it. Yet it is not inconceivable that, as so many a scholar thinks, some extinct Scandinavian tale may lurk in the background. It may have fused in England with somewhat similar Celtic folktale elements and possibly elements of Anglo-Saxon folklore ... to provide the basic plot of the Grendel story; and, just conceivably, this story may then, to the further bedevilment of the *Beowulf* student, have travelled to Iceland to fuse there with an offshoot of its partial ancestor from Scandinavia, thus rearing its bewildering head in *Grettis saga*. All this complication seems to me altogether unlikely – yet, who truly knows?[12]

The debate between proponents of the English Hypothesis and those who favoured a common origin of some sort – either as Guðbrandur Vigfússon had originally proposed or by viewing *Beowulf* and *Grettis saga* as different versions of the same folktale (the Bear's Son Tale), as Friedrich Panzer maintained[13] – soon turned into a quarrel over what oral transmission could or could not preserve. Oral transmission was, of course, the vehicle on which all theories of common origin had to rest, and this is what Carl W. von Sydow, who emerged as a leading critic of such ideas, chose to focus his attention on.

Von Sydow had earlier believed that both *Beowulf* and *Grettis saga* went back to a common but now lost Irish source which had contained the original version of the poem; however, he later modified his position and formulated his own version of the English Hypothesis.[14]

In his criticism of theories that postulated a common origin, von Sydow's basic line of argument was that the process of oral transmission was incompatible with the nature of various key analogues that it was supposed to have delivered to different countries and thereby into different languages. To demonstrate his case, von Sydow singled out three analogous points of contact between the saga and the poem: the *hæftmece-heptisax* parallel, the runes on the handle of the giant sword and Grettir's rune staff, and Lawrence's thesis of confused and clear landscape descriptions in the two branches of the old legend. In respect to the analogy between *hæftmece* and *heptisax*, von Sydow found it highly improbable that the latter word – an unimportant term for a weapon – could have been passed on for six hundred years or so within an oral tradition, only to surface once in an insignificant episode of *Grettis saga*. As a result, he felt that the analogy between the two words could only point to direct or indirect literary borrowing.[15] Concerning the issue of runic messages in both works, von Sydow maintained that in *Beowulf* the runes on the handle of the giant sword played absolutely no role in the series of events that are described in the poem. To him it was a clear example of a motif that the author of *Grettis saga* had reworked into a rune staff carrying a message to Steinn the priest in order to make it meaningful.[16] Finally, von Sydow turned to Lawrence's waterfall theory and rejected it on general grounds. An oral tradition, he argued, could not contain at one and the same time two conflicting descriptions of a landscape, one clear and the other one confused, as Lawrence had postulated. Given enough time, one of the two would always be obliterated by the other within the tradition.[17]

The Irish-English Hypothesis is still being kept alive, by scholars such as Martin Puhvel, for example, but it has always been a version of the English Hypothesis that only a minority of scholars, most of them Irish, have embraced. There are great many 'ifs' in this approach, and one has to agree with Anatoly Liberman when he says in his criticism of it that 'the Irish-English hypothesis should be rejected not because the Old English and Icelandic texts use nearly the same word in the same situation, but because none of its theses can be proved.'[18]

Whatever version of the English Hypothesis its proponents chose to embrace, a means of ferrying the Beowulf story across the ocean to Iceland had to be found. It goes without saying that scholars had to resort to pure guesswork when it came to this part of the effort to bridge the gap between the poem and the saga, but vacuums of knowledge in medieval studies have never failed to attract attention, and there has been no lack of solutions proposed in this area either. Kemp Malone suggested that the legend could have reached Iceland through bilingual Viking settlers in England, and that 'through those who spoke both languages English tales like the Grendel story could spread all over the Scandinavian world.'[19] Douglas Stedman and Alois Brandl favoured the idea that the Beowulf legend had been brought to Iceland by Anglo-Saxon missionaries who had indeed worked there in the early decades of the eleventh century,[20] and, as I have already mentioned, Carl W. von Sydow and Hermann Schneider believed that an Icelander travelling in England had brought the legend home with him.[21] By far the most ambitious piece of speculation however, came from Eiríkur Magnússon who went so far as to discover the person responsible for the introduction of the Beowulf legend into Icelandic culture. According to his biographer, Magnússon suggested 'that the tales from *Beowulf* had been brought to Iceland from the British Isles with a settler named Auðunn Skökull, whose kin lived in the same district and was related by marriage to that of Grettir.'[22]

It is not an understatement to say that the English Hypothesis has been under constant attack since Sophus Bugge first suggested it, and nowadays it seems to have very few spokesmen among *Beowulf* scholars. Critics who subscribed to a common origin for *Beowulf* and *Grettis saga* quickly discovered several weak spots in the process that the English Hypothesis implicitly postulated and wasted no time in hammering away at them. One of the first targets was the fact that Old English and Old Norse are obviously different languages. As early as 1909, in his *Studier i Beowulfsagan*, Henrik Schück categorically stated that Old English would have been incomprehensible in thirteenth-century Iceland, so that even if the *Beowulf* poem had somehow found its way to the country, it could still not have been a source for *Grettis saga*.[23] R.W. Chambers, in an article entitled 'Beowulf's Fight with Grendel and its Scandinavian Parallels,' took up this argument and added several others to show that Old English was not likely to have been much understood in medieval Iceland:

My reasons for thinking that a thirteenth century Scandinavian could not have drawn from a MS of *Beowulf* are (1) the absurd blunders made when Icelanders drew from the Old English genealogies; (2) the difficulties which Thorkelin, despite his acquaintance with Icelandic and many years of study, found in understanding *Beowulf;* (3) the fact that, already in the early twelfth century, a writer like Henry of Huntingdon, who can understand Anglo-Saxon prose, finds the poetry difficult and its terms strange (*extranea*). For these and other reasons, the idea of an Icelander about the year 1300 reading a MS of *Beowulf* seems to me fantastic.[24]

And Chambers concluded this train of thought in his book on *Beowulf* by dryly remarking that if the Sandhaugar episode was derived from the poem, 'we have an interesting literary curiosity, but nothing further.'[25]

Another glaring weakness in the English Hypothesis is its failure to explain exactly how *Beowulf* could have inspired the supposed analogues in *Grettis saga*, in particular the Sandhaugar episode. W.W. Lawrence attacked this flaw in an article entitled 'The Haunted Mere in *Beowulf*' published in 1912: 'It is clear that the Anglo-Saxon *Beowulf*, in anything like the form in which we have it at present, could not have given a hint for the description of Grettir's adventure at the waterfall.'[26] In *Beowulf and Epic Tradition*, Lawrence comes back to this point and is even more critical of the English Hypothesis than before: 'One thing is obvious: that the straightforward account in the saga cannot have been derived, even indirectly, from the epic. The saga is clear where the epic is confused.'[27] In his book on *Beowulf* Chambers continued Lawrence's line of attack and singled out landscape descriptions in the poem and the saga as evidence against the possibility of an English origin for the latter:

> Now it is in the highest degree improbable that, after the landscape had been blurred as it is in *Beowulf*, it could have been brought out again with the distinctness it has in the *Grettis saga*. To preserve the features so clearly the *Grettir*-story can hardly be derived from *Beowulf*: it must have come down independently.[28]

More recently, the issue of landscapes and settings has been raised by Joan Turville-Petre, who also rules out direct influence of the poem on the author of the saga: 'Even if he could have read the poem, the saga writer could not possibly have constructed his account from this source,'[29] and also by J. Michael Stitt, who concurs with the critics of the English Hypothesis that *Beowulf* cannot be the only source for the Sandhaugar episode of the saga.[30]

In his criticism of the possibility that *Beowulf* might have directly or indirectly influenced the author of *Grettis saga*, Chambers also used literary arguments. In 'Beowulf's Fight with Grendel, and its Scandinavian Parallels,' he wonders aloud why the saga author chose not to make use of the finer points of the Grendel section of the poem:

> Now, when we turn to the *Sandhaugar* episode, we find that the heroic epic setting has absolutely disappeared. There is nothing even corresponding to it, *except for the things in which the Danes take over functions from folk tale*: the only sufferings or doings of the Danes which have their counterpart in the *Sandhaugar* episode are things like their victimization before Beowulf appears, and their departure leaving Beowulf in the water. But, apart from this, the whole Danish setting is wanting; even the motive of the ven-

geance for Æschere, which would have appealed to an Icelandic audience of the thirteenth century. In the *Sandhaugar* episode there is no second raid of the monster-brood, although this would have supplied what is so obvious a fault in that episode, a reason why Grettir, whose fear of the dark is haunting him, should nevertheless have felt bound to go out of his way to seek the monster in the cavern. If the compiler of the *Grettis saga* knew the story in the *Beowulf* form, why should he have reverted to the looser construction of the folk tale? For the Danish setting, which places the combat in a royal hall, makes a fine tale, eminently suited to Grettir's early adventures at the court of a king. Why abandon the courtly setting? And, above all, why abandon the vengeance motive? Is it likely that an Icelandic saga-man, borrowing his tale from *Beowulf*, would have omitted a detail so entirely congenial to him?[31]

In the final analysis the English Hypothesis must be rejected. It is clear that it fails to account properly for how *Beowulf* is supposed to relate to the saga, and proponents of this thesis have never managed to defend it successfully against the criticisms of Chambers, Lawrence, and other scholars. Furthermore, I agree with Richard L. Harris when he calls the idea of the saga's dependence on *Beowulf* 'naive.' 'Too many stories,' he adds, 'once told have been long forgotten, and the conflagrations damaging the Cotton and Arnamagnaean collections should be sufficient lessons in the uncertainties of preservation of the written word.'[32]

7

Panzer's 'Bear's Son' Thesis

In 1910 there appeared in Munich a remarkably ambitious and impressive work under the innocuous title of *Studien zur germanischen Sagengeschichte I. Beowulf.* The author, Friedrich Panzer, had collected and collated more than two hundred versions of a particular folktale, known as 'The Bear's Son Tale,'[1] from a variety of different languages and cultures. From these Panzer reconstructed in the first part of his book what he believed to be the original elements of the different versions of the tale. In the second part, he turned his attention to *Beowulf* and proceeded to argue that both the Grendel section of *Beowulf* and the Sandhaugar episode of *Grettis saga* were to be regarded as mutually independent versions of the Bear's Son Tale and related only insofar that they were two branches on the same stem.[2] Panzer was not the first critic to note similarities between *Beowulf* and the Bear's Son Tale, this had been done by Ludwig Laistner some twenty years earlier.[3] What was original about his theory was the revolutionary way that it proposed of linking *Beowulf* and *Grettis saga*, a way that was incompatible both with Guðbrandur Vigfússon's ideas of an old Scandinavian legend shooting its branches to England and Iceland and with the different versions of the English Hypothesis.

The folktale that Panzer believed to be the missing link between *Beowulf* and *Grettis saga* exists in several different versions, but the main outline of the story is something like this: The hero sometimes has an animal, usually a bear, as his ancestor, or he is raised by bears. He is often immensely strong and performs incredible feats of strength, but is otherwise an unpromising youth. He leaves home, or his master, and gathers around him two or three strong companions that he meets along the road. The companions often turn out to possess some special powers as well. Together, the hero and his companions come upon a deserted dwelling place, sometimes a castle, in the woods. The hero and his companions cook food, but an evil supernatural being steals it. The hero's companions fight the demon unsuccessfully, but the hero himself prevails against the monster, wounds it, and ties it to a tree, often by its beard. The wounded demon flees to his subterranean lair, tearing off a part of himself in the process of escaping and leaving a trail of blood behind him. The hero follows the trail and usually lowers himself by a rope into the underworld. There he beheads his supernatural enemy or enemies, a male and in some cases a related female as well, sometimes with a magic sword that he discovers in the demon's lair. After that he frees a princess or princesses (usually three) who have been held captive by the demon and has them and much treasure pulled up to the world above. His companions, who have been watching over or holding the rope, covet the princesses and the treasure and betray the hero by leaving him in the underworld, sometimes by cutting the rope, as soon as the princesses and the treasure have been pulled up. The hero eventually makes his way up, sometimes aided by a surviving demon or a magic bird, hunts down and punishes the treacherous companions and marries one of the princesses.[4]

In examining the Grendel section of *Beowulf*, Panzer noted a number of points where he thought that the poem followed the pattern of the folktale:

- Hroðgar's splendid hall matches the house in the woods.[5]
- Grendel compares with the 'Earthman' demon (*Erdmann*) in the folktale.[6]
- Like the demon in the folktale, Grendel appears at night, provoked by the merry noises of Hroðgar's court.[7]
- Beowulf's youth, unusual strength, early heroic deeds (such as the swimming match with Breca), and lack of promise as a boy all match the characteristics of the hero in the Bear's Son Tale.[8]
- The poem's description of Beowulf lying awake to wait for the monster while his companions sleep, the fight itself, the demon's immunity to weapons, the wounding of the demon and his escape as his arm is torn off, and finally, the display of Grendel's severed limb as a trophy, were all, according to Panzer, motifs which were to be found in the different versions of the folktale as well.[9]
- In the folktale the demon also leaves a bloody track, which the hero follows, and he sometimes has a mother, although revenge of the kind that we find in *Beowulf* does not occur in any versions of the folktale.[10]
- Unferð is cast in the mould of the Bear Son's cowardly retainers.[11]
- The demon's treasure-filled underwater lair in *Beowulf*, the fire burning in the cave, the hero's battle against Grendel's mother, his discovery of a magic sword, the killing of the demon with her own weapon, and Beowulf's attack on the already dead Grendel and the Danes who leave the mere were all items that matched the folktale in Panzer's view. He had to admit, however, that in *Beowulf* no princesses are rescued by the hero.[12]

Panzer then turned to the account of Beowulf's fight against the dragon and, as he had done previously with the Grendel section, found it to contain essential folktale elements, although he did not find them to stem from the Bear's Son Tale.[13]

In his analysis of *Grettis saga*, Panzer determined that the folktale had left the same unmistakable marks on it that he had discovered in *Beowulf*:

- As in the folktale, the demon appears three times at Sandhaugar and is attacked by the hero on her third visit.[14]
- The troll-woman, her knife, and her trencher all have their counterparts in the different versions of the Bear's Son Tale, and so does her disappearance following the loss of her arm.[15]
- Steinn, the priest, corresponds to the companions of the folktale in his failure to guard the rope properly. His name is also close to that of the *Steinmensch* in a Faroese version of the folktale.[16]
- In some versions of the Bear's Son Tale the hero must pass through water to reach the abode of the monsters. The cave, the fire, the sword on the wall, and the discovery of treasure are all familiar features, although the author of the saga is not keeping to the pattern of the folktale when he has Grettir kill the giant with his own weapon instead of with the sword for which the giant reaches during his encounter with the hero. The bones that Grettir carries from the cave do not fit the folktale pattern either; however, Panzer believed that they played a role in shaming the priest for his cowardice.[17]
- Although, unlike the Bear Son's unfaithful companions, Steinn is not directly punished, he is reprimanded by Grettir.[18]
- There are, of course, no princesses in the Sandhaugar episode, but Steinvǫr, the lady of the farm, is certainly a lady in distress. The affair that she has with Grettir, and the son that they have together, easily casts her into the role of one of the princesses of the Bear's Son Tale in Panzer's view.[19]
- Panzer also believed that as a hero Grettir conformed with the model of the strong but unruly and unpromising boy of the folktale who, like Grettir, performs various feats of strength, although he has no taste for ordinary work.[20]
- Grettir's adventure in the gravemound of Kárr the Old, Panzer considered to be a variant of the Bear's Son Tale. It included standard elements such as entry into the underworld, an unfaithful companion watching over a rope, and the presence of a treasure, and, in addition, Panzer felt that Þorfinnr's calm reaction to Grettir's breaking into his father's burial place made no sense unless versions of the folktale in which a boy goes out in search of treasure for his master were taken into account. In other words, Panzer believed the Kárr episode to be a substitute for an earlier passage of the Bear's Son

type in the saga, of which Þorfinnr's emotional tranquility over Grettir's breaking into his father's burial mound was a relic.[21]

- Grettir's fight with the bear, his swimming trips to fetch fire while in Norway and in Drangey, and many of the various feats of strength that the saga ascribes to him, as well as the story of the maiden who sees Grettir naked on the beach, were all features for which Panzer found corresponding episodes in some version of the folktale.[22]

In comparing *Beowulf* and *Grettis saga* in terms of how well each work had preserved the original folktale, Panzer found the Old English poem, generally speaking, closer to it than the saga. He noted that in the Sandhaugar episode the troll-woman should not be out of her lair, that the motivation given by the saga for Grettir's journey into the gorge is poor, that a lame sword motif is present in the episode which occurs once he is inside the giant's cave, and that the wounded troll-woman is completely absent from the cave. On the other hand, however, he believed that *Grettis saga* had preserved features from the original tale such as the threefold appearance of the unknown demon, her arrival at midnight armed with a sword and a trencher, the cutting off of the demon's arm, the descent to the underworld by means of a rope, and the discovery of the giant alive once the hero is inside his cave.[23] It may also be noted that in spite of his initial categorical insistence that *Beowulf* and *Grettis saga* were independent versions of the same folktale,[24] Panzer appears to have revised his ideas on this subject towards the end of his book, where he allows for the possibility of some form of contact either with an early Scandinavian version of the *Beowulf* story or with a poem close to the version of *Beowulf* we now have.[25] Perhaps he made this unexpected concession in order to defend himself against foreseeable criticism, because in his discussion of *Beowulf* and *Grettis saga* hardly a word had been said about the literary parallel upon which so much of the debate in previous scholarship had focused – namely the famous *hæftmece-heptisax* pair – and this allowed Panzer to get past that obstacle.

In the decades that followed the publication of his book, many *Beowulf* scholars accepted Panzer's ideas, either partially or fully. It is for instance obvious from Chambers's work on *Beowulf* that, although it did not quite convince him, Panzer's theory gave him much case for thought. Chambers was prepared to accept that bits and pieces of the Bear's Son story had influenced the common ancestor of *Beowulf* and *Grettis saga*, and he was even willing to admit that a version of the tale might have left its mark on the Sandhaugar episode.[26] But he was, at the same time, critical of Panzer's method,[27] and he did not agree with him that the Bear's Son story formed the core of both works or that no further connection between them need be postulated. After having considered the elements of the folktale, Chambers argued his case against Panzer as follows:

Now it may be objected, with truth, that this is not like the *Beowulf*-story, or even particularly like the *Grettir*-story. But the question is not merely whether it resembles these stories as we possess them, but whether it resembles the story which must have been the common origin of both. And we have only to try to reconstruct from *Beowulf* and from the *Grettis saga* a tale which can have been the common original of both, to see that it must be something extraordinarily like the folk-tale outlined above.

For example, it is true that the departure of the Danes homeward because they believe that Beowulf has met his death in the water below, bears only the remotest resemblance to the deliberate treachery which the companions in the folk-tale mete out to the hero. But when we compare the *Grettir*-story, we see there that a real breach of trust is involved, for there the priest Stein leaves the hero in the lurch, and abandons the rope by which he should have drawn Grettir up. This can hardly be an innovation on the part of the composer of the *Grettis saga*, for he is quite well disposed towards Stein, and has no motive for wantonly attributing treachery to him. The innovation presumably lies in the *Beowulf*-story, where Hrothgar and his court are depicted in such a friendly spirit that no disreputable act can be attributed to them, and consequently Hrothgar's departure home must not be allowed in any way to imperil or inconvenience the hero. A comparison of the *Beowulf*-story with the *Grettir*-story leads then to the conclusion that in the oldest version those who remained above when the hero plunged below *were* guilty of some measure of disloyalty in ceasing to watch for him. In other words we see that the further we track the *Beowulf*-story back, the more it comes to resemble the folk-tale.[28]

Chambers expanded on this view later in his book and added that the chosen retainers whom Beowulf has taken with him on his journey to combat Grendel 'could not be represented as unfaithful, because the poet was reserving the episode of the faithless retainers for the death of Beowulf.'[29] He also pointed to the *hæftmece-heptisax* parallel and the strange conclusion drawn by the watcher(s) in *Beowulf* and *Grettis saga* from the blood-stained water as elements that were altogether absent from Panzer's folktale.[30] Chambers's final verdict on Panzer's theory was that he had indeed shown that the Grendel episode of *Beowulf* was an epic glorification of a folktale motif, but the absence of the three princesses in the poem made it impossible to regard it as one of the different versions of Panzer's Bear Son's Tale. 'At most,' Chambers concluded, 'it is a version of a portion of them. The omission of the princesses in *Beowulf* and the *Grettis saga* is fundamental. With the princesses much else falls away. There is no longer any motive for the betrayal of trust by the watchers. The disguise of the hero and his vengeance are now no longer necessary to the tale.'[31]

Chambers was not the only critic to give Panzer's work a mixed review. Carl W. von Sydow failed to see much of a comparison between Steinn's leaving the rope in *Grettis saga* and the treason of the Bear's Son's companions in the folktale.[32] Von Sydow was, like Chambers, inclined to think that the saga had borrowed both Steinn and the rope that he is supposed to watch over from the folktale; however, the two parted company over Chambers's supposition that the Bear's Son Tale might have influenced the common ancestor to *Beowulf* and *Grettis saga*, a theory that von Sydow rejected completely.[33] Fernand Mossé, in the introduction to his French translation of *Grettis saga*, included a brief chapter devoted to explicating Panzer's analysis of the saga which Mossé, for the most part, accepted. Mossé thought that Panzer had gone too far, though, in trying to discover stolen princesses in the Sandhaugar episode; it did not have any, and Steinvǫr would not do as a substitute.[34]

Nevertheless, many critics have been prepared to accept Panzer's theory with all of its ramifications. In America, W.W. Lawrence hailed it as 'a landmark in the investigation of *Beowulf*,'[35] and, on the other side of the Atlantic, Walter J. Sedgefield, in his 1935 edition of *Beowulf*, also praised Panzer's contribution: 'The great merit of Panzer's exhaustive study is that it throws new light upon the development of those Scandinavian sagas which deal with strong men fighting with monsters, and enables us to view the Beowulf story in something like a proper perspective.'[36] In recent years Panzer's line of investigation has been defended and continued by scholars such as E.E. Wardale,[37] Gwyn Jones,[38] Joaquín M. Pizarro,[39] Richard L. Harris,[40] and Peter A. Jorgensen.[41]

In their efforts to keep Panzer's ideas alive, these and other sympathetic scholars have, however, had to fight a constant battle against the tide of criticism to which Panzer's book has been exposed ever since its publication. First of all, his basic method has certain disturbing implications. Panzer collected relatively modern versions of the Bear's Son Tale, and in using them to construct an ancient original version and for comparison with *Beowulf* and *Grettis saga*, he obviously had to assume that the basic story had remained unchanged in its structure for more than a thousand years. Although folklorists like Vladimir Propp, Antti Aarne, and Stith Thompson insist on the relative stability of the folktale as a form of narrative,[42] their views hardly justify Panzer's assumption.[43] Secondly, Panzer's method of reducing different versions of the story to schematized summaries has come under intense criticism. Decades ago, Carl W. von Sydow pointed out that two very different stories can be made to produce the same composite pattern, and argued that a pattern which is obtained in this manner proves nothing about a relationship between the stories in question. He also drew attention to how different the narrative elements of the Bear's Son Tale are from the Grendel episode, although structurally they might be made to appear similar:

- In the different versions of the Bear's Son Tale, the demon most commonly only inhabits the house in the woods during the day.
- The demon is almost always a little dwarf with a long beard.
- The hero always uses a rope to get to the demon's under-ground lair.
- In most versions of the folktale there is no water that the hero has to pass through in his quest of the demon, and hence no swimming either.
- A princess or all three princesses are present in 190 of the 200 variants of the story.
- The hero's discovery of the princesses is always what motivates his helpers to betray him.

Von Sydow also pointed to several essential elements of the Grendel episode that are completely missing in the Bear's Son Tale:

- The king is harassed by the demon in his palace until the hero comes to his aid.
- The warriors who are supposed to keep watch have fallen asleep when the demon attacks.
- The hero tears off the demon's arm.
- Revenge is exacted by the demon's mother.
- No rope is used to reach the demon's abode.
- The magic sword is only discovered by the hero when it looks as though he will succumb to the demon in the fight against her.
- One of the demons is beheaded in order to bring its head back as a trophy.
- The demon's sword melts.
- The demon's blood on the water leads the hero's companions to think that it is the hero who is dead.[44]

In this comparison von Sydow came to the same conclusion as Klaeber, namely that similarities between the Bear's Son Tale and the Grendel episode were 'remote and generally vague.'[45] R.C. Boer went even further by accusing Panzer of assembling unrelated bits and pieces, particularly in *Grettis saga*, to make the Sandhaugar episode fit into the narrative pattern of the folktale.[46]

Furthermore, von Sydow and Chambers were critical of Panzer for his lack of geographical discrimination or attention to landscape in his comparisons of the Bear's Son Tale with *Beowulf* and *Grettis saga*.[47] It was also pointed out that Old English literature on the whole showed no signs of being influenced by this folktale.[48] The same may be said about early Scandinavian literature. J. Michael Stitt, who surveys the Scandinavian versions of the folktale in his book *Beowulf and the Bear's Son*, notes that only two motifs from it – those of treacherous abandonment and the abduction of women – are present in two late medieval Icelandic sagas, and that there is no firm evidence of the actual presence of the Bear's Son Tale in Scandinavia until the beginning of the eighteenth century.[49] Stitt also notes that in Scandinavian versions of the folktale, the hero is never associated with water.[50]

In conclusion, it must be said that, all in all, the criticism against Panzer's 'Bear's Son' theory outweighs his evidence concerning the supposed relationship between *Beowulf* and *Grettis saga* as two versions of the Bear's Son Tale. The basic shortcomings of Panzer's thesis, particularly the alleged connection between the folktale and the Sandhaugar episode, have, in the decades that have passed since his book appeared, not been repaired by anything that his followers have had to offer. The great weakness in Panzer's theory is that several of the motifs that he found in the three stories and used as special evidence to connect them – for example, the unpromising youth, great feats of strength, and the abandonment of the hero by his companions – are commonly found in medieval texts that have nothing whatsoever to do with the Bear's Son Tale.[51] As Theodore M. Andersson has recently pointed out, the folktale context that Panzer insisted on using as a basis for his comparison is simply 'too universal.'[52] In his investigation of the two hundred variants of the tale, Panzer never succeeded in finding a single version that corresponded motif by motif to the saga episode, and only a discovery of that kind would have been the sort of proof that might have clinched his argument. The few real similarities that are to be detected between the Grendel episode of *Beowulf*, the Sandhaugar episode of *Grettis saga*, and the different versions of the Bear's Son Tale can only be a coincidence that has probably come about because all three share a basic theme in the sense that they describe a hero's destruction of an evil being.

8

The Common Origin Theory

Among the different theories that compete to offer an explanation as to how *Grettis saga* and *Beowulf* might be related, there is no question that the original one suggested by Guðbrandur Vigfússon more than a century ago has always been the most popular among medievalists. As with the English Hypothesis, the Common Origin Theory is here used as an umbrella term, because there are, as we shall see in this chapter, considerable differences in how Vigfússon's followers imagine contact between the poem and the saga to have come about. However, the core of agreement that all variants of this theory share is that they postulate a common ancestor for the two works: Vigfússon's 'old legend.' In its most conservative form, the Common Origin Theory has it that the author of *Grettis saga* knew poems or stories related to the Old English epic.[1] Most Common Origin Theory critics, however, are not this modest. They usually work on the assumption that both the saga author and the composer of *Beowulf* had access to and used the same form of the 'old legend' and, armed with this conviction, they have mercilessly used *Grettis saga* to emend *Beowulf* or vice versa.

What commonly characterizes critics who have embraced this theory is a desire to find rational solutions to problems in both the saga and the poem. It is to this group that we owe the myth about the so-called realism of the Sandhaugar episode. Their line of approach demands *a priori* that the saga preserve a clearer version of the 'old legend' than *Beowulf*. This attitude is particularly explicit in W.W. Lawrence's *Beowulf and Epic Tradition*: 'One thing is obvious: that the straightforward account in the saga cannot have been derived, even indirectly, from the epic. The saga is clear where the epic is confused; it preserves the original form of the story so much better that it may even be used to explain obscure incidents and description in the Anglo-Saxon.'[2]

Along with W.W. Lawrence, R.W. Chambers gradually emerged as the chief promoter and defender of the Common Origin Theory. Chambers rejected the English Hypothesis on the grounds that Old English had been unintelligible in medieval Iceland and that the Sandhaugar episode could not have been constructed from *Beowulf.* He also rested his case on the strong cultural ties between England and Scandinavia:

> Other stories which were current in England in the eighth century were also current in Scandinavia in the thirteenth. Yet this does not mean that the tales of Hroar and Rolf, or of Athils and Ali, were borrowed from English epic accounts of Hrothgar and Hrothulf, or Eadgils and Onela. They were part of the common inheritance – as much so as the strong verbs or the alliterative line. Why then, contrary to all analogy, should we assume a literary borrowing in the case of the *Beowulf-Grettir* story?[3]

As for the logic behind the Common Origin Theory, Chambers believed that Lawrence's landscape theory had proven once and for all the validity of Vigfússon's original hypothesis.[4] However, Chambers must have found the Sandhaugar episode a meagre tale, because gradually he began to look for other Icelandic materials that could qualify as *Beowulf* analogues and make it possible for him to put together an outline of what he believed to be the original story. Eventually, his reconstruction of the 'old legend' rested not only on *Beowulf* and *Grettis saga*, but also on two other late sagas, *Samsons saga fagra*[5] and *Gull-Þóris saga*, and on an Icelandic folktale, *Gullbrá og Skeggi*. What Chambers distilled from these raw materials to 'reconstruct' his 'old legend' we shall see later in this chapter.

On most aspects of the Common Origin Theory, Lawrence and Chambers were in perfect agreement, but as we saw in the previous chapter, they – and Common Origin Theory critics in general – disagreed on the question as to how much the Bear's Son Tale was supposed to have influenced the 'old legend.' The location of the homeland of the 'old legend' was another issue on which Common Origin Theory critics have traditionally differed. Some, like Lawrence and Chambers, preferred a solution based on Vigfússon's idea:

> A widespread *märchen*, in a form determined by the mountainous country of the Scandinavian peninsula, was attached, in Scandinavian territory, to the hero Beowulf, and placed in a historical setting. In one incident of this story, the hero fought with a supernatural being in a cave under a waterfall. Brought to England, still in the form of lays, it was ultimately worked over, with other material, into the present epic ... The tale continued to live on in Scandinavia, both in its independent *märchen*-form, and as united with *Beowulf*. In a version pretty close to that taken to England and made the basis of the Anglo-Saxon epic, it was added to the exploits of Grettir Asmundarson, a historical per-

sonage of the eleventh century. The *Grettissaga*, which preserves much of original form of the story, thus enables us to see more clearly what was the original setting of the second adventure in *Beowulf*.[6]

Henrik Schück, on the other hand, imagined an even more complicated scenario:

1 / In its earliest form the 'old legend' is Danish but has no attachments to historical figures or events.

2 / In the next stage the legend incorporates historical material in Denmark. That version of the story is brought to England, but the unhistorical form of the story also lives on in Denmark.

3 / In Denmark the unhistorical version of the legend also eventually becomes a historical epic and is again brought to England, where in the meantime the legend has degenerated to an unhistorical folktale which, in that form, spreads to Scandinavia where it ultimately links up with stories about Grettir.[7]

Daring as Schück's proposed meandering of the 'old legend' may seem, he is still not nearly as imaginative as an earlier critic, John Earle, who gives the transmission of the 'old legend' a fixed date in his *Anglo-Saxon Literature*:

The identity [of events in the Sandhaugar episode and in *Beowulf*] is so manifest that we only have to ask which people (if either) was the borrower, the English or the Danes. And here comes in the consideration that the geography of the 'Beowulf' is Scandinavian. There is no consciousness of Britain or England throughout the poem. If this raises a presumption that the Saxon poet got his story from a Dane, we naturally ask, When is this likely to have happened? and the answer must be that the earliest probable time begins after the Peace of Wedmore in 878.[8]

Other critics have been more careful about committing themselves to a specific set of circumstances. Thus Klaeber, in his edition of the poem, merely states that 'a genetic relation of some kind must clearly be admitted between the *Beowulf* and certain Scandinavian stories, in particular the one attached to Grettir the Strong.'[9] H. Munro and Nora Chadwick are uncommitted about the location of the 'old legend' over and above placing it somewhere in the North,[10] and Eugen Mogk also belongs to this moderate camp, in the sense that he does not believe that it is possible to decide whether the story ultimately had a Danish or an English origin.[11]

There is also disagreement among whose who subscribe to the Common Origin Theory over the Glámr episode in *Grettis saga*. As we saw in chapter 1, some critics accept it as a bona fide genetically related analogue to *Beowulf* while others have rejected it. Scholars who accept Glámr usually maintain that his fight with Grettir corresponds to Beowulf's struggle against Grendel in Hroðgar's hall. It then follows that the first fight in the Sandhaugar episode loses its primary status since it is only an echo of a previous chapter of the saga. C.S. Smith, who argues along these lines, presents his case as follows:

Comparing now the descriptions in Gretti [i.e., *Grettis saga*] of his two encounters in the hall, first with Glám and second with the evil-spirit, we shall find them to be identical. The same incidents are repeated in the same order. It is a trait well known to Icelandic students that the same incident is made at times to do double duty in the same saga. Hence in our mind there rests little doubt as to the identity between Glám and the hall-haunter of the second tale, for the difference in the catastrophe does not, to our view, entitle the latter to other distinction than that of being regarded as another form of the same legend. But how much more graphic, more masterly in all its parts, is the story of the wrestling with Glám. Unquestionably that is the original, and the other the copy.[12]

But on the status of Glámr, Smith is probably only speaking for a minority of Common Origin Theory critics. Most of them seem to have accepted Chambers's argument that the double fight of the Grendel story only compares to the double fight at Sandhaugar.[13]

Common Origin Theory critics have also disagreed on the question as to how to view the female monsters in the poem and the saga. On this issue Chambers maintained – with a curiously anti-feminist slant – that *Beowulf* preserved the original story while *Grettis saga* had altered the roles of the male and the female monsters:

in the *Grettis saga* it is the female monster who raids the habitation of men, the male who stays at home in his den. In this the *Grettis saga* probably represents a corrupt tradition: for, that the female should remain at home whilst the male searches for his prey, is a rule that holds good for devils as well as for men. The change was probably made in order to avoid the difficulty – which the *Beowulf* poet seems also to have realized – that after the male has been slain, the rout of the female is felt to be a deed of less note – something of an anti-climax.[14]

In *The Art of Beowulf*, Arthur Brodeur contradicts this view and comes to the aid of the ladies. Brodeur believes that *Grettis saga* preserves the original conception of the female as the more dangerous adversary and finds Grettir's battle with the giant in the Sandhaugar episode to be an anti-climax.[15]

The main conflict among Common Origin Theory followers has, however,

always been over the nature and shape of the 'old legend,' and this issue has
been hotly debated ever since Guðbrandur Vigfússon announced his discovery
of *Grettis saga* as a genetically related *Beowulf* analogue. Vigfússon never
speculated much about the nature or the form of the 'old legend' that he had
postulated, and quite possibly, he expected that it would eventually be found
somewhere. After a few decades of fruitless searching, Common Origin Theory
critics had to come to terms with the fact that if they wanted the legend, they
would have to invent it themselves. One of the earliest such 'reconstructions'
was offered by Chambers in 1929. Chambers culled his ingredients from *Sam-*
sons saga fagra, in addition to *Beowulf* and *Grettis saga* and produced from
these three sources the following summary of the 'old legend,' which he characterized as the 'residuum which is left when we have eliminated from each
version what is peculiar to itself':

A creature with supernatural powers ravages a place and carries off human beings. In
Beowulf the victims are the retainers from the King's Hall: in the *Sandhaugar* episode,
the goodman and his servant: in the *Samsons saga* the Princess Valintina. In the first two
cases the victims are taken by force from the hall, in the third case the Princess is enticed
further and further into the forest. The ravager himself wanders abroad, but he has a
mother who lives in a cave. (In the *Sandhaugar* episode the sexes have been reversed:
but we have seen that this is probably a corruption.) This cave is situated behind a waterfall. This is expressed quite clearly in the *Grettis saga* and *Samsons saga*, for in Scandinavian lands vast waterfalls are familiar things, and the word *foss* is there to hand. In the
Old English we have mention of the 'mountain torrent descending,' the 'mingled water
rising up' (apparently the spray), and the 'water below the level of the ground': all pointing to a waterfall, although the position of the cave relative to the waterfall is not
defined.

A champion arrives from a far distance, he has come purposely to the rescue. This
must be an original feature of the story: for in the *Grettis saga* it persists, although quite
inappropriate. Grettir, since his struggle with Glam, has been haunted by 'Glam's eyes,'
and he fears the dark above all things: yet he is represented as seeking deliberately to
encounter these dwellers in darkness. In *Beowulf* and the *Sandhaugar* episode the champion awaits the attack of the ravisher within the house, wrestles with and defeats him. In
the *Samsons saga* Kvintalin does not come in at this stage, as he is reserved for another
fate. In *Beowulf* and the *Sandhaugar* episode the hero is not completely successful: the
enemy gets away with the loss of an arm, and, though this proves fatal, the conqueror has
not the satisfaction of showing the corpse. Subsequently the hero plunges (in *Samson*, is
plunged) into the water, where he grapples with a creature who is the mother of the ravisher. (In the *Grettis saga* the relations of male and female are of course reversed, as
stated above.) The hero then penetrates into a cave behind the waterfall. (In *Beowulf* the

account is ambiguous: at one time the monster appears to have carried the hero to the bottom, at another he seems to enter the cave and grapple with her. In the *Grettis saga* the hero enters the cave before he attacks his foe: in the *Samsons saga* the fight takes place at the bottom of the water: thus each of the two Scandinavian sagas follows one of the versions which seem to be combined in *Beowulf*.) In all versions a special point is made of the blood or entrails of the foe falling into the water. The hero finds treasure in the cave, but the story emphasises his taking things interesting rather than rich. (In *Beowulf* he takes nothing but Grendel's head and the hilt: in the *Grettis saga* emphasis is placed upon the bones: in the *Samsons saga* upon the personal trinkets of the Princess Valintina.) A watcher or watchers above (in *Beowulf* there are many) believe the hero to be dead. In all three cases the watchers above are led to believe that the hero is dead by observing the blood-stained water. The hero returns back in safety.[16]

In this first attempt at a reconstruction, Vigfússon's favourite element, the *hæftmece-heptisax* parallel, is noticeably absent, but Chambers, who later emended his summary in his book on *Beowulf*,[17] eventually found a way to include it: 'In *Beowulf, Grettir* and *Gull-Thorir* the sword which the hero meets below is characterized by its *haft* or *hilt*.'[18] The emended summary also has it that the gold in the monster's cave is cursed, and that the hero leaves the treasure behind for that reason.[19] Despite these improvements, Chambers's summary is quite vague. The Sandhaugar trolls and Grendel now descend from 'a creature with supernatural powers,' and there is no motivation for his attacks. By the same token, Beowulf and Grettir are made to hearken back to a champion from afar. Chambers and all subsequent reconstructors of the 'old legend' consider the monster's loss of an arm to be a key element which the original story contained. This is, as James Carney has pointed out, a double-edged piece of evidence:

Only in *Beowulf* and in the *Grettissaga* is there no logical reason why the arm should be hewn off. So far from proving independent origins rather does comparison point to the following conclusion: *the hewing off of the monster's arm in Beowulf must have been motivated in the original source by the arm being exposed when the rest of the body was hidden.* The *Beowulf* poet has here departed from the general picture, and the fact that the *Grettissaga* agrees with *Beowulf* in this innovation, like the *haeftmece*/*heptisax* agreement, points to borrowing rather than remote inheritance from a common Germanic original.[20]

These and other weaknesses in Chambers's reconstruction are understandable; he never attempts to use *Grettis saga* and *Beowulf* alone, and the outcome of trying to squeeze a common summary out of four texts is pretty bland prose.

Still, Chambers's reconstruction draws praise from Klaeber in his edition of the poem: Chambers has 'managed to reconstruct what may be considered the outlines of the original form of the Grendel story, in particular of the second adventure.'[21]

In 1950, Felix Genzmer offered a completely different version of the 'old legend' using the Bear's Son Tale, *Beowulf*, *Grettis saga*, and *Hrólfs saga kraka*[22] as his sources. Genzmer's reconstruction, which he calls 'The Geatish Saga of Biulf the Bear's Son' ('Die Gautische Saga von Biulf dem Bärensohn') is much more ambitious than Chambers's, as may be seen from the following summary:

Chapter 1: Beowulf ('Biulf') is born to a farmer's daughter. The father is a prince, Björn, whom a sorceress stepmother whose sexual advances the prince rejected turned into a bear. The boy is an unpromising but a very strong youth.

Chapter 2: Beowulf is taunted by Breki for his slackness and challenged to a swimming match. To everyone's surprise Beowulf outswims Breki. The king, Gauti, discovers that the boy is his grandson. The sorceress wife is killed.

Chapter 3: A giant who is a killer of men and cattle inhabits an island. Beowulf swims to this island and kills the giant.

Chapter 4: Beowulf turns the coward Wött into a hero by making him drink a wolf's blood.

Chapter 5: King Gauti builds himself a splendid hall. One Christmas night, when the king's retainers sleep, the hall is attacked by a troll. One of them is snatched away by the monster, who leaves bloody tracks behind. Next Christmas, King Gauti orders his men to keep watch, but towards midnight they all fall asleep, and again one of them is taken by the troll. On the third successive Christmas night, Beowulf offers to keep watch with twelve companions. The companions fall asleep, but Beowulf stays awake and fights the troll when it appears. They have a hand to hand struggle, the troll tries to get away but is held tight, and Beowulf's companions hack at it with their weapons but to no avail. Beowulf eventually rips the troll's arm off, and the monster escapes, leaving a trail of blood behind him.

Chapter 6: Beowulf, carrying his sword, Heptisax, follows the bloody trail to a waterfall. He lowers himself down by means of a rope. Behind the waterfall he discovers a cave where a fire is burning. By the fire he sees a huge troll-woman who is the mother of the attacker. Beowulf attacks her with his Heptisax, but the sword will not wound her, and he throws it down. He then catches sight of a giant sword, Gullinhjalti,[23] hanging on the wall in the cave, wrests himself free from the embrace of the troll-wife, seizes the sword, and decapitates her. She falls to the ground and her blood runs into the river.

Beowulf then proceeds to explore the cave, finds the wounded male troll, decapitates him as well, and then leaves the cave, taking Gullinhjalti with him. Above the cave the men who were supposed to be watching the rope see blood on the water, assume that Beowulf is dead, and leave. Only Wött remains. Beowulf returns in triumph to King Gauti's palace, presents the giant sword to him, and receives lands and honours in return.

Chapter 7: A dragon inhabits a cave full of cursed treasure. A golden cup is stolen from the treasure and presented to Beowulf. Beowulf, again with twelve companions, sets out to fight the dragon. The retainers, except Wött, flee the scene of battle, Beowulf is killed in the fight, Wött kills the dragon. A funeral pyre is erected, and people mourn Beowulf's death.[24]

Genzmer believed this version of the 'old legend' to have been current in Scandinavia from the sixth century onward, and to have spread from there to England and Iceland where all but the troll fight and the swimming competition in the story was lost.[25] This basic assumption is probably the weakest link in Genzmer's theory. It is also unlikely that 'Heptisax' was the name of the sword in the original story. As Chambers points out in his book on *Beowulf*, the name of the sword would have to have been very important in the 'old legend' to survive in its two late descendants, *Beowulf* and *Grettis saga*,[26] whereas in Genzmer's reconstruction 'Heptisax' as a name has no special function or meaning. In respect to the Grendel story and the Sandhaugar episode, Genzmer – as opposed to Lawrence and Chambers – believed *Beowulf* to retain more original features of the story than *Grettis saga*.[27]

Twenty years after the publication of Genzmer's hypothesis, Larry D. Benson proposed yet another version of the 'old legend' in his article, 'The Originality of *Beowulf*':

A hero hears of a strange monster who regularly attacks and carries off the inhabitants of some dwelling. The hero agrees to remain all night in that dwelling while its owner stays away. He is attacked by the monster, who tries to drag him away. He manages to detach an arm from the monster, and the monster falls into some inland body of water where he lives. The hero dives into the water, while one or more of his friends wait above. Beneath the water he finds a dwelling place, where he encounters another monster, of opposite sex from the first, who has treasure, the body or bodies of those he has slain, and a valuable sword (perhaps magical in an even earlier version). After a fierce struggle, the hero manages to stab the monster. His friend or friends waiting above see the blood in the water and leave, concluding that he has been killed. But he emerges from the water with some token of his adventure, and those who thought he was dead rejoice. This is accounted a great deed, for it purged the land of the monsters that afflicted it.[28]

'We could quibble,' writes Benson, 'about some of the details of this reconstruction, but I think all could agree that it does account for both the episode in the Norse saga and the central fable of the Old English poem.'[29] This simply is not true. As we have already seen, Beowulf does not dive into an 'inland body of water'; the giant's cave in the Sandhaugar episode is not 'beneath the water,' it is behind it; Beowulf does not discover any 'body or bodies' of those the monster has slain in the monster's lair; *Grettis saga* says nothing about 'a valuable sword' in the giant's cave; and finally, it would take a great deal of literary imagination to be able to call Grettir's fight with the giant in the cave 'a fierce struggle.'

The latest reconstruction effort to date comes from Anatoly Liberman in his article 'Beowulf-Grettir,' published in 1986:

The hero kills a cannibal devastating a large area. The cannibal is described as an evil spirit, so the hero assumes the role of an exorcist, a shaman, and not only rids the people of a monster but cleanses the area of a demon. This demon is proof against all swords except his own or against all weapons in general, but in his combat with the hero he is unarmed only because he does not anticipate resistance. Having no other choice, the hero crushes his opponent by main force. However, the misfortunes of the people soon begin anew, because the cannibal's mother or dam attempts to avenge her son or mate. The monster's habitat is a cave at the bottom of the sea or lake. The hero arms himself with a sword, a gift from his host or simply a sword of great renown, and descends to the bottom. He is attacked by the female monster but is unable to injure her, because his sword unexpectedly fails him and because she fights with her own magic sword, the only one that can bring her death; the magic is contained in the haft. The hero wrests the *hæftmece/heptisax* from the monster and kills her with it. (But this sword can be used only once: when the hero wants to take it as a trophy, it melts, and nothing remains but the magic haft.) The hero returns to the shore where no one expects to see him alive.[30]

This fantasy is so far removed from events as they actually transpire in the Sandhaugar episode that it could never be its literary ancestor. But Liberman's attempt is neither better nor worse than those of Chambers, Genzmer, or Benson. All four base their reconstructions on different sources, and the outcome is four very different versions of the 'old legend.' As the reconstruction efforts of these critics show, the Common Origin Theory has given its followers a chance to be creative in the highest degree and ample opportunity to invent bits and pieces of the 'old legend' – to make it as it should have been – even if it meant that they had to emend both the poem and the saga in doing so. This cannot be an acceptable working method, and the results are not impressive. An enthusiastic Common Origin Theory follower, Óskar Halldórsson, had to admit reluctantly as late as 1982 that the 'old legend' had, for more than a century, eluded scholars in their attempts to reconstruct it,[31] – and one might add that it will most certainly continue to do so.

In addition to feuding over the contents and structure of the 'old legend,' Common Origin Theory scholars have had to defend their theories against criticism from sceptics who, not surprisingly, consist mainly of those who favour the English Hypothesis. The Achilles heel of Guðbrandur Vigfússon's idea is obviously that the 'old legend' is nowhere to be found, and scholars who are critical of the Common Origin Theory were quick to point this out.[32] The Lawrence–Chambers approach also asks us – against all common sense – to believe that the Icelandic *Grettis saga* analogue, which is anywhere from three hundred to five hundred years later than *Beowulf*, preserves the basic outline of the Grendel story better than the Old English poem. We are furthermore told that in the comparison of these analogues some features, for instance the nature of the heroes and the monsters, are completely interchangeable, whereas others, such as landscapes, settings, and various details are preserved more or less intact by both *Beowulf* and *Grettis saga*. One would expect heroic exploits of the kind that the 'old legend' is presumed to have described to be linked to a specific, named hero, and a glance at *Beowulf* is enough to show us that heroic deeds are always linked to someone's name. If this was the case, was the hero's name forgotten, whereas the tale of his adventure survived in the Old English poem and the Icelandic saga? Not very likely.

Critics were also sceptical about the reluctance of Common Origin Theory scholars to discuss the origin of their 'old legend.' In his *Germanische Heldensage*, Hermann Schneider asked Chambers three questions that Chambers had carefully avoided dealing with in his book on *Beowulf*. Specifically, Schneider wanted to know where the 'old legend' had come from, how old it was supposed to be and how it might have come about.[33] Understandably, Chambers had little to say about these issues, except to hazard a guess that perhaps the 'old legend' went back to the sixth century.[34] Klaeber, however, in an uncharacteristic flight of fancy, provided Schneider with some answers:

On the whole, it seems safest to attribute the undeniable parallelisms to the use of the same or similar Scandinavian sources both in the Old English and the Old Norse accounts. There existed, we may assume, on the one hand a tale – made over into a local legend – of the freeing of the Danish court from a strange monster through the prowess of a mighty warrior, and another one – like the former going back to a primitive folk-tale – about a similar adventure expanded to a fight with two monsters and placed in picturesque Scandinavian surroundings. Both kinds of narrative circulated orally in the North. In the course of time they were attached to various persons (two of whom are unquestionably historical characters), Bǫðvarr, Grettir, Ormr, Bēowulf respectively. A comparatively early combination of the two sets was perhaps effected in Scandinavia, though it is actually traceable in the Anglo-Saxon epic only. The artistic *Beowulf* version represents the final result of this formative process.[35]

It goes without saying that this theory does not rest on anything other than Klaeber's imagination.

To show that the Common Origin Theory really does prove that a relationship exists between *Beowulf* and *Grettis saga*, one would ideally want the 'old legend' or something resembling it to be discovered. A fruitless search of more than a century has not turned up anything, and it must be said that there is something very strange about the fact that only the authors of *Beowulf* and *Grettis saga* appear to have known the 'old legend.' Writers in medieval Iceland would not have ignored a story of the calibre that Common Origin Theory critics postulate, and in addition the Common Origin Theory asks us to believe that the author of *Grettis saga* – who supposedly knew the whole story – only used bits and pieces of it and buried them in an unimportant chapter of his saga to boot. This simply is not a very believable scenario.

In the absence of finding the legend, one might apply the usefulness of this theory as a criterion of its validity. Can the poem be used to explicate the saga or vice versa? Here the answer is no: all such attempts have in the end done more harm than good for the study of the two works. It has contributed nothing that could verify the validity of this approach. What is perhaps worst about the Common Origin Theory is its total disregard for the very different literary characteristics of *Beowulf* and *Grettis saga*. The *Beowulf* poet cares little about verisimilitude, or about being consistent, or about making the supernatural look natural. He paints with words, so to speak, and is first and foremost a creator of mood and atmosphere. The saga author, by contrast, is for the most part consistent, and he nearly always presents his material in a realistic, matter-of-fact fashion and with an eye for detail. As W.S. Mackie warned sixty years ago in his article 'The Demons' Home in *Beowulf*,' 'we should be cautious before filling ... gaps, or interpreting ... obscurities, with the aid of the *Grettissaga*. Otherwise we may, as it were, be attempting to complete *Kubla Khan* with the help of *Robinson Crusoe*.'[36]

In view of these shortcomings the great popularity which the Common Origin Theory enjoys in *Beowulf* studies is nothing less than amazing. And its power is not to be underestimated, as the following example demonstrates. In a recent bilingual edition of the poem, the editor informs his readers – as a statement of fact – that the poem and the saga 'both go back independently to a common original.'[37] He then has the audacity – presumably on the strength of the poem's secure ties to *Grettis saga* – to translate *hæftmece* as 'the sword with a long wooden hilt.'[38] Faith of this kind in the Common Origin Theory can only be defined, to borrow one of H.L. Mencken's phrases, as an illogical belief in the existence of the improbable.

9

The Big Bang Theory

The history of twentieth century research into the supposed genetic relationship of *Beowulf* and *Grettis saga* falls into two clearly marked stages. During the first half of the century, critics applied old-fashioned philological methods and presented their results in a careful, almost defensive, manner. They generally looked to *Grettis saga* for something that could match the double fight of the Grendel story, and only the Sandhaugar episode was generally accepted as a candidate that could meet that demand. Only the most daring researchers were prepared to admit the possibility that the 'old legend' might somehow have split into two, and only critics who thought along those lines included the Glámr episode as a genetically related *Beowulf* analogue. This was the critical landscape of Beowulf–Grettir studies until the 1950s, when two articles on the subject – Arnold Taylor's 'Two Notes on *Beowulf*' and Nora K. Chadwick's 'The Monsters and Beowulf' – appeared and changed it for good. What was revolutionary about these articles, particularly Taylor's, was that the relationship between the poem and the saga was no longer regarded merely as a likely possibility; it was now accepted as a proven fact. Once this line had been crossed, there was no longer any need to restrict one's search for analogous material to whole sections of the saga that resembled some part of the Grendel story; bits and pieces of the 'old legend' might be anywhere in the saga, and for that matter, anywhere in Old Norse literature. Although Taylor never said it in so many words, the underlying assumption of this new approach was that the 'old legend' had somehow exploded and left literary debris all over the place. And as Big Bang Theory explained the origin of the universe, so this new approach explained the fate of the 'old legend' and its relationship to *Grettis saga*. Critics who have followed this new line of approach have not produced uniform results in their research, so in this chapter, as before, the phrase the 'Big Bang Theory' is used as an umbrella term.

Chadwick's contribution lay mostly in her extremely liberal interpretation of what elements in the poem and the saga might be considered analogous and in her purely speculative arguments – arguments which the old philological school would never have found acceptable. The following statement, in which Chadwick equates the encounter with Glámr, the Sandhaugar episode and the Grendel story, may be taken as an example of her methodology:

I regard it as immaterial that the adventure against the trolls of Sandhaugar is represented as taking place some years later than the encounter with Glámr, and that some of the details of the two encounters have been interchanged ... The visit of Glámr's ghost, the *draugr*, corresponds to that of Grendel; and this is followed, as in *Beowulf*, by the visit of the *draugr's* mother, while Grettir's encounter with the *jötunn* under the waterfall, clearly represents the quietus of the *draugr* Glámr, and, as in *Beowulf*, the final episode.[1]

It was also Nora Chadwick who inserted the unfortunate Norse term *draugr* ('ghost') – meaning, as she uses the word, an evil supernatural being of any kind – into the Beowulf–Grettir debate. In doing this, Chadwick casually wipes out all distinctions between the various monstrous opponents of Beowulf and Grettir. Although this cannot be regarded as an acceptable methodology, her opinions on the subject of *draugar* in *Beowulf* and *Grettis saga* have clearly influenced a number of *Beowulf* scholars.[2] In a recent book on *Beowulf*, George Clark, who accepts most of Chadwick's theory and has himself applied it to unearth an extremely deeply buried *Beowulf* analogue in *Njáls saga*,[3] explains how her article of 1959, 'The Monsters and Beowulf,' was years ahead of its time and therefore failed to convince most *Beowulf* critics:

The closest parallels to *Beowulf* are neither Panzer's folktales nor Fontenrose's myths but the various recreations of a traditional story that Nora K. Chadwick treated in a learned but knotty, and often neglected, article of 1959. In these stories, the adventure seems an inheritance to which various members of a noble family of the Gautar (the 'Geatas,' or Geats of *Beowulf*) or members of 'the Hálogaland family of Ketill Hængr' succeed. The heroes carry on a feud with three great enemies who are frequently themselves related: 'The *draugr* Agnarr and his variants; the dragon Hárekr; and an evil supernatural woman,' a triad clearly paralleling Grendel, Grendel's mother and the dragon. Though all the texts exemplifying this recurring story are later than *Beowulf*, it seems unlikely that the Anglo-Saxon poem is their source. A common tradition older than *Beowulf* must lie behind the Anglo-Saxon poem and the various versions of Chadwick's story of the noble hero and the three monsters, or, as she puts it, 'The theme is an old one, of a high and ancient literary lineage.'

For a variety of reasons, Chadwick's paper has not much influenced the consensus of opinion on the origins of *Beowulf*: in 1959 her conclusions did not fit the dominant critical movements; her article makes hard reading; and in 1959 only two of the sagas she cites were readily available in English translation – even published editions of the Old Norse texts themselves were not widely available. Moreover Chadwick's case seems liable to some objections. The sagas she cites are much later than *Beowulf* (but earlier than most of the folktales cited by Panzer). The hero's feud with the triad of enemies paralleling Grendel, Grendel's mother, and the dragon frequently come as episodes in stories of lives filled with supernatural encounters – hence skeptical readers might have concluded that the combination was merely accidental, not a connected and recurring theme. Moreover, only two of the texts she cites include a treasure-guarding, tomb-dwelling dragon, and neither of those were available in English.[4]

Arnold Taylor – and those critics who accepted the Glámr episode as an analogue before him – assumed that bits of the 'old legend' had been used and reused by the saga author, and on the basis this approach, Taylor proposed Grettir's fight with the brown bear and his breaking into the gravemound of Kárr the Old as new *Beowulf* analogues.[5] As we shall see in this chapter, later critics have found it unnecessary conservatism to limit their search for analogous bits to *Grettis saga*, or even to postulate any well defined relationship between the saga and *Beowulf*. Richard Harris, in his article 'The Deaths of Grettir and Grendel: A New Parallel,' pauses to reflect on this issue, and what he says is quite typical of an attitude that has characterized the last forty years in Beowulf–Grettir studies:

For the purposes of this study, it will be assumed that *Beowulf* and *Grettis saga* do possess versions of a portion of the folk-tales representative of The Bear's Son Tale but that the two works [i.e., *Beowulf* and *Grettis saga*] are more closely related to each other than to the Bear's Son Tale itself ... speculation on the precise relationship between *Beowulf* and *Grettis saga* appears idle and unproductive. It is enough to conclude, as nearly all have, that some connection exists between the two works, most likely involving an indirect common source.[6]

In recent decades, Peter Jorgensen has emerged as the main advocate for the Big Bang Theory. In his work on *Beowulf* and *Grettis saga*, he favours Panzer's theory concerning the origin of the 'old legend,' but not, of course, Panzer's view of how the poem and the saga are related. In an article entitled 'Additional Icelandic Analogues to *Beowulf*,' Jorgensen describes how the state of affairs in Beowulf-Grettir studies looks to him as a critic who favours the Big Bang Theory:

Since the flurry of investigations a half century ago, the ensuing years have produced a remarkably small number of Icelandic sagas with analogues to *Beowulf*. Flateyjarbók yielded *Þorsteins þáttr uxafóts* and a single family of heroes was discerned in *Herrauðs saga*, *Þorsteins þáttr bœjarmagns*, *Hálfdanar saga Eysteinssonar*, and *Harðar saga ok Hólmverja*. *Njáls saga* was added in 1971, and the numerous parallel motifs in *Hálfdanar saga Brönufóstra* were presented in 1975. It is appropriate that the beginning of the second centenary of scholarship on this particular connection between Old English and Icelandic literature should bring forth another group of analogues. With over two dozen works attesting to the popularity of the Bear's Son Folktale in Icelandic, it should almost be expected that bits and pieces of the story would surface elsewhere in the extensive corpus of Icelandic literature, often in much reduced form. It is immaterial here whether the tale arrived from England, Ireland, or Norway, in written or in oral form, or in any combination of the above, for only after all the parallels have been enumerated and studied will conclusions about the story's genesis gain added importance.[7]

Concerning the relationship between *Beowulf* and *Grettis saga*, Jorgensen assumes that a poem about the Grendel legend existed in Iceland before the saga was written.[8] But he does not think that *Grettis saga* should have the seat of honour as the best genetically related Icelandic analogue to *Beowulf*. According to Jorgensen, a late *fornaldarsaga*, *Hálfdanar saga Brönufóstra*, is even closer to the Old English epic,[9] both on 'points of correspondence ... which can be pointed to as hard facts as well as those which conjure up remembrances and feelings of the Old English version.'[10] Furthermore, Jorgensen believes that once all the bits and pieces left by the 'old legend' in variously mutated forms have been rounded up and collated, the story itself may be reconstructed from them:

Much as philological reconstruction reaches a point where an inductively arrived at system is used deductively to explain previously anomalous phenomena, so too, has research on the Bear's Son Folktale developed to the stage at which variants of the story known in post twelfth-century Iceland can be established. The motifs examined above [i.e., in late sagas such as: *Gunnars saga Keldunúpsfifls*, *Sörla saga sterka*, *Gríms saga loðinkinna*, *Örvar-Odds saga*, *Hjálmþés saga ok Ölvis*, etc.] have not been used in such reconstructions, but their affiliation by similarity of type, place of occurrence and by sequence cannot be denied. Their value lies in what they can tell us about the composition of a saga, for they show us the saga writers, as far back as *Grettis saga*, consciously altering a well-known story in order to create one or more additional adventures for the hero. One is able to discern authors of different abilities and inclinations, sometimes being very adept at incorporating pre-existing material (as in numerous passages in *Grettis saga*), sometimes poorly motivating the episode (as in *Ólafs saga Tryggvasonar*,

Þórodds þáttr Snorrasonar), sometimes reversing the roles of hero and monster (as in *Gunnars saga Keldunúpsfífls, Hálfdanar saga Eysteinssonar, Egils saga einhenda*), often becoming trapped into *non sequiturs* (as in *Göngu-Hrólfs saga, Hrana saga hrings*) and finally, even copying verbatim from their archetype (as in *Ála flekks saga*).[11]

What Jorgensen actually discovers in these sagas are, as remains of the 'old legend,' indeed items 'in much reduced form.' In another article entitled, 'The Two-Troll Variant of the Bear's Son Folktale in *Hálfdanar saga Brönufóstra* and *Gríms saga loðinkinna*,' Jorgensen finds no less than twenty-three 'hard facts' pointing to the 'old legend' in the first of these sagas:

To begin with, the hero, Hálfdan (#1) literally 'half-Dane,' is the son of Hring, king of Denmark, which dimly echoes the location of the hall in Denmark, Heorot, ruled over by the son of Healfdene, 'half-Dane,' who was king of the Hringdenes. Hálfdan, too, has sailed from home with some companions as has Beowulf, but the Icelandic version then shifts directly to the tracking down of the monsters' lair, which also corresponds to that arduous journey in *Beowulf*. Hálfdan's is a day-long trip, along an *einstigi* (#2), a way where one must proceed single file, finally overcoming a section so steep (#5) that he is obliged to pull himself up by his axe-handle. Beowulf, too, must master steep rock faces and stretches of path which can only be taken single file. Just as Beowulf is outfitted with a weapon given to him by the king's follower, Unferth, so too, Hálfdan is equipped with a weapon given him by earl Óttarr (#3). In both the epic and the saga a tracking down of the cave is involved, and the saga differs only apparently when the tracks are said to be chiseled into the mountain (#4), for the use of the word *spor* for a niche in stone in Icelandic is strange, the expected form being *skor*. It is likely that the original *spor*[,] meaning footprints[,] has been preserved from an older version, but given the difficult ascent of the hero up the face of a mountain and the phonetic similarity to *skor*, it was left unchanged but reinterpreted in the saga to mean niche or handhold. The large size of the adversaries is not specifically mentioned in the Icelandic, but it, too, can be deduced from the tracks being spaced four yards apart. Upon arriving at the well-known large cave (#6) Hálfdan perceives the inevitable bright fire or light (#7).

Since *Hálfdanar saga* has omitted the first wrestling match with the male giant, it is not surprising that he finds both the male and the female sitting by the fire (#8). (But Hálfdan still challenges the monsters one after the other, taking on the male first and decapitating it in the cave.) That the monsters in the saga are cannibalistic as in *Beowulf* is shown by the fact that they had a kettle over the fire containing horse meat and human flesh (#9), and the carrying off of people to their lair has been replaced by their being brought to the cave by the use of magic (#11). The female's name, Sleggja (#10), meaning a large hammer, especially one to use on iron or stone, may possibly be connected semantically with a proposed etymology for Grendel as the 'destroyer,' from the Old

English verb *grindan* 'to grind,' and her return to the main cave carrying a man under each arm (#12) reminds one of Grendel's[12] lumbering away bearing the body of Æschere and the arm of her son.

Thereupon Hálfdan rushes in and challenges the male giant first (#13), but beheading it in a manner reminiscent of Beowulf's violent decapitation of the already-dead Grendel deep in the cave (#14). In a small way it lends support to the theory that the second 'battle' with Grendel is a remnant of the common folktale version in which the giant first loses his arm in the wrestling match in the house, is chased into the cave and defeated again. Sleggja's recognition of the hero she has never met (#15) is not unknown in folktales, but here it is noteworthy because the bear's son folktale has the two-troll variant which allows the return of the male monster to the female and presumably the chance to relate the outcome of the first battle. The result in the Old English epic is the revenge sought by Grendel's dam.

During the battle down in the cave, there is evidence that the motif of the ogre vulnerable only to a special sword has not been lost in the saga, for it is implicit that the axe used to decapitate Járnnefr was useless against the female, just as Beowulf's sword could not pierce Grendel's mother. As the armed hero is standing opposite the defenseless ogress, the text has him 'draw back' [*sic*], his axe is never mentioned again and his opponent has enough time to attack him 'until she reached a sword' (#16)! In the epic poem it is Beowulf who throws away his sword to begin a wrestling match, while in the saga it is the giantess who has been left holding the useless motif, throwing it down in order to initiate hand-to-hand combat (#17). As in *Beowulf* the struggle is hard and long, with the giantess enjoying a slight advantage (#18) until they come to the edge of a gorge (#19), the presence of which may be related to the gorge *under næssa genipu* into which the *fyrgenstrēam* plunges in the distorted and much-discussed scenery of the Old English epic. In the saga the troll's feet are pulled out from under her and she falls down into the gorge (#20), while the hero throws the monster to the ground in *Beowulf*. Divine intervention plays a major role, too, in both versions of the battle, allowing Beowulf to draw a golden-hilted sword from the equipment of the ogress and to decapitate her with it, while Hálfdan finds a sword which mysteriously appears, also adorned with gold, and uses it to behead the ogress (#21).

Slightly further on in the saga narrative (#22) the reader is informed that Hálfdan's men were *hugsjúkir*, 'sick at heart,' just as Beowulf's men were *mōdes sēoce*, 'sick at heart' at his absence, but the epic hero returns with valuable booty and the saga hero also comes back to camp with gold, silver, and jewels from the cave (#23).[13]

This long list of parallels is undeniably very impressive, but it is also quite misleading. Read in context, the very short chapter of *Hálfdanar saga Brönufóstra* that describes these events[14] does not – not even remotely – resemble the Grendel episode of *Beowulf*. The differences between the two stories are far too great: Hálfdan is looking for food when he chances upon the trolls, he climbs a glacier and then a rock to reach them, no particular type of relationship is indicated between the trolls, the ogress dies by falling into a gorge, and after the battle with the trolls Hálfdan frees a girl and her two brothers, who have been held captive by the trolls.

Other *fornaldarsǫgur* have not proved to be quite so full of fragments of the 'old legend' as *Hálfdanar saga Brönufóstra*, but among other discoveries Jorgensen has found:

- that the 'old legend' contained a swimming match,[15] which he then discovers to have 'parallels' in *Hálfdanar saga Brönufóstra*, *Örvar-Odds saga*, *Vilmundar saga viðutan*, *Finnboga saga*, *Hemings þáttr*, and *Egils saga einhenda*, in addition to *Grettis saga*, of course.
- that it also had 'the arrival of the hero at a court of a nobleman and his clash with an antagonistic liegeman there.'[16] Jorgensen also finds this motif in *Hálfdanar saga Brönufóstra*.[17]
- that the 'old legend' contained the gift of a useless weapon to the hero.[18] Jorgensen finds this attested in *Grettis saga*, *Hrólf's saga*, *Þorsteins þáttr uxafóts*, *Hálfdanar saga Eysteinssonar*, and *Gunnars saga Keldunúpsfífls*, among others.
- monsters attacking human dwellings, arms that are chopped off, the presence of water, single footpaths (*einstigi*), bright lights, cave battles, external aid, and treasure in a number of *fornaldarsǫgur*.[19]

These various fragments of the 'old legend' that Jorgensen has discovered in sundry sagas inevitably call attention to the methods that he uses to find them. Jorgensen's singular practice of identifying 'altered analogues' goes straight back to Nora Chadwick's tactics. Its main attraction is, of course, that it is extremely good for business, in the sense that it ensures that one's supply of eligible analogue materials will never run dry. But it is Jorgensen's tool box, as a critic in search of analogues, which is his most amazing characteristic. Things 'which conjure up remembrances and feelings of the Old English version' we have already seen, but Jorgensen also finds items 'which dimly echo' others,[20] 'role reversals,' 'deviant versions,' and the 'telescoping' of people and places in his quest for new analogues.[21] With a methodological arsenal of this kind, any critic who is worth his salt could, of course, prove that the telephone book is directly descended from the Bible, and armed with it, Jorgensen finds yet another parallel to *Beowulf* in *Grettis saga*:

In this vein it should be remarked that there occurs in *Grettis saga* an attack at night on the hero by twelve berserks. Only two survive, but flee the farmstead. The next morning all the men go out to trail the two and find them beneath a rock, dead from their wounds and the cold. Ordinarily, this passage could not be connected with the Bear's Son Folktale, except that it occurs in a saga which has varied the folktale on no less than six other occasions,[22] excluding Grettir's swimming adventures! It should also be noted that the attack was at Christmas, and the very next chapter of *Grettis saga* has the hero, at Christmas, kill a marauding bear, whose cave was under an overhanging rock (approachable by an *einstigi*, once again). Both the attacks by Glámr and by the ogress in the Sandhaugar episode are also said to take place at Christmas.[23]

Richard Harris, another Big Bang Theory critic, describes his discovery of the fifth analogue in *Grettis saga* and the saga author's working method in musical terms:

It is as if these five episodes of *Grettis saga* formed a set of fugue-like variations on a single theme, the theme found in the first part of *Beowulf* and, to some extent, in Panzer's variants of the Bear's Son Tale. Beginning with the relative simplicity of the visit to the *haugr* of Kárr inn gamli, they vary in complexity and intensity, the central confrontation, ending with Glámr's curse, being the most drastic single event in Grettir's career. When Þorbjörn comes for him in the fifth episode as he lies in a weakened state in his retreat, the details of the end are predictable, for we have already been told the story several times, but with Grettir as hunter instead of as quarry.[24]

Harris is also well informed about the intentions of the author of *Grettis saga*, and he even knows that this author was familiar with the materials on which the 'old legend' drew. 'I think it may be concluded,' Harris writes, 'that the saga's author knew more of the material, in some form or other, upon which Grendel's story is based, than could be assumed without an awareness that Grettir's death does indeed offer another parallel to the narrative in *Beowulf*.'[25] In short, both Jorgensen and Harris read *Grettis saga* as a multiple repetition of the Grendel story, the saga author sometimes directly repeating it, but more often presenting it in variously disguised forms.

As we shall see in the next chapter, it is perfectly true that *Grettis saga* contains a variety of literary patterns, including repetitions and recombinations of motifs. But so far no one has discovered anything quite so spectacular as the fivefold exegesis that Jorgensen and Harris propose. Harris's thesis presupposes that the author of *Grettis saga* was somehow obsessed by the Grendel story, and that it meant something very special to him. Why else would he want to use it and reuse it five or six times in his saga, adding new details and new characters to it at every turn? Did his audience also know the 'old legend,' and did they appreciate this peculiar handling of it, or has it – as one suspects – taken seven hundred years to fully understand what the saga author was up to? And if the 'old legend' was such an important piece of literature, why was it preserved in its entirety – or something close to it – in only one Old English poem and a single Icelandic saga? It also remains unexplained why the author of *Grettis saga* buried the fullest version of his favourite story – i.e., the Sandhaugar episode – in a late and relatively unimportant chapter of his saga. If the Sandhaugar episode appeared early in *Grettis saga* and described something really important in Grettir's life, it would not be so far-fetched to look for echoes of it later in the saga, but this is not the case, and Harris's thesis is therefore very improbable.

In chapter 37 of the book of Ezekiel, the Lord sets the prophet down in a valley full of dry bones and asks him: 'Son of man, can these bones live?' The same question may be asked of Big Bang Theory critics: do these fragments that they keep unearthing constitute the remains of something that was once a full-fledged story? The dry bones of the Old Testament are of course Israel, and the answer is yes, they can live; however, with the fragments of the scattered legend that the Big Bang Theory postulates, the answer has to be no. The main problem is, as we have seen in this chapter, the basic assumption of a proven relationship between *Beowulf* and *Grettis saga*, on which the whole Big Bang Theory argument rests. This relationship has never been satisfactorily demonstrated. It has also never been shown why the 'old legend' – over and above other stories that were current in Northern Europe during the Middle Ages – should have left the profound influence on Old Norse literature that Jorgensen and others have wanted to maintain. If the story was so important, we would expect to have more complete versions of it in Icelandic instead of late and scattered fragments. And finally, it must be said that the 'anything goes' methodology of most Big Bang Theory critics is simply not acceptable.

As we have seen in this and in the previous three chapters, none of the four theories that have been proposed to link the saga and the poem really succeeds in doing so. All four are badly flawed, and these flaws are serious enough to undermine their credibility completely. All the wishful thinking that scholars have poured into trying to establish a link between *Beowulf* and *Grettis saga* throughout the past century has, regrettably, been work in vain.

PART III

THE GENETICALLY RELATED *BEOWULF* ANALOGUES IN
GRETTIS SAGA IN VIEW OF ICELANDIC SOURCES

10

A Saga Author Shops Around: The Eclectic Composition of the Glámr and Sandhaugar Episodes

It is, of course, no good to reject the various theories that attempt to explain the origin of the supposed genetically related *Beowulf* analogues in *Grettis saga* if no alternative explanation can be offered instead. In this chapter I shall, accordingly, try to do so. I shall, however, concentrate exclusively on the Glámr and the Sandhaugar episodes, because it is on their 'proven' existence as genetically related *Beowulf* analogues that other episodes of the saga that have been thought to be related to the Old English poem must rest.

It has been shown that the author of *Grettis saga* was very well versed in Icelandic histories and sagas that had been written prior to his own, and that he frequently refers to them or borrows from them in the course of putting together his own story. According to Guðni Jónsson, who edited the saga in the *Íslenzk fornrit* series, the author of the saga knew and used the following texts:

1 / *The Book of Settlements (Landnáma)*
2 / *The Saga of the People of Laxárdalur (Laxdæla saga)*
3 / *The Saga of the Confederates (Bandamanna saga)*
4 / *The Saga of Bjorn, Champion of the Hítardalers (Bjarnar saga Hít-dælakappa)*.
5 / *The Saga of the Sworn Brothers (Fóstbrœðra saga)*
6 / *The Saga of the Battle on the Heath (Heiðarvíga saga)*
7 / *The Saga of the People of Eyri (Eyrbyggja saga)*
8 / *The Saga of Christianity (Kristni saga)*
9 / *The Book of the Icelanders (Íslendingabók)*
10 / *Egil's Saga (Egils saga)*
11 / *Njal's Saga (Njáls saga)*
12 / *The Saga of the People of Vatnsdalur (Vatnsdæla saga)*
13 / *Kormak's Saga (Kormáks saga)*
14 / *The Story of Arrow Odd (Örvar-Odds saga)*[1]

We may rightfully suspect that the author of *Grettis saga* knew and used even more texts, but what can be deduced from this long list of books? It tells us two things: in the first place, we are looking at a very 'literary-minded' author, and secondly, if all these texts have left their mark on *Grettis saga*, we may assume that he liked to decorate his saga with bits and pieces from books that he had read, or books that he had heard read, or stories that he knew in an oral form, perhaps to impress his readers, but more likely because he thought that they blended nicely with his own product. The first assumption is also backed by the number of literary patterns that we find in *Grettis saga* in the form of doublets and triplets and, strangely enough, repetitions and recombinations of motifs. Characters in the saga often come in identical pairs or play the same role: for example, the half-trolls Þórir and Hallmundr, the obnoxious pair Bjǫrn and Þorbjǫrn ferðalangr, and Grettir's rope watchers, the farmer Auðunn, and the priest Steinn. The berserks, Þórir þǫmb, Ǫgmundr illi, and Snækollr are all more or less cast in the same mould, and so are the would-be assassins of Grettir, Þórir rauðskeggr and Grímr skógarmaðr. Grettir twice swims to obtain fire, once in Norway and once in Iceland; like Glámr, Þorbjǫrg the sorceress lays a curse on Grettir; and twice someone is sent to kill Grettir. Finally, the saga frequently repeats certain phrases and parts of sentences.[2]

The Glámr Episode

As one of the few things that scholars investigating *Grettis saga* have been able to agree on is that there is a link between the Glámr and the Sandhaugar episodes; one of them must be primary, and the other a recipient. But which is which? Once this question is posed, the critical consensus ends. C.S. Smith, who was the first scholar to address the issue, was not in any doubt as he compared the Sandhaugar and the Glámr episodes: 'how much more graphic, more masterly in all its parts, is the story of the wrestling with Glam. Unquestionably that is the original, and the other a copy.'[3] R.C. Boer, in an article entitled 'Zur Grettissaga' published in 1898, concurred with Smith. Furthermore, he argued that in the composition of the Sandhaugar episode the saga author had merely combined a number of elements from Grettir's fights with Glámr and Kárr the Old. From the Glámr episode Boer believed that he had taken:

- The mysterious disappearance of people.
- Drops of blood by the doorstep.
- Most of the details of Grettir's fight with the troll-woman.

From the Kárr episode the saga author had repeated:

- Details concerning Grettir's cave fight, such as the rope, and the flight of the watchman.[4]

The counter-argument to these ideas came from Friedrich Panzer. In his book on *Beowulf* Panzer completely rejected Boer's theory, and maintained that both in the Glámr and the Sandhaugar episodes the author of *Grettis saga* had borrowed a ghost story featuring a living dead ghost called Þórólfr bægifótr, from *Eyrbyggja saga*.[5] Panzer furthermore argued that the Sandhaugar story was primary, and that as a character, Glámr was fashioned merely by combining features from the description of the troll-woman at Sandhaugar and the above-mentioned Þórólfr bægifótr from *Eyrbyggja saga*.[6]

A third theory concerning the origin of Glámr was offered by Heinz Dehmer, who suggested that his relationship to Þórólfr bægifótr did not involve a literary borrowing by the saga author. According to Dehmer, many Icelandic ghost stories in the sagas shared a certain number of elements, and similarities in the description of Þórólfr bægifótr and Glámr might simply be the result of a common tradition rather than a conscious borrowing.[7] In a later article Dehmer listed what he believed to be the common characteristics of the Icelandic tradition of describing battles within a haunted house:

- The hero wraps himself in a cloak.
- He has a tug of war with the ghost over the cloak.
- A wrestling match between them follows.
- The demon is much stronger than the hero.
- A second fight in the demon's lair is never a part of this formula.[8]

Dehmer maintained that the Sandhaugar episode was not a ghost story, and was therefore not really related to the Glámr story. It featured neither a cloak nor a tug of war, and although the troll-woman is much stronger than Grettir – as is the case with fight descriptions in genuine ghost stories – he does not kill her in the traditional and decisive ghost story manner, i.e., by cutting her head off and placing it against her buttocks, which is the way in which Glámr is put to permanent rest.[9]

The most convincing analysis of the Glámr episode was, however, submitted by another German scholar, Wolf von Unwerth, in a book bearing the long and esoteric title, *Untersuchungen über Totenkult und Ódinnverehrung bei Nordgermanen und Lappen – mit Excursen zur altnordischen Literaturgeschichte* (*Studies in the Worship of the Dead and the Veneration of Odin among the North Germanic Peoples and the Lapps – with a Digression into the History of Old Norse Literature*), which he published in 1911. The Glámr episode had always been thought to go back to an oral folktale, but von Unwerth argued that both the ghost himself and his story had distinctive literary traits. It was, according to von Unwerth, a collection of literary motifs commonly found in the Icelandic saga ghost stories that he had been investigating. Such motifs included:

• a ghost who makes an entire region desolate,
• drives a few people mad,
• breaks people's bones, and
• rides roof-tops,
• kills animals,
• and after he has been 'killed,' is finally disposed of by putting his head against his buttocks.[10]

In *Eyrbyggja saga* (chapter 34), we are told that Þórólfr bægifótr drove many people away from the farm that he haunted, and killed others who stayed behind. *Laxdœla saga* (chapter 17 and subsequent chapters) tells of the evil ghost Hrappr, who also killed people. *Svarfdœla saga* (chapter 32) has the ghost Klaufi, who hurts people and animals, and *Þorsteins þáttr bæjarmagns* (chapters 12–13) features the ghost Agði, who has murderous intentions. *Eyrbyggja saga* (chapter 34) also tells us that Þórólfr bægifótr drove some people to madness. In *Heiðarvíga saga* (chapter 9) the ghost of Víga-Styrr drives a girl to madness and death. Ghosts who fight with humans – Hrappr (chapter 24) and Hallbjǫrn (chapter 38) – appear in *Laxdœla saga*. A description of a wrestling match between a human and a ghost inside a house, and of the damage done to it in the process, is found in *Hrómundar saga Gripssonar*,[11] (chapter 4), and in *Grettis saga*'s account of the hero's fight with the farmer Auðunn, we see the same type of wrestling match that causes great damage as we see in the Glámr episode a few pages later.[12] Fight descriptions quite similar to Grettir's struggle against Glámr occur in *Flóamanna saga* (chapter 13) and in *Hávarðar saga Ísfirðings* (chapter 2). Ghosts ride roof-tops in *Eyrbyggja saga* (chapter 34) and *Flóamanna saga* (chapter 13). The ghost kills animals (birds that touch down on Þórólfr bægifótr's gravemound) in *Eyrbyggja saga* (chapter 34). In disposing permanently of a ghost, one needs to cut off its head and place it somewhere a good distance away from where it belongs, preferably by the feet of the ghost or against its buttocks. This method is followed in *Áns saga bogsveigis* (chapter 5) to prevent a dead man from adopting a career as a ghost, and of course in the Glámr episode of *Grettis saga*.[13] As a further precaution, the body of the ghost may be burnt to cinders and the ashes securely buried, as we find in chapter 32 of *Svarfdœla saga* and in the final disposal of Glámr. It is, of course, impossible to prove that the Glámr episode consists to a large extent of a string of motifs borrowed from older sagas, but as we know that the author of *Grettis saga* was familiar with many of them, it undeniably strengthens von Unwerth's theory.[14]

Von Unwerth also demonstrated that the Glámr episode has an unmistakable connection with a little-known and highly problematic saga called *Hávarðar saga Ísfirðings*.[15] As Theodore M. Andersson has put it, *Hávarðar saga Ísfirðings* 'enjoys a particular disrepute among scholars because of evidence that it is a late reconstruction of an earlier saga and because it contains demonstrable historical errors and unprepossessing stanzas.'[16] In the form that we now have it, this saga was according to its editors in the *Íslenzk fornrit* series, originally composed sometime during the first half of the thirteenth century – some decades earlier than *Grettis saga* – and based on old legends from the Westfjords. The editors of this saga, Björn K. Þórólfsson and Guðni Jónsson, think that an older version of *Hávarðar saga Ísfirðings* had been lost by the time that the later version was composed and find it most likely that the author had either read the older version or heard it read. At one point he had known the story, but by the time that he recomposed *Hávarðar saga Ísfirðings*, he had become rusty concerning various details, such as the names of people and places.[17] Sigurður Nordal, however, does not rule out the possibility that the later redactor still had access to and used the original saga which would mean that the older version was not lost until some time after the later one had come to be written.[18] The earliest extant copies of the saga as we now have it are paper manuscripts that go back to the seventeenth century. These in turn appear to derive from a single manuscript, now lost, which is thought to have been written about 1450.[19]

In *Hávarðar saga Ísfirðings*, the hero, Ólafr, fights with a ghost named Þormóðr, who visits his widow's bed every night and who is about to frighten everyone off the farm. Von Unwerth demonstrated that a comparison of this fight with Grettir's fight against Glámr shows such an unmistakable resemblance both in the events described and in terms of language that one of the two sagas must have borrowed the episode from the other.[20] In English translation, the examples from these two sagas that von Unwerth compared are as follows:

Hávarðar saga Ísfirðings (Chapter 2)	*Grettis saga* (Chapter 35)
Ólafr was lying on a gable-end bed near the door ...	[Grettir] lay down on a bench opposite the farmer's bed closet ...
A light was burning in the hall ...	A light was burning in the hall ...
Ólafr lay down in his shirt and pants ...	Grettir did not want to take his clothes off ...

he covered himself with a cloak	he covered himself with a shaggy fur cloak ...
Þormóðr entered the hall and wagged his bald head backwards and forwards ...	Grettir saw that the thrall stretched his head inside ...
He saw that an extra bed was occupied ...	Glámr saw that some sort of heap was lying on the bench ...
he approached and pulled hard at the cloak ...	[Glámr] moved further inside the hall and pulled hard at the cloak ...
they divided the cloak between them ...	they tore the cloak apart between them ...
Þormóðr sensed that he was up against a strong man ...	[Glámr] wondered who could have pulled so hard against him ...
Þormóðr leapt under his arms ...	Glámr leapt under his arms ...
they fought hard ...	They fought very hard ...
they broke most things that were in their way ...	they smashed everything that was in their way ...
Þormóðr attacked fiercely, and in the end they fought their way outside ...	Glámr now seemed more powerful and clutched Grettir in his grip as they moved into the vestibule ...[21]

In *Hávarðar saga Ísfirðings*, however, the end of the fight has none of the high drama of the Glámr episode. Once the fight has moved out of the hall, the ghost stumbles over a piece of wood and falls on his back. The saga then merely relates that Óláfr disposed of Þormóðr in a fitting manner.

Von Unwerth thought that his comparison showed that of the two sagas, *Hávarðar saga Ísfirðings* contained the original story, and that the author of *Grettis saga* had borrowed its ghost fight and incorporated it into his description of Grettir's fight with Glámr.[22] On this issue I am convinced that von Unwerth is right, as it is very difficult to imagine that *Hávarðar saga Ísfirðings* could have borrowed this scene from *Grettis saga*. In the first place, the fight scene in *Hávarðar saga Ísfirðings* is very straightforward, almost crude in its simplicity, and it shows all the signs of going back to a local ghost story. The *Grettis saga* version is, by contrast, a more polished and more 'literary' narrative and it is considerably longer. Secondly, certain details have been embellished; the simple 'cloak' in *Hávarðar saga Ísfirðings* has, for example, become 'a shaggy fur cloak' in *Grettis saga*. And there are other ways as well in which the author of *Grettis saga* magnifies and intensifies events that take place during the fight. In *Hávarðar saga Ísfirðings* the ghost and Óláfr 'fight hard'; in *Grettis saga* they fight 'very hard.' In *Hávarðar saga Ísfirðings* they first 'divide the cloak between them' and then 'break most things that are in their way;' in *Grettis saga* Grettir and Glámr 'tear the cloak apart' and then 'smash everything that is in their way.' If the author of *Hávarðar saga Ísfirðings* had borrowed this section from *Grettis saga*, he would have had to simplify it considerably and leave out the climax of the fight, including Glámr's famous curse, his decapitation, and his burial. This is unlikely, for why would an author want to borrow a description of something from another book only to leave out the best part? This would not make too much sense.

Although it has been an established fact for decades in Old Norse studies that some kind of relationship existed between this scene from *Hávarðar saga Ísfirðings* and the Glámr episode of *Grettis saga*,[23] for some strange reason this knowledge has never entered the debate over the assumed presence of genetically related *Beowulf* analogues in *Grettis saga*. Chambers, who carefully recorded all publications that he considered relevant to these and other subjects of concern to the poem in the bibliography of his life-long and cumulative study, was obviously not aware of von Unwerth's book,[24] nor do other *Beowulf* scholars appear to have taken note of it. Had they done so, they might well have had some second thoughts about the Glámr episode being a genetically related *Beowulf* analogue. If von Unwerth is right, and we have reasonable evidence to assume that the author of *Grettis saga* borrowed his description of the hero's fight with Glámr inside the farmhouse from *Hávarðar saga Ísfirðings*, this factor alone makes it unlikely that the Glámr episode is a genetically related *Beowulf* analogue. Furthermore, we only need to add a few more sagas to the list of works that are known to have influenced *Grettis saga* and deduce that the author borrowed bits and pieces from them to have much of the Glámr episode as *Grettis saga* relates it:

- the various elements that relate Glámr's career as a ghost before he tangles with Grettir could to a large extent have come from *Eyrbyggja saga* (riding rooftops, driving people crazy or killing them, and making a region desolate).
- the parts of the fight scene and its immediate aftermath that do not come from *Hávarðar saga Ísfirðings* could have been borrowed from *Flóamanna saga* (the description of the fight after Glámr falls out of the door), and from *Svarfœla saga* (the final disposal of the ghost by burning its body and disposing securely of the ashes).

If the author of *Grettis saga* did in fact work along these lines – as indeed seems entirely possible – it goes without saying that the Glámr episode can under no circumstances be a genetically related *Beowulf* analogue, no matter how closely scholars think that it matches the Grendel story.

The Sandhaugar Episode

Any critic who believes that both the Glámr and the Sandhaugar episodes go back to the same 'old legend' has a good deal of explaining to do concerning the odd manner in which the author of *Grettis saga* relates these stories. In the first place, it would be interesting to know why he only uses half of the story in the Glámr episode, which is unquestionably the more important of the two, and then decides to give a fuller version of the Grendel story in a late and relatively obscure chapter of his saga. Secondly, it would appear that the saga author has been struck with complete amnesia over what has happened so far in his own story, when he sends Grettir to do battle at Sandhaugar. Ever since Glámr's curse, the governing theme of the saga has been Grettir's fear of the dark and of the creatures that inhabit it, and the last thing that a reader would expect is to see him voluntarily go out of his way to seek a battle with supernatural creatures. The third curious thing about the Sandhaugar episode is its picaresque nature. It is literally an adventure which is – except for Grettir's presence in it – completely independent of the rest of the saga. When the adventure is over Grettir moves on, and every single character that we met in the Sandhaugar chapters vanishes for good from the saga.

The author of *Grettis saga* wanted to write a long story about his hero.[25] We know this from the fact that after Grettir's death in chapter 82 of the saga, he adds to the story a longish appendix (eleven chapters) that describes the revenge taken for Grettir, but he does not stop even when Grettir's half-brother, Þorsteinn drómundr, has carried out his duty in Constantinople. After killing Þorbjǫrn ǫngull there, a brief fabliau-like story relating Þorsteinn's rescue from prison and his affair with a married lady is thrown in as a finale to the saga. This last part is so loosely connected to the main body of *Grettis saga* that it is commonly known by its own title: *Spesar þáttur*. If we consider the Sandhaugar episode in light of these above-mentioned points, it is very difficult to avoid the impression that it was conceived as a 'filler' by a saga author who was running low on things to do for his hero. Within the saga as a whole, one of the main characteristics of the Sandhaugar episode is that it kills time in Grettir's life. He arrives at the farm at Christmas and stays there for the remainder of the winter, and yet the only adventure that the saga author can assign to him during all this time is his early fight with the two trolls. The rest of the hero's stay at the farm – a period of four or five months – is completely uneventful and is summed up by the saga in one sentence: 'Grettir stayed at Sandhaugar during the winter in disguise.'[26]

My guess is that the troll adventure which the author of *Grettis saga* gives to his hero at Sandhaugar has its origin in a troll fight story that he knew as a legend associated with the part of the country where this farm is situated, and that he decided to use it in an amended form as a part of his own story.[27] Why else would the first fight have two different endings, and why else would the saga author have to tell us that the local population knew a version that had the troll-woman turn into a stone at sunrise? The original ending, however, was of no use to our author because it gave the real victory to the appearance of daylight rather than his hero, and he therefore changed it.

It is a curious coincidence – if, indeed, it is a coincidence – that in the Sandhaugar episode there is not a single feature which is not to be found either earlier in the saga itself or in other sagas, some of which we know the author of *Grettis saga* to have been familiar with, and others that he might have known in an oral or a written form. As to the broad structure of the first fight, I agree with R.C. Boer that it is most likely that the author of *Grettis saga* refashioned the Glámr episode into Grettir's fight with the troll woman,[28] or – as might be equally plausible – he retold an already existing regional troll fight story, inserted Grettir into it, and gave it a new ending. In the process of doing this, however, the saga author embellished his story with numerous features that he probably borrowed from other works:[29]

- A raid by a supernatural being (a dragon) on a human habitation occurs, for instance, in *Hrólfs saga kraka* (chapter 35), and a princess is abducted (by an enormous vulture) at Christmas in *Egils saga einhenda ok Ásmundar ber-serkjabana* (chapter 2).[30]
- The troll-woman in the Sandhaugar episode is most likely inherited from the original troll fight story. A troll-woman armed with a long knife and a tren-cher appears to someone in a dream in *Haralds saga harðráða* (chapter 80), and – also in a dream – in *Laxdæla saga** (chapter 48).
- The indoor fight scene is, as in the Glámr episode, borrowed from *Hávarðar saga Ísfirðings*.
- In *Örvar-Odds saga** (chapter 19) we meet a troll-woman who lives in a waterfall.
- Wrestling matches against trolls on the edge of a chasm are known from *Sörla saga sterka* (chapter 3), and *Hálfdanar saga Brönufóstra* (chapter 4).
- A hip throw by the hero occurs as a decisive move in his wrestling match with the troll in *Hálfdanar saga Brönufóstra* (chapter 6), and in *Gríms saga loðinkinna* (chapter 1).
- The arm that Grettir cuts off the troll-woman may be compared to several incidents earlier in the saga where people lose their heads, arms, or hands: Qnundr tréfótr (Grettir's great grandfather) cuts off Vígbjóðr's arm (chapter 4); Grettir cuts off the arm of Hjarrandi, and both hands off Gunnarr (brothers

of Bjǫrn, who taunted Grettir in the bear episode and was later killed by him), as they try to avenge Bjǫrn (chapter 24); Grettir cuts the hand and the head off Þorbjǫrn ferðalangr (chapter 37); and the berserk Snækollr and the would-be assassin Þórir rauðskeggr lose their heads to Grettir's sword (chapters 40 and 56). If the saga author was not simply recycling some of these incidents in the Sandhaugar episode, he might have looked to various *fornaldarsǫgur* and *þættir* in which trolls lose their hands or arms, for example: *Egils saga einhenda ok Ásmundar berserkjabana* (chapter 10); *Þorsteins þáttr uxafóts* (two trolls, male and female, in chapter 10); *Hjálmþés saga ok Ölvis* (chapter 12); *Jökuls þáttr Búasonar* (chapter 2); and *Ketils saga hængs* (chapter 2).[31]

As for Grettir's cave adventure, certain features, such as the rope, the cowardly watchman, and the presence of treasure show striking similarity with his break-in into the gravemound and subsequent fight with Kárr the Old earlier in the saga. Boer noted this resemblance before the turn of the century,[32] and some critics, at least – including Guðni Jónsson, who, like Boer, edited *Grettis saga* – have concurred with him that these episodes must be related.[33] In the second fight, as in the first one, it is the familiarity of the various motifs that characterizes the narrative:

• Panzer points out that the name of Steinn, the watchman, and the use of a rope to reach the abode of the monster are familiar elements in different versions of the Bear's Son story, and thinks that the author of *Grettis saga* was familiar with that story and used it in the second part of the Sandhaugar episode.[34] Chambers, who on the whole rejects Panzer's theory, is inclined to agree with him on this point.[35]
• In *Þorsteins saga Víkingssonar* one of hero's opponents is described as jumping overboard from ship in terms similar to those used to depict Grettir's dive into the chasm: i.e., 'you could see the soles of his feet.'[36]
• In *fornaldarsǫgur*, it is quite commonplace to find giants living in large caves in which fires are kept burning. This occurs, for example, in *Hjálmþés saga ok Ölvis* (chapter 9), in *Örvar-Odds saga* (chapter 6), in *Hálfdanar saga Brönufóstra* (chapter 4), and in *Gríms saga loðinkinna* (chapter 1).
• A weapon with a wooden handle (*atgeirr*) fails its owner in *Njáls saga* (chapter 30).[37]
• A sword hangs on the wall in the cave of a giant in *Hjálmþés saga ok Ölvis* (chapter 9).
• Gore on the water appears in *Samsons saga fagra* (chapter 7), and in *Þorsteins saga Víkingssonar* (chapter 23).

- A watchman or watchmen who leave the rope that they are supposed to guard is a standard motif in different variants of the Bear's Son folktales.[38]
- The hero discovers human bones or finds living prisoners in the troll cave in, for example, *Hálfdanar saga Brönufóstra* (chapter 4),[39] and in *Bósa saga ok Herrauðs* (chapter 8).[40]
- It is a common expectation that the hero will find treasure in the caves of trolls, regardless of whether his encounter with them is of a friendly or a hostile nature. The following four sagas are only a small sample of the host of troll stories that follow this pattern: *Hálfdanar saga Brönufóstra* (chapter 5), *Sörla saga sterka* (chapter 4), *Jökuls þáttr Búasonar* (chapter 2), and *Hjálmþés saga ok Ölvis* (chapter 9).

If these commonplace motifs were removed from the story of Grettir's cave adventure there would not be much left of it, and the Sandhaugar episode as a whole, could never be noted for its originality.

A problem such as the one of trying to decide whether there is a literary relationship between two works must in the final analysis come down to the question of probability; there simply cannot be any other criterion upon which to base one's conclusions. Assuming influence from contemporary Icelandic sources on *Grettis saga*, particularly when they are as glaringly obvious as in the Glámr and the Sandhaugar episodes, is certainly an easier solution than accepting the existence of an 'old legend' that would have had to survive centuries of oral transmission, not to mention migration from country to country, intact. It is also simpler than tackling the thorny problem of attempting to explain how *Beowulf*, directly or indirectly, could have influenced the saga. In this case, the simplest explanation must be the most likely one.

11

Conclusion

Three centuries ago the great manuscript collector and antiquarian, Árni Magnússon, observed that there were only two kinds of scholars in the world: those who devoted themselves to helping spread errors in their field, and those who trailed after the first lot and cleaned up their mistakes. This scheme of things ensured, according to Magnússon, that both groups had something to keep themselves busy.[1] This was probably a sound assessment of the state of affairs in Old Norse scholarship in Magnússon's time, and I do not think that *Beowulf* studies have reached such a level of perfection in our day that his theory no longer applies. Of course experimentation and new ideas are necessary in the field, but so are counter-arguments and debate. Unfortunately, however, this way of looking at scholarly work seems to have become somewhat unfashionable in *Beowulf* studies in recent decades. 'Negative criticism,' i.e., the refutation of theories of other scholars, is at the moment not considered a very constructive form of research. Scholarly flights of fancy, where common sense and logic are tossed aside, have – at least as far the subject of this book is concerned – become dangerously acceptable. But if scholarly imagination is not checked by logic and common sense, and if certain theories are allowed to become such sacred cows that they are beyond criticism, then *Beowulf* studies, as a subject, will soon be at an intellectual level closer to comic books and science fiction than to other academic disciplines.

Although I have, in the previous ten chapters, argued against a generally accepted opinion concerning the supposed genetic relationship between *Beowulf* and *Grettis saga*, I am perfectly aware of the fact that it is impossible to determine with any absolute certainty whether or not the two works are indeed related. In the final analysis, the question of a relationship between the poem and the saga boils down to three possible answers:

1/*Grettis saga* is closer to the 'old legend' than *Beowulf*. Hence we are allowed to use the saga to reconstruct the Old English poem, as Chambers, Lawrence, and others have done.

2/*Grettis saga* is no closer to the 'old legend' than *Beowulf*. The saga only relates and reworks bits and pieces of the original story. As a result, it cannot be used to clarify any unsolved problems in *Beowulf*.

3/*Beowulf* and *Grettis saga* are not related in any way, although parts of each work may – on the surface at least – appear to be similar. This possibility obviously rules out the presence of an 'old legend' or a common ancestor for both the saga and the poem.

In this situation, it can only be the weight of the evidence that determines which of these possibilities appears to be the most likely one, and with that in mind, the third one should not be ruled out quite so casually as we saw C.S. Smith and Larry Benson do in the introduction to this book. It is perhaps well to remember that 'there is nothing more deceptive than an obvious fact,' as Arthur Conan Doyle has Sherlock Holmes observe in 'The Boscomb Valley Mystery.'[2]

So far, the evidence that we have examined has not suggested any form of contact between *Beowulf* and *Grettis saga*, but one area, the question of a mutual *genre*, remains unexplored. In the past, the debate over this has always focused on the Grendel story, on the one hand, and on one of the five supposed analogues in *Grettis saga*, the Sandhaugar episode, on the other, and in the following discussion I shall do the same.

What kind of story was the 'old legend' that Vigfússon thought that he had discovered over a century ago? Vigfússon never seems to have given much thought to this question, but others soon did. The trio of Klaeber, Lawrence, and Chambers – in addition to Panzer, of course – were all agreed that originally the Grendel story had to have been a folktale or a *Märchen*.[3] And there was no doubt that the Sandhaugar episode was also a folktale; after all, the saga all but said so. The tacit assumption upon which this conclusion had to rest was that it was possible to peel the Old English poem like an onion, until one came upon some kind of a reognizable folktale-like 'kernel' from which the poem as we now have it had presumably later developed. This explanation of the poem's growth and development from its humble origins was, however, always a bit dubious, and Klaeber clearly had reservations, which he voiced quietly in the introduction to his first edition of *Beowulf*:[4]

There is no evidence to show that 'a Bēowulf legend' had gradually grown up out of popular stories that had been brought over to England by the migrating Angles. If such

were the case, it would be inexplicable why the exclusive interest in Scandinavian legends remained virtually unimpaired, and why in particular such a minute attention to the
fortunes of Northern dynasties continued to be manifested in the epic.[5]

In his book on *Beowulf*, WW. Lawrence felt compelled to take issue with the
unorthodox opinion that his friend and colleague was spreading: 'The answer
seems clear. Interest in Scandinavian legend remained unimpaired, just as it did
in Germanic legend generally. How keen this interest was, all the remains of
pagan verse in Anglo-Saxon illustrate – *Widsith, Deor, Waldhere*, the Northum-
brian lyrics.'[6] This is not a very satisfactory reply to Klaeber's doubts. In the
first place it is rather dubious to equate, as Lawrence does, the common Germanic literary heritage with a remote and relatively provincial Scandinavian
past; and secondly, none of Lawrence's examples show any signs of having a
folktale origin.

The debate between Klaeber and Lawrence on the folktale origin of *Beowulf*
went no further than this, insofar as I know. Perhaps they did not think that the
subject matter was important enough to have a full-scale scholarly debate.
Lawrence, at least, did not think very highly of folktales as a literary *genre*. In
his book on *Beowulf* he characterized the folktale kernel from which he
believed the poem had grown as 'a tale told among simple people with childlike
imaginations.'[7] As for the competing viewpoints that were offered by the two
scholars there is little doubt as to which of the two won the day. Lawrence's
ideas – or Panzer's, to be exact – are repeated by *Beowulf* scholars from time to
time,[8] whereas Klaeber's objections are all but forgotten.

Recent work by *Beowulf* scholars on the question of the possible folktale origin of the poem has been heavily influenced by the ideas of the Russian folklor-
ist Vladimir Propp. Some years ago, Daniel R. Barnes investigated the poem
closely from a Proppian viewpoint, with the debate between Klaeber and
Lawrence in mind. He concluded that the tale that may be extracted from
Beowulf by applying Propp's system offers 'additional support' for the folktale
origin theory, but 'is not of itself sufficient "proof" that *Beowulf* is essentially a
folktale.'[9] Barnes's methods and conclusion have, however, come under criticism. Bruce A. Rosenberg replied to his article shortly after its publication and
dryly observed that 'the poem that has come down to us on Cotton Vitellius A
XV is not a folktale,' and proceeded to take Barnes to task for the questionable
methodology that he felt that his colleague had used:

we should be suspicious when we are told that 'I have applied Propp's theory to *Beowulf*
by testing the poem against the structural model presented in *Morphology of the Folktale*.' And we should proceed with extreme caution when the author asserts that one of

his premises is 'that examination of the poem in terms of a synthetic structural theory which attempts to describe the principles common to *all* folktales – *independent of content similarities* – offers, if not a less hypothetical means than the comparative method, at least a radically new approach to the question of the "folktale element" in *Beowulf* ' ... [Barnes] admits that *Beowulf* bears 'obvious traces' of literary artistry, yet he examines the poem as though it were a folktale. Literary history is ignored, and I believe to the detriment of the author's argument.[10]

Icelandic scholars have, with the exception of Óskar Halldórsson and Vésteinn Ólason, always considered the Sandhaugar episode to be a genuinely indigenous folktale. Björn M. Ólsen thought that the saga author had merely embellished – for instance by adding the two stanzas – an already existing folktale and then attached it to Grettir's name.[11] Other critics, such as Jónas Kristjánsson and *Grettis saga*'s editor, Guðni Jónsson, have, for the most part, expressed the same opinion.[12]

If we close the circle and come back to the starting point of this debate, I think that the evidence – when considered in its entirety – confirms Klaeber's scepticism. There neither is, nor has there ever been, any reasonable evidence to suggest that the Old English poem originated as a folktale, and it is my belief that if the Grendel story had never been thought of as an analogue genetically related to the Sandhaugar episode, it would never have occurred to anybody to suggest the singular development theory that Lawrence postulated for *Beowulf*. Of course, the classification of the Sandhaugar episode and the Grendel story as different *genres* does not in itself rule out their kinship, as the 'old legend' could have taken on different shapes in different countries. But it would undeniably have strengthened the possible ties between these two stories – as Panzer, Chambers, and Lawrence indeed believed – if they could be shown to belong to the same type.

In conclusion, I want to emphasize that I do not rule out the possibility that the Sandhaugar episode and the Grendel story have a common Indo-European ancestor somewhere in the dark and distant past,[13] but if they do, that ancestor is beyond recovery. I do not think, however, that this is very likely. If we take the texts of *Grettis saga* and *Beowulf* and compare them without any wishful thinking or *a priori* notions of one being analogous and genetically related to the other, one can only conclude that any likeness that we find in the two works is accidental, because as we have seen in the previous chapters, the trail always goes cold if we try to go beyond the surface of the two texts, and – for all the scholarly ink that has been spilled on the matter – it is impossible to come up with a reasonably convincing theory to explain how the two texts are supposed to be linked. These are my two main reasons for believing that the two are not related. 'The arm of coincidence is ... long'[14] as Chambers once remarked, and ironically, the author of *Grettis saga* has his hero voice the same thought: 'many things look alike.'[15] As far as *Grettis saga* and *Beowulf* are concerned, I find myself in complete agreement with Kemp Malone's view when he observes that 'the Icelandic sagas are masterpieces of literary art but they have little in common with *Beowulf*.'[16]

Notes

Introduction

1 For a brief summary of the relevant passages see Klaeber 1950, ix–xi and xiv–xvii. Full translations of the two most widely recognized genetically related analogues from *Grettis saga* are provided, e.g., in Garmonsway, et al., 1968, 302–16, and Chambers 1959, 163–82.

2 Smith 1881, 65.

3 Benson 1970, 26. It may be added that in the years that have passed since Benson wrote his article, complete faith in a link between *Grettis saga* and *Beowulf* has been reiterated by every publication that has concerned itself with the poem and the saga. The latest such study, Andersson 1997, informs its readers, for example, that 'Among the Norse analogues only *Grettis saga* seems convincing to most students,' (125) and goes on to add that 'there is not much doubt of some connection between *Beowulf* and *Grettis saga*' (131).

4 Shippey 1978, 59.

5 Powell 1901, 395–6. Chambers 1959, 481, also notes this analogue and finds striking resemblance to *Beowulf* in the rescue of the grisly arm by the demon in female disguise.

6 Von Unwerth 1911, 167–73. Von Unwerth believes that in the first part of the Sandhaugar episode the author of *Grettis saga* borrows from his own description of Grettir's fight with Glámr, which in turn is a story made up of various literary motifs from other Icelandic texts.

1: Determining Analogous and Genetically Related Material

1 Because the word 'analogue' can both denote a general similarity between two texts and imply that the texts in question are genetically related, I want to make it very clear at the outset of my discussion that I am concerned solely with the latter use of

the word. In the chapters that follow, I am interested in *Beowulf* and *Grettis saga* analogues only as evidence that either links or fails to link the two works.

2 Guðni Jónsson, ed., *Grettis saga, Íslenzk fornrit*, 7, 1936, chaps. 64–6. All references to the saga in this book are to this edition. For an English translation see, e.g., Chambers 1959, 175–82, or Garmonsway 1968, 312–16.

3 Vigfusson 1878, vol. 1, xlix.

4 Vigfusson 1878, vol. 1, xlix, n. 1.

5 *Mece* in Old English denotes a certain type of sword, but it is not clear to what precisely the prefix *hæft-* is supposed to refer. *Grettis saga*, chap. 66, explains *heptisax* as a weapon with a wooden handle that could be used both for stabbing and cutting. Both words are discussed in detail in chap. 4.

6 Vigfusson and Powell 1883, vol. 2, 502.

7 See, e.g., Gering 1880, 85.

8 Smith 1881, 66: *Beowulf*, lines 1539–40: 'brægd þa beadwe heard, þa he gebolgen wæs, / feorhgeniðlan, þæt heo on flet gebeah.' *Grettis saga*, 212: 'bregðr hann flagðkonunni til sveiflu.'

9 Klaeber 1950, xv n. 1.

10 Halldórsson 1982, 20.

11 Malone 1958, 307.

12 Garnett 1880, 492.

13 Finnur Jónsson, 1923, 745n. 1, questions the relationship between the Sandhaugar episode and *Beowulf* that Chambers postulates in the first edition of his book on the poem (see Chambers 1959, 50) on the grounds that he assumes a common source but fails to show how the two texts are related ('han antager en fælles kilde, men ingen ligefrem sammenhæng'). Chambers eventually attempted to provide such a context; see Chambers 1959, 451–78. According to Anatoly Liberman (1986, 385), Steblin-Kamenskij, in his 1976 Russian edition of *Grettis saga* 'ascribes all the convergencies between the poem and the saga to the inevitable loci communes and peculiarities of oral transmission.'

14 Chambers 1959, 49–50.

15 Klaeber 1950, xviii.

16 Stedman 1913, 13–14.

17 *Grettis saga*, chaps. 32–5. For an English translation see, e.g., Chambers 1959, 163–75, or Garmonsway 1968, 302–12.

18 Not all critics are convinced that the text (lines 433–40b and 798–805b) actually indicates that Grendel had magical powers that made him immune to weapons. Laborde 1923, 203–4, thinks that the monster's skin was so tough that Beowulf's companions could not injure him. Boer 1900, xlii n. 1, and von Unwerth 1911, 171–2, stress the loss and the strange recovery of the horses that belong to Þórhallr on the occasion when he meets and employs Glámr as a shepherd (chap. 32) as an example of Glámr's use of magic before he utters his famous curse on Grettir.

19 Vigfusson and Powell 1883, vol. 2, 502.
20 Vigfusson and Powell 1883, vol. 2, 502.
21 Chadwick 1959, 190. The idea of linking Glámr and the troll-woman at Sandhaugar was originally proposed by Carney 1955, 95.
22 Gering 1880, 86n. 2.
23 See Boer 1898, 60; Bugge 1887, 57n. 1; Lawrence 1928, 187; Jónsson 1936, xlix (and the fact that he excludes Glámr in his discussion of the Sandhaugar episode, li–lv); and Turville-Petre 1974–7, 349.
24 See Chambers 1959, 48, and 1929, 87.
25 Smith 1881, 66–7.
26 Stedman 1913, 9. This observation is clearly based on a misunderstanding of the Icelandic text. In *Grettis saga*, chap. 32, 111, Glámr is described as 'ósǫngvinn ok trúlauss,' which must refer to his refusal to sing religious hymns, and therefore to his anti-Christian attitude. See Lie 1939, 134, for a further discussion of the meaning of *ósǫngvinn*.
27 Stedman 1913, 8–13.
28 Mossé 1933, xxxiii.
29 Smith 1881, 67, held Grendel and Glámr to be of widely different nature, whereas Stedman and many later critics thought that certain details in their description pointed to a common origin.
30 Klaeber 1950, xvii.
31 *Grettis saga*, chap. 18. Neither this episode nor the two that follow are included in the standard handbooks on *Beowulf*, such as Chambers 1959, and Garmonsway 1968. Those who wish to view the full text in English should consult a translation of the saga, e.g., Fox and Pálsson, 1974.
32 Jónsson 1936, 57. It is more likely, however, that the real function of Grettir's companion is that of a one-member dramatic audience, and it is worth noting that a page later the author seems to assume that he is there to pull Grettir out of the gravemound ('varð hann þá að handstyrkja sig upp festina').
33 Klaeber 1950, xvi n. 1.
34 Taylor 1952, 13–14.
35 McConchie 1982, 482–3.
36 Jónsson 1936, chap. 21.
37 Klaeber 1950, xiv n. 3.
38 Lawrence 1928, 187.
39 Taylor 1952, 15–17.
40 Arent 1969, 190–1. Some years later Arthur A. Wachsler, who seems to have been unaware of the work of Taylor and Arent, repeated some of these points and added others; see Wachsler 1985, 381–90.
41 Halldórsson 1982, 14.
42 Harris 1973, 31 and 52.

43 See, e.g., Jorgensen 1978, 55 and 1979, 86.
44 Jónsson 1936, chaps 70–82.
45 Harris 1973, 34.
46 Harris 1973, 52.
47 Harris 1973, 37–41.
48 Harris 1973, 50.
49 Liberman 1986.
50 Liberman 1986, 388.
51 Jorgensen 1986, 203.
52 Mitchell 1991, 59.
53 Halldórsson 1982, 34.

2: The Making of Heroes and Monsters

 1 Vigfusson and Powell 1879, 404, and 1883, 502.
 2 Gering 1880, 87, wonders aloud how earlier scholars like Grímur Thorkelin, N.F.S. Grundtvig, Eiríkur Magnússon, and W. Morris – all of whom knew both *Beowulf* and *Grettis saga* – could have failed to see the connection between them.
 3 Jónsson 1936, lv.
 4 See, e.g., Powell 1901, 396.
 5 See the discussion of the Sandhaugar episode and Grettir's fight with the bear in chap. 1.
 6 See, e.g., Stedman 1913, 26 and 17, and Benson 1970, 28.
 7 Vigfusson and Powell 1883, 502 and n. 2 on the same page.
 8 See Panzer 1910, 32–9 and 44–66, on how this feature is expressed in various tales, and 268–9 and 322–4 on his attempt to apply the idea to Beowulf and Grettir. Panzer's theory is discussed in chap. 7.
 9 Jónsson 1936, 42.
10 The first section definitely relates Beowulf's exploits as a boy, but no chronology is given for the second, which may or may not refer to the same event.
11 See, e.g., Chambers 1959, 65 and Klaeber 1950, 207 (note on line 2183).
12 Arguments to this effect are summed up by Wrenn 1953, 218 (note on lines 2183–9), and Kuhn 1984, 245n. 11.
13 Seven days according to Unferð (line 517a).
14 Even Fred C. Robinson's well-known article, 'Elements of the Marvellous in the Characterization of Beowulf,' in which the author finds ways of rationalizing Beowulf's dive into Grendel's mere, his swimming contest with Breca, and his return by water from Frisia, does not alter this fact. I prefer the more traditional reading of the above-mentioned episodes of the poem, not just because it suits my argument, but because I find it futile to try to rationalize the main hero of a poem which

is neither consistent nor rational, and which asks us to believe that this same hero fought and defeated a number of supernatural enemies. In short, I prefer the mystery in a mysterious poem like *Beowulf*, and taking it away feels like being told that the parting of the Red Sea took place because of strange and unusual weather conditions.

15 See, e.g., chaps. 38, 58, and 75. Grettir's most famous water adventure, his swim from the island of Drangey to the shore of the mainland of Iceland, has been repeated several times during this century by lesser mortals.

16 Benson 1970, 28.

17 Guðni Jónsson believes Hallmundr to be a half-troll as well; see his introduction to *Grettis saga*, l. The exact nature of Hallmundr is left undefined in the saga.

18 Vigfusson 1878, xlix, and Vigfusson and Powell 1883, 502.

19 See, e.g., Chadwick, 1959, 178–91; Chadwick's use of the term *draugr* for all kinds of supernatural beings is now widely accepted.

20 See Lehmann 1901, 191–2. Early theories on the origin of the Grendels are summed up, e.g., by Kögel 1892, 274–6, and Wardale 1965, 92–3.

21 'The Haunted Mere in Beowulf.' Lawrence developed his ideas on the subject further in a later study entitled *Beowulf and Epic Tradition*.

22 Lines 1359b and 2128b. Lawrence interpreted the Old English term *fyrgenstream*, 'mountain stream,' to mean a waterfall.

23 Lawrence 1912, 241–5, and 1928, 162.

24 Lawrence 1912, 240.

25 See, e.g., Chambers 1959, 461–4; Liestöl 1930, 371–2; Fontenrose 1959, 527n. 12 and Kennedy 1940, xxi.

26 For a further discussion of this point see, e.g., von Sydow 1923, 31.

27 This has presented a dilemma to critics who look for rational explanations of everything in the poem. Klaeber 1950, 181 (note on lines 1282 ff.), for instance, offers the far-fetched but amusing theory that the reference to her weakness is 'evidently to be explained as an endeavor to discredit the unbiblical notion of a woman's superiority.'

28 See Lawrence 1928, 181–2, and Goldsmith 1970, 104.

29 See Wrenn 1953, 209.

30 See Lawrence 1928, 163–4.

31 For further reference see Klaeber 1950, xxviii–xxix, and Chambers 1959, 309–10. 'Grendel' also surfaces in English place names, often attached to water, but apart from that they throw no light on the meaning of the word according to Chambers. On the place name 'Grendill' in Iceland, see Einarsson, 1956, 79–82. He believes that the name is modern, probably given by a recent surveyor.

32 *Mære mearcstapa*. It has also been suggested, first by Edv. Lehmann 1901, 189, and later by Kiessling 1968, 191, that *mære* (with a long 'æ') – normally taken to be an adjective – might be a noun, *mære* (with a short vowel), meaning an incubus or a night monster (Old Norse *mara*).

33 See Jónsson 1936, 123–4n. 2; Janzén 1947, 51; Magnússon 1989, 252; and Jónsson 1954, 209 and 311.
34 See Boer 1898, 57–8, and 1900, xlii.
35 See von Unwerth 1911, 171–2. Von Unwerth also points to the presence of a giant named Glámr in *Bárðar saga*, chaps. 13–14.
36 See Boer 1900, xlii n. 1, and von Unwerth 1911, 171–2.
37 Carney 1955, 94–5.
38 It has been argued (see, e.g., Hume 1975, 473) that there is a causal relationship between Glámr's becoming a ghost and the fact that his death is caused by some kind of a monstrous creature. There is nothing in the text of *Grettis saga* which confirms (or denies) this view.
39 Gordon 1927, 83. Gordon, it may be added, sees little ingenuity in Glámr's behaviour as a ghost and suspects that his habit of riding the house-top 'may have been suggested originally by the cattle of Iceland getting on the turf roof to nibble the grass.'
40 See von Unwerth 1911, 167–9, and Jónsson 1936, xvii–xxxi.
41 Pálsson 1980, 98–9.
42 Pálsson 1980, 98: 'sýnast þeir með svo stórum líkömum, að höfuð ber herbergjum hærra.'
43 It appears both in *Eyrbyggja* and *Laxdæla saga*.
44 Carney 1955, 96.
45 Kiessling 1968, 200.
46 See, e.g., Halvorsen 1974, 656.
47 Christmas is very often the time when such attacks occur, but here there is nothing in the text to indicate that these particular raids are inspired by animosity towards Christianity, like the account of Grendel's ongoing strife against God.
48 There is no single word in English for this vessel. *Trog* is a cross between a tray and a trough.
49 See, e.g., Jónsson 1936, 30n. 1, and Shetelig 1937, 378.
50 See Klaeber 1950, xv n. 2.
51 See, e.g., Motz 1982, 72–3.
52 Garmonsway et al. 1968, 316.
53 Jorgensen 1973, 56. The compounds *ástvinr* and *málvinr*, which occur in the kennings for lovers that Jorgensen found ('*ástvinr meyja*' and '*ekkju málvinr*'), indicate more than just a friendship. It is difficult to see how they can be used as evidence of the semantic range of the uncompounded form *vinr* in Old Norse.
54 See, e.g., Malone 1958, 307.
55 Like the Sandhaugar episode, chap. 18 of the saga is somewhat inconsistent. The story of the high-handed practices of Kárr and his son does not accord well with the description of Þorfinnr's character, and his reaction to Grettir's robbing Kárr's gravemound makes little sense.

56 McConchie 1982, 482–3.

57 It is a fire burning on a promontory on the island that first attracts Grettir's attention, and he immediately interprets what he sees as a sign of a buried treasure. After having broken into the gravemound, Grettir pays no attention to the presence of Kárr; he merely assembles his booty and is about to leave when Kárr attacks him (cf. Jónsson 1936, 57–8). McConchie's statement (p. 484) that 'Grettir's interest in the gravemound is not given a precise motivation' is only true in the sense that the saga author does not spell it out any clearer than this.

58 Wachsler 1985, 382–3.

59 Taylor 1952, 17.

60 It is very uncertain what *þyle* really means and what Unferð's role in Heorot is. See, e.g., Rosier 1962, 1–8, and Eliason 1963, 267–84.

61 For further discussion see Hughes 1977 and Rosenberg 1975.

62 Wachsler 1985, 386.

63 Chadwick 1959, 193.

64 Chadwick 1959, 192.

65 Chadwick 1959, 193.

66 It is not clear what meaning Chadwick wants to assign to this form.

67 Arent 1969, 184–5.

68 Janzén 1947, 155. ('*Belsheim* menar mansnamnet vara samma namn som den i Normandie starkt utbredda *Grente*. Han förmodar namnet ha uppstått på "et sted i Vesten, og mindst et par generationer førend det første gang viser sig paa Isl.," och att det möjligen är ett främmande namn av oviss innebörd.')

69 Liberman 1986, 389–90.

70 For discussion along these lines see, e.g., Arent 1969, 184–5, and Chadwick 1959, 193.

71 Harris 1973, 40.

72 Harris 1973, 36.

73 Anatoly Liberman's objections to Harris's methods were noted in chap. 1.

74 Cf., e.g., item 6 regarding Grettir's death and items 6 and 7 from *Beowulf*.

75 Harris 1973, 43–4.

76 For a thorough investigation of the different roles that Grettir is made to play in the saga itself and in later tradition see Hastrup 1990, 154–83.

3: The Hero's Fight against the Monsters

1 Jónsson 1936, lv.

2 See Klaeber 1950, 155 (note on lines 736b–8).

3 German scholars have normally been more discriminating on this point than their English and American colleagues. In German these two kinds of fights are usually

called *Zerrkampf* (tug-fight) and *Ringkampf* (wrestling match). Old Norse has no term for the first type but knows the second as *glíma*.

4 In this passage the difficulty concerns the interpretation of line 749b: 'ond wið earm gesæt,' which Klaeber (1950, 155) and many other editors and translators read to mean that Beowulf sat up supporting himself on his arm. Wrenn, on the other hand, believes that the arm in question is Grendel's and that Beowulf 'sat right up violently ... so as to drive back Grendel's arm.' For further discussion of this line see Wrenn 1953, 198 (note on lines 745–9).

5 It was Heinz Dehmer who first called attention to this peculiarity of fighting with the demon's arm rather than with the demon himself. He traced the motif to Irish sources. For further discussion, see Dehmer 1928.

6 See, e.g., Whitbread 1949, Rosier 1963, and Carens 1976.

7 It should be noted that some critics believe that the best first battle analogue in *Grettis saga* is Grettir's fight with Glámr. Consequently, they see the battle against the troll-woman as an analogue to Beowulf's fight against Grendel's mother. See, e.g., Gordon 1927, 83, and Chadwick 1959, 190.

8 According to Grettir, she perished when she fell into the ravine, but the local inhabitants of Bárðardalur claim that troll-woman was caught by the light of dawn as they wrestled. She died when he cut her arm off and a stone in her likeness still stands there at the edge of the cliff. See *Grettis saga*, chap. 65.

9 See, e.g., Lawrence 1912, 234n. 1, and Puhvel 1979, 120–1.

10 See Puhvel 1979, 115.

11 See, e.g., lines 750–3a, 765b–6 and 805b–7a. Klaeber 1950, lii, complains that the fight is 'too short and easy' for Beowulf.

12 See Jónsson 1936, 212.

13 Benson 1970, 28.

14 Jónsson 1936, 120–1, 212, and 215.

15 Jónsson 1936, 120–1.

16 Chambers 1929, 87.

17 Jónsson 1936, xlix.

18 See, e.g., Dehmer 1928, 207.

19 Earle 1884, 137.

20 See, e.g., Boer 1923, 107–12, Leach 1921, 299, and Goldsmith 1970, 100.

21 See Dehmer 1927, 40–1.

22 Dehmer 1927, 41.

23 Jorgensen 1979, 84.

24 Jónsson 1936, 121.

25 Puhvel 1979, 119.

26 See chapter 9, 'The Big Bang Theory.'

27 Goldsmith 1970, 100.

28 The Devil was commonly held to have flaming eyes during the Middle Ages. See, e.g., Russell 1984, 68: 'his eyes are saucerlike and glow or shoot fire.'

29 For further discussion of these points see Taylor 1952, 15–17, Arent 1969, 190–1, and Wachsler 1985, 381–90.

30 I follow Fred C. Robinson's reading of line 1545a: *ofsæt þa þone selegyst*. For a further discussion of the meaning of the Old English verb *ofsittan*, see Robinson 1994, 1–7.

31 It is a matter of punctuation of line 1555 whether this happens through divine intervention. See Klaeber 1950, 187 (note on lines 1555 ff.).

32 It is not entirely clear whether Beowulf does this with Hrunting or the giant sword (see, e.g., Eliason 1963, 279), nor does the poem tell us why Grendel is decapitated. Klaeber 1950, xviii, finds it hard to accept that the hero would be wasting his time killing dead monsters, and proposes that in the original form of the story 'the male demon had been merely wounded; when the hero had made his way to the dwelling place of the monsters, he put the wounded enemy to death (and afterwards killed the mother).'

33 Cf. Jónsson 1936, 216: 'It is not said how much money he got from the cave, but people assume that it was a fair amount.' (Translation mine.)

34 Parks 1993, 12 and 13.

35 Chambers 1929, 85.

36 Klaeber 1950, 186 (note on lines 1506 ff.). Klaeber here accepts Lawrence's idea that *Samsons saga fagra* is yet another version of the 'old legend.' On this theory see Lawrence 1929, 172–81.

37 See McConchie 1982, 483.

38 Adapted from Stitt 1992, 155. For further discussion see his chapter 'The Gravemound Battle Tradition,' 129–69.

39 Arent 1969, 195.

40 See, e.g., Stedman 1913, 13–17.

41 Chadwick 1959, 190.

42 *Beowulf*, see, e.g., lines 194–5 and 409b–32.

43 Wardale 1965, 94.

44 Jónsson 1936, 209–10: 'Þorsteinn hvíti hét maðr, er bjó at Sandhaugum ... Þar þótti mǫnnum reimt mjǫk sakar trollagangs.'

45 Jónsson 1936, 215, explains *heptisax* as a weapon with a wooden handle that could be used both for stabbing and cutting. This now famous word, the nature of the weapon in question, and the relationship of both to Old English *hæftmece*, will be discussed in detail in the next chapter.

46 See, e.g., Brodeur 1959, 95; Chambers 1929, 91, and Lawrence 1928, 182.

47 Lawrence 1912, 234n. 1.

48 Brandl 1901–9, 994: 'Grettir erlegt ihn [i.e., the giant] mit einem Schwerthieb in die Brüst, ungefähr wie Beowulf die Grendelin.'

49 In prose word order: *ek lét heptisax hǫggva harðeggjar af skepti. See Jorgensen 1973, 54–61, and 1979, 88.
50 Liberman 1986, 391n. 3.
51 Stitt 1992, 205.
52 The motif of the gore-stained water also occurs in two Icelandic texts recorded later than *Grettis saga: Samsons saga fagra* and *Þorsteins saga Víkingssonar.*
53 Chambers 1959, 63. In the folktale, now identified as AT301, the hero goes into the lower world to rescue stolen maidens. The maidens are pulled up by the hero's companions, who in turn steal them and betray the hero by leaving him behind. He usually makes his way to the upper world through some sort of magic, finds the maidens, and punishes the treacherous companions.
54 Benson 1970, 32.
55 See Danielli 1945.

4: A Sword by Any Other Name

1 See chap. 1.
2 Chickering 1977, 133, lines 1455b–6a. Klaeber 1950, 350, simply glosses *hæftmece* as a 'hilted sword.' For the definition that *Grettis saga* gives of *heptisax*, see chap. 1, n. 4.
3 Davidson 1962, 140.
4 See Falk 1914, 10.
5 See Boer 1898, 60 and 1900, lxiii. In his 'Beowulf och Bjarke,' C.W. von Sydow also voices similar scepticism. A case for transmission through an oral tradition is made by Chambers 1959, 474, and more recently by Stitt 1992, 95–6.
6 Schneider 1934, 26–7.
7 Von Sydow 1923, 29–30.
8 Turville-Petre 1974–7, 352.
9 Taken from Chambers 1959, 180. The text in Jónsson 1936, 215, reads: 'En er Grettir kom at honum, hljóp jǫtuninn upp ok greip flein einn ok hjó til þess, er kominn var, því at bæði mátti hǫggva ok leggja með því; tréskapt var í; þat kǫlluðu menn þá heptisax, er þann veg var gǫrt.'
10 Earle 1892, 159.
11 See, e.g., Dehmer 1927, 58; von Sydow 1923, 30 and Puhvel 1979, 118.
12 See Jorgensen 1973 and Halldórsson 1982, 26.
13 Translation mine. For the original text, see Jónsson 1936:
     Þá hét konungr á berserki sína til framgǫngu; þeir váru kallaðir úlfheðnar, en á þá bitu engi járn; (5)
     Þorgeirr var fyrir búi þeira brœðra í Reykjarfirði ok reri jafnan til fiska, því at þá váru firðirnir fullir af fiskum. (26)

Skip þat, er kaupmenn hǫfðu gǫrt, var mjǫk breiðvaxit; þat kǫlluðu menn Trékylli, ok þar er víkin við kennd. (32–3)

Þorsteinn hafði látit gera kirkju á bœ sínum. Hann lét brú gera heiman frá bœnum; hon var gǫr með hagleik miklum. En útan í brúnni undir ásunum, þeim er upp heldu brúnni, var gǫrt með hringum ok dynbjǫllur, svá at heyrði yfir til Skarfs-staða, hálfa viku sjávar, ef gengit var um brúna; svá hristusk hringarnir. Hafði Þorsteinn mikinn starfa fyrir þessarri smíð, því at hann var járngǫrðarmaðr mikill. Grettir var atgangsmikill at drepa járnit, en nennti misjafnt ... (173)

14 See Jónsson 1936, xxxi–xxxvii.

15 Jorgensen 1973, 55: '... the scrambled syntax of the second stanza contains a number of details which are also found in the fight with Grendel's dam in *Beowulf*, but not in the corresponding prose version of *Grettis saga*. It is known that writers of the thirteenth century used in their prose redactions pre-classical or Old Norse verses which they no longer completely understood, and if this can be shown to be the case in *Grettis saga*, then the existence in Iceland of a poem older than the saga treating the Grendel legend must be assumed.'

16 Jorgensen 1973, 56–7.

17 Turville-Petre, 1974–7, 352.

18 In the preamble to Jorgensen's argument two other points also merit attention. It is an overstatement to maintain that *hæftmece* and *heptisax* occur 'at precisely the same point' in the relevant episodes of *Beowulf* and *Grettis saga*. The sword Hrunting is called a *hæftmece* before and not during Beowulf's battle with Grendel's mother, and the sword also has various other appellations. The issue of whether *hæftmece* and *heptisax* can be considered as cognate words will be dealt with later in this chapter.

19 Shetelig and Falk 1937, 385–6. See also Falk 1914, 68.

20 In addition to *hæftmece, beado-leoma, hilde-bil(l),* and *wæg-sweord* are also applied to Hrunting, and these terms occur only in *Beowulf*. The same is true of the giant sword that Beowulf discovers during his battle with Grendel's mother, the *hilde-gicel* – also called *ealdsweord* and *wigbil(l)* – whose blade melts.

21 Cf., e.g., Chambers 1959, 469: 'This casual use of the word *hæft-mēce* would not have attracted attention or called for any remark, were it not for its counterpart the *hepti-sax* in the *Grettis saga*.'

22 Brady 1979, 93.

23 Beowulf's own sword is said to be 'the best of blades' (*irena cyst*) in line 673a, and lines 1023a and 2154a describe Hroðgar's gift as famous, precious, and richly adorned.

24 For a summary of early suggestions concerning the etymology of Hrunting, see Liberman 1986, 390.

25 Malone 1944 and 1946.

26 Eliason 1963, 278n. 40 and 284.

27 Shetelig and Falk 1937, 386.
28 Klaeber 1950, 360.
29 Klaeber 1950, 429.
30 Brady 1979, 101.
31 Klaeber 1950, 301.
32 Brady 1979, 101.
33 Lehmann 1967, 230.
34 See Davidson 1962, 129, and Lehmann 1967, 227–8.
35 Chambers 1959, 473–4.
36 See, e.g., Klaeber 1950, 185 (note on line 1457): 'It appears that in the original story much was made of a sword with a wonderful "haft" (or "hilt"), which later, as a result of the fight, was detached from the blade ... It was a part of such a marvelous sword, we imagine, to bring about the hero's victory. This feature is obliterated in the *Grettis saga*; in the *Beowulf*, the term *hæftmēce* has been transferred to an entirely different sword'; and also Jorgensen 1979, 89: 'It is very likely that the nonce epithet itself, i.e., *hæftmēce*, was a transferal by the *Beowulf* poet from the sword in the cave to the hero's weapon ...'
37 See Puhvel 1979, 117.
38 The traditional interpretation of *fetelhilt* has been questioned by H.R. Ellis Davidson, who points to stories about swords that are secured in some way that makes it impossible for anyone except the hero to draw them. 'It is thus possible that this unique term *fetelhilt* is not a descriptive one but one arising out of a traditional element in the story, though its significance is no longer apparent in the poem as we have it.' Davidson 1962, 142.
39 See Klaeber 1950, 189, and Wrenn 1953, 212.
40 Davidson 1962, 139.
41 Davidson 1962, 141.
42 Evison 1963, 138–9.
43 Taylor 1952, 16.
44 He referred to *hæftmece* and *heptisax* rather mysteriously as 'one word,' as we saw in chap. 1.
45 See, e.g., Jorgensen 1973, 56–7.
46 See, e.g., Chambers 1929, 94, and Puhvel 1979, 116.
47 See, e.g., Halldórsson 1982, 23: 'Augljósasta bendingin um skyldleika Bjkv. og Grettlu er hið samkynja vopnsheiti sem kemur fram í báðum verkum ... En þótt orðin samsvari hvort öðru hafa vopnin hvorki sama snið né hlutverk.'
48 Evison 1963, 138.
49 Liberman 1986, 380 and 383.
50 Mastrelli 1985–6, 405–20.
51 See Schück 1909, 18–19n. 1.

52 Arent 1969, 195. Arent's criticism rests on her belief that both words refer to a weapon which may 'merely belong to the paraphernalia of trolls and giants.'

5: Hell and High Water

1   See von Sydow 1923, 31–2.
2   See Klaeber 1950, xiv n. 3.
3   See, e.g., Arent 1969, 191, and Jorgensen 1975. It should be noted, however, that Arent believes that the scenery of the bear analogue in the saga recalls the dragon's lair rather than the surroundings of the mere.
4   Smith 1881, 65: 'In both cases we find the hero engaged in strife with two superhuman beings of different sexes, inhabiting a cave 'neath a force.'
5   Lawrence 1912, 218–19.
6   Lawrence 1912, 235–7. Lawrence later expanded his ideas on this subject in *Beowulf and Epic Tradition*, where he maintains, for instance, that the muddled picture which the author of *Beowulf* gives of a waterfall might have come about because he had never seen the real thing. See Lawrence 1928, 184–6.
7   Klaeber must have had some doubts, however, because the reference to Lawrence which follows the gloss begins with a question mark.
8   Chambers 1959, 464.
9   See, e.g., Schlauch 1956, 42–3; Chadwick 1959, 186; Jorgensen 1973, 54; Harris 1973, 41; Chickering 1977, 334; and Jack 1994, 117.
10 Mackie 1938, 457. For further a discussion of *fyrgenstream* as an epithet for 'ocean' in Anglo-Saxon literature, see also Sarrazin 1910, 5.
11 Lawrence 1939, 479.
12 Malone 1932, 192.
13 Malone 1958, 298. Malone's article is presented as a criticism of Klaeber's handling of the mere scene in his edition of *Beowulf*. However, Klaeber's notes and glosses in this section of the poem are simply an echo of Lawrence's theories concerning the landscape of the mere and its connection with *Grettis saga*.
14 This is not entirely without exception. Andersson 1997, 131, notes the findings of Mackie and Malone in their argument against Lawrence's waterfall theory, but he dismisses their impact on the question of a genetic relationship between the poem and the saga: 'Despite this curious debate over landscape features, there is not much doubt of some connection between *Beowulf* and *Grettis saga*.'
15 See, e.g., Lawrence 1912, 240: 'It is clear that the Anglo-Saxon *Beowulf*, in anything like the form in which we have it at present, could not have given a hint for the description of Grettir's adventure at the waterfall. The situation is obscure in Anglo-Saxon; it is crystal-clear in Scandinavian. The fact that the *Grettissaga* explains so well the obscurities of the Anglo-Saxon version prevents us from concluding that the

main outlines of the Scandinavian account represent a late rationalization or alteration of the original situation'; and Lawrence 1928, 182–3: 'The saga is clear where
the epic is confused; it preserves the original form of the story so much better that it
may even be used to explain obscure incidents and description in the Anglo-Saxon.
As an illustration, let us see how the tale of Grettir serves to show the original conception of the demon lair ...'

16 Neither Mackie nor Malone questioned this assumption in their objections to
Lawrence's theory. For later reiterations of the clarity and realism of the waterfall
scenery in the saga see, e.g., Arent 1969, 196; Halldórsson 1982, 32; and Liberman
1986, 374.

17 Lawrence 1912, 239: 'It is very significant, then, that the idea of a cave under a
waterfall, in a precipitous country, adhered so strongly to the story that the natural
scenery was disregarded in order to retain it.' The possibility that the saga author had
an actual waterfall in mind should, however, not be altogether discarded. In his edition of the saga Guðni Jónsson suggests the possibility that another waterfall
(Goðafoss) in a nearby river (Skjálfandafljót) may have been what he had in mind.
See Jónsson 1936, 213n. 1. Halldór Laxness, in a humorous article on Icelandic out-
laws, reports that in the 1940s the inhabitants of Bárðardalur believed the saga
description to be accurate; the waterfall had simply changed since Grettir's time.
Laxness 1949, 87–8.

18 Jónsson 1936, 214: 'en er þeir kómu til forsins, sá þeir skúta upp undir bergit; þat var
meitilberg svá mikit, at hvergi mátti upp komask, ok nær tíu faðma ofan at vatninu.'
The key word here is *skúta*, which in this context can either be a noun (acc. sing. or
pl.) meaning 'cave(s),' or a verb meaning 'to overhang.'

19 Panzer 1910, 315, takes the ten fathoms as the distance from the top of the cliff to the
cave below the fall; Boer 1900, 238n. 8, as the distance from the cave to the surface
of the pool; and Lawrence, 1912, 234n. 2, rounds up the remaining possibility by
taking them as the distance from the top of the cliff to the pool beneath. Lawrence, in
the last-mentioned article, does not seem to have realized that *skúta* was a problem,
as he only addresses the issue of the 'ten fathoms' in a footnote and concludes –
quite erroneously – that it is 'not important' for the purpose of his argument.

20 See Chambers 1959, 179. His translation of the passage reads: 'But when they came
to the waterfall they saw that the sides of the gorge hung over: it was a sheer cliff so
great that one could in nowise come up, and it was nearly ten fathoms from the top to
the water below.' Chambers further explains his vision of the waterfall landscape in
n. 2 for this page: 'The translators all take *skúta* as acc. of *skúti*, which is quite possible: but they are surely wrong when they proceed to identify the *skúti* with the *hellir*
[i.e., 'cave'] behind the waterfall. For this cave behind the waterfall is introduced in
the *saga* as something which Grettir discovers *after* he has dived beneath the fall, the
fall in front naturally hiding it till then.' It may be added that Heinz Dehmer reads

this passage to mean exactly the opposite; i.e., that Grettir sees that there is cave behind the waterfall: 'Nach Weihnachten holt Grettir Stein ab, um mit ihm nachzusehen, ob seine Ansicht richtig sei. Sie kommen an den Wasserfall und sehen eine von überhängenden Felsen gebildete Höhle, die sich weiter unter den Felsen hinzieht.' Dehmer 1927, 57.

21 See Jónsson 1936, 216–17. Stanza 60: 'fast lá framan at brjósti / flugstraumr í sal Naumu,' 'the flowing current beat against my breast in the hall of the ogress.' Stanza 61: 'Ljótr kom mér í móti / mellu vinr ór helli,' 'the ugly giant came out of his cave to meet me.'

22 Lawrence 1912, 225.

23 Lawrence 1912, 222–3.

24 Lawrence 1912, 241.

25 Lawrence 1912, 226–7.

26 See Hulbert 1929, 193–4. Mackie later argued along similar lines: 'The poet of *Beowulf* ... cares little about verisimilitude, and does not greatly trouble to be consistent; his purpose is not to make the supernatural appear natural, but to invest his narrative with an eerie atmosphere of strangeness and horror.' Mackie 1938, 456.

27 See, e.g., Goldsmith 1970, 113–14, and Niles 1983, 16.

28 Mackie 1938, 458.

29 Malone 1958, 301–2.

30 Malone 1958, 306.

31 Malone 1958, 298–9.

32 Both texts describe downward-flowing water, a grey rock, frosty woods, dark mists, and an abyss.

33 For a short summary of different theories on this subject see, e.g., Jack 1994, 110. Wright 1993, 106–74 contains a detailed and thorough discussion of St. Paul's vision and its relationship to *Beowulf*.

34 The main weakness in Malone's theory is, as Margaret Goldsmith has pointed out, that 'the place [i.e. the cave of Grendel's dam] is not in the least like hell when Beowulf arrives there.' Goldsmith 1970, 116.

35 Wright 1993, 132.

36 Chickering 1977, 334.

37 Klaeber 1950, 186 (note on lines 1506 ff.).

38 Malone 1958, 303.

39 See, e.g., Benson 1970, 28, and Turville-Petre 1974–7, 351.

40 Rosier 1963, 12. A similar argument is also presented by Dragland 1977, 614: 'If Heorot contains the symbolic darkness of Grendel, the mere-cave has something of the hall about it, described as it is as a kind of underground Germanic dwelling.'

41 Turville-Petre 1974–7, 351.

42 Klaeber explains the phrase *fyrleoht geseah* as: 'The light in the "hall" (which

enables Béowulf to see his adversary).' Klaeber 1950, 186. The suggestion that *fyrleoht* should be translated as 'fiery light' was originally proposed by W.S. Mackie. See Mackie 1938, 461.

43 See Klaeber 1950, 188, and Mackie 1938, 461.
44 See Lawrence 1939, 478n. 2 and Chambers 1959, 466–7.
45 Mackie 1938, 461.
46 Puhvel 1979, 115.

6: The English Hypothesis

1 Vigfusson 1878, vol. 1, xlix n. 1.
2 Vigfusson and Powell 1883, vol. 2, 502.
3 Bugge 1887, 58: 'Ich vermute, dass die hier besprochene isländische sage [i.e., *Grettis saga*] aus einer nordenglischen stammt. Diese nordenglische sage ruhte, wie ich annehme, auf einem alten liede, das mit demjenigen, aus welchem der dichter des epos geschöpt hat, identisch oder nahe verwant war.' Without noticing that he was contradicting himself, Bugge completely changed his mind a few pages later and then argued that the sagas that he had been discussing did not go back to *Beowulf*, but were derived from a Danish or an English folktale that had nothing to do with the epic (see Bugge 1887, 66–7). It was, however, only Bugge's original suggestion that caught the attention of other scholars, and, as Liberman points out: 'his authority stood so high that his tentative hypothesis immediately became dogma.' Liberman 1986, 355–6.
4 Liberman 1986, 355.
5 See, e.g., Schück 1909, 20–2.
6 Liberman, in his article, mentions Bernhard ten Brink, Karl Müllenhoff, and Thomas Arnold as early supporters of Bugge. See Liberman 1986, 356.
7 See Boer 1898, 65, and his remarks in the preface to his edition of the saga: 'der interpolator hat die geschichte mit einer Beowulf-überlieferung, welche er in einer englischen fassung kennen gelernt hatte, zusammengeworfen ... Zwei strophen dichtete er hinzu; das wort *heptisax* ... verrät die englische quelle der erzählung.' Boer 1900, xliii.
8 See Olrik 1903, 248.
9 See Heusler 1911–13, 246.
10 See von Sydow 1923, 29–30, and Schneider 1934, 27.
11 Harris 1973, 28. Many prominent scholars have argued for an Irish influence on *Beowulf*, e.g., Heinz Dehmer, Max Deutschbein, Carl W. von Sydow, Gerard Murphy, James Carney, and Martin Puhvel.
12 Puhvel 1979, 137–8.
13 Friedrich Panzer's ideas are discussed in the next chapter.

14 Carl von Sydow wrote in Swedish, and not much has been done to introduce his ideas concerning the relationship between *Beowulf* and *Grettis saga* to English-speaking readers. It should therefore be noted that the latest effort to do so, *Beowulf and the Bear's Son*, by J. Michael Stitt, ascribes the notion of a common Irish source to von Sydow but omits to mention that he later changed his mind. See Stitt 1992, 95. The relevant passage in von Sydow's article, 'Beowulf och Bjarke' reads as follows: 'Beträffande förhållandet mellan Gr [i.e., the Grendel episode] och Grettis-sagas trollepisod, har jag tidigare ansett dem båda härstamma frän en gemensam irisk källa, men det har länge förvånat mig och gjort mig tveksam, att man i Grettis-saga ej, såsom i Ormsþáttr, finner något irisk drag som ej också finns i Gr under det att Gr har många sådana som ej finns i Grettissaga. Då jag nu blivit övertygad om att Beowulf-sången indirekt är källan för Grettissaga, beror detta dels på nyssmämnda faktum, dels på de båda motiven hæftmece-heptisax och runinskriften.' Von Sydow 1923, 45.

15 See von Sydow 1923, 28–9. This argument has recently been contradicted by Stitt: 'Von Sydow argued that oral tradition is incapable of preserving a specific term in a foreign language over a span of several centuries. But while the compound noun *hepti-sax* is unique each root [i.e., *hæft-* and *hepti-*] is a common word. Oral transmission is not impossible.' Stitt 1992, 95.

16 See von Sydow 1923, 30.

17 Von Sydow 1923, 31: 'En muntlig prosatradition kan ej samtidigt innehålla två sinse-mellan stridande uppgifter av detta slag, utan det ena byts fullständigt ut mot det andra, om den har någorlunda god tid att utkristalliseras.' In his book *Beowulf and the Bear's Son*, J. Michael Stitt criticizes this passage in von Sydow's article with the following cryptic remark: 'Von Sydow's argument would be more convincing if the two descriptive passages [i.e., in *Beowulf* and *Grettis saga*] had detailed similarities, but the similarity here barely extends beyond the motif of a water(fall)-dwelling hag.' Stitt 1992, 95–6.

18 Liberman 1986, 383.

19 Malone 1958, 307.

20 Stedman 1913, 23, and Brandl 1901–9, 995–6.

21 Von Sydow 1923, 29–30, and Schneider 1934, 27.

22 See Einarsson 1938, 290. See also Einarsson 1933, 175.

23 Schück 1909, 21: 'Att den på angelsaksiskt språk affattade dikten om Beowulf skulle hafva varit känd på Island omkring år 1300, kan svårligen antagas, och äfven om så varit, torde språket hafva varit obegripligt. Beowulfdikten kan således icke hafva varit den omedelbara källan till de islandska sagorna.' The question as to whether speakers of Old English and Old Norse could have communicated is an issue that is still debated among medievalists. See, e.g., Fjalldal 1993, 601–9.

24 Chambers 1929, 88n. 2.

25 Chambers 1959, 50.
26 Lawrence 1912, 240.
27 Lawrence 1928, 182.
28 Chambers 1959, 53. See also pages 461–72.
29 Turville-Petre 1974–7, 347.
30 Stitt 1992, 96.
31 Chambers 1929, 91.
32 Harris 1973, 30–1.

7: Panzer's 'Bear's Son' Theory

1 In modern folklore studies this story is now known as AT 301, or 'The Three Stolen Princesses.'
2 Panzer 1910, 319: 'Es ist durch diese Ausführungen, glaube ich, der Nachweis erbracht, daß die Erzählung der Saga von Grettirs Abentauer in Sandhaugar in letzter Linie auf dem Bährensohnmärchen beruht. Damit aber rückt ihr Verhältnis zur Beowulfsage in ein ganz neues Licht. Denn damit ist offenbar die Möglichkeit gegeben, daß beide Überlieferungen durchaus selbständig nebeneinander stünden, indem beide unabhängig voneinander aus der gemeinsamen Märchenquelle sich ableiteten.'
3 See Laistner 1889, 15–34.
4 For a more detailed summary and a comparison of the different versions of the story see, e.g., Pizarro 1976–7, 265–9.
5 Panzer 1910, 257.
6 Panzer 1910, 263.
7 Panzer 1910, 264.
8 Panzer 1910, 268–72.
9 Panzer 1910, 274–6.
10 Panzer 1910, 278.
11 Panzer 1910, 280.
12 Panzer 1910, 284–90.
13 Panzer 1910, 305–13.
14 Panzer 1910, 316.
15 Panzer 1910, 317.
16 Panzer 1910, 317.
17 Panzer 1910, 318.
18 Panzer 1910, 318–19.
19 Panzer 1910, 319.
20 Panzer 1910, 322–4.
21 Panzer 1910, 326–7.
22 Panzer 1910, 327–32.

23 Panzer 1910, 319–20.

24 Panzer 1910, 319.

25 Panzer 1910, 402: 'Daneben finden sich jedoch in der Grettis saga ... eine Reihe von Zügen, die auffällig mit dem Beowulf zusammentreffen und, da sie beidenmal auch formale Elemente einschließen, tatsächlich literarische Einwirkung voraussetzen. Diese Beeinflussung aber wäre auf zwei Wegen zu denken: es könnte (mittelbar) die skandinavische Vorlage des Beowulf oder aber eine mit dem Beowulf stofflich und teilweise formal identische englische Dichtung die isländische Überlieferung beeinflußt haben: beides wäre nach den allgemeinen Kultur- und den besonderen literarischen Verhältnissen an sich gleich denkbar.'

26 Chambers 1959, 478.

27 See, e.g., Chambers 1959, 380, where he refers to Panzer's elements of the different versions of the folktale as 'an artificial, theoretical composite.'

28 Chambers 1959, 62–3.

29 Chambers 1959, 380.

30 Chambers 1959, 68n. 1.

31 Chambers 1959, 380–1. For criticism of Panzer's theory in this vein see also Mogk 1919, 115.

32 Von Sydow 1923, 28: 'löftesbrott – knappast förräderi! – vilket ytterligare framhäver Grettes styrka.'

33 Von Sydow 1923, 28: 'Även om Grettissagas trollepisod kunde föras tillbaka till en med Beowulfsången gemensam källa, kan den alltså icke ge något stöd åt teorien att denna källa skulle ha tillkommit under påverkan av björnsonsagan.'

34 Mossé 1933, xl n. 2: 'C'est peut-être aller un peu loin que de voir comme le fait Panzer, (l. c., p. 319) un souvenir de ce motif [i.e., the stolen princesses] dans les rapports de Grettir avec Steinvor, la femme du bondi, assaillie par les monstres.'

35 Lawrence 1928, 171. Like Chambers, however, Lawrence has some concerns about Panzer's working method: 'What is of importance is to show that, in spite of all divergences, a common pattern is really visible. Panzer's method is to construct this common pattern, and to illustrate it, incident by incident, from his collections. This is obviously somewhat dangerous, and may lead to false conclusions. By taking many different colors and lines from many different pictures one can put together almost any kind of picture that one pleases. That this would be an unjust criticism of Panzer's book is evident when the tales themselves are read.' Lawrence 1928, 172–3.

36 Sedgefield 1935, xxviii.

37 Wardale 1965. Wardale explains differences between the Bear's Son Tale and Beowulf and Grettis saga by arguing that 'it is possible that the North-West of Europe had evolved a special form of the tale for itself.' Wardale 1965, 98.

38 See, e.g., Jones 1972, 10–11.

39 See, e.g., Pizarro 1976–7, 263: 'Friedrich Panzer's theory about the folktale of the

Bear's Son as a source of *Beowulf* and of various Icelandic sagas has met much scepticism and neglect in recent years. Klaus von See recently declared Panzer's views to be "heute zu den Akten gelegt." This dismissal of a painstaking study seems to me premature. It has often been caused by an excessively vague idea of the Bear Son's tale and of the episodes that it involves.'

40 See Harris 1973, 30.

41 See, e.g., Jorgensen 1975, 35–6.

42 See Propp 1968, 23–4, and Aarne and Thompson 1961, 7.

43 For further reading see, e.g., Rosenberg 1991, 41–6, where Panzer's methods and conclusions are critically summarized.

44 Von Sydow 1923, 25–6. See also Puhvel 1979, 86–90.

45 Klaeber 1950, xiv.

46 Boer 1912, 167.

47 See von Sydow 1923, 34, and Chambers 1959, 369.

48 See Schneider 1934, 20.

49 See Stitt 1992, 123. Women are abducted in *Egils saga einhenda*, and treacherous abandonment occurs in *Flóres saga konungs*.

50 Stitt 1992, 36.

51 Take, e.g., *Egils saga*.

52 Andersson 1997, 133.

8: The Common Origin Theory

1 See, e.g., Ólason 1993, 147: 'Augljós eru kynni Grettluhöfundar af fornaldarsögum, og væntanlega hefur hann þekkt meira af slíku efni, skráðu eða óskráðu, en varðveist hefur því að bæði í lýsingu á viðureign Grettis og Gláms og í frásögn af viðureign hans við ófreskjur í Bárðardal norður eru mikil líkindi við Bjólfskviðu. Hlýtur höfundur Grettis sögu eða fyrri sagnamenn íslenskir að hafa þekkt sagnir eða kvæði sem hafa verið skyldari Bjólfskviðu en nokkrar varðveittar fornaldarsögur.'

2 Lawrence 1928, 182–3.

3 Chambers 1959, 51–2.

4 See, e.g., Chambers 1929, 88–90.

5 See Chambers 1959, 476–7. *Samsons saga fagra* was originally proposed as an analogue by W.W. Lawrence; see Lawrence 1929, 172–81. Summaries of these stories may be found in Garmonsway 1968, 322–4, 324–7, and 328–331.

6 Lawrence 1912, 241–2. See also Chambers 1959, 51: 'it is certain that these stories – like all the subject matter of the Old English epic – did not originate in England, but were brought across the North Sea from the old home. And that old home was in the closest connection, so far as the passage to and fro of story went, with Scandinavian lands. Nothing could be intrinsically more probable than that a story current in

ancient Angel and carried thence to England, should also have been current in Scandinavia, and thence have been carried to Iceland.'

7 Schück 1909, 21.

8 Earle 1884, 139.

9 Klaeber 1950, xiv.

10 H.M. and N.K. Chadwick 1932, 437.

11 Mogk 1919, 116.

12 Smith 1881, 66.

13 See Chambers 1929, 87.

14 Chambers 1959, 49–50.

15 Brodeur 1959, 101.

16 Chambers 1929, 97–8.

17 See Chambers 1959, 476–7.

18 Chambers 1959, 477.

19 Chambers 1959, 477.

20 Carney 1955, 100, n. 1 from previous page.

21 Klaeber 1950, xx n. 1a.

22 English translations of the relevant parts of this saga are given in Garmonsway 1968.

23 Genzmer borrows this name of the sword from Chambers. See Chambers 1959, 473–5.

24 Genzmer 1950, 20–3.

25 See Genzmer 1950, 24 and 61–2.

26 See Chambers 1959, 472–3.

27 See Genzmer 1950, 30–3.

28 Benson 1970, 27.

29 Benson 1970, 28.

30 Liberman 1986, 380.

31 Halldórsson 1982, 17: 'Við rannsóknir þeirrar þjóðsögu sem hér er til athugunar hefur í heila öld verið beitt sögubundinni aðferð. Samt verður að telja að enn hafi ekki tekist að finna eina ákveðna frumsögu né teikna ættartré hennar.'

32 See, e.g., Deutschbein 1909, 110: 'Aber vergebens hat man sich in der altnordischen Literatur nach unabhängigen Spuren von Grendelkämpfen umgesehen ... An selbständigen Zeugnissen für die Existenz einer Beowulf-Grendelsage im skandinavischen Norden fehlt es bis jetzt.'

33 Schneider 1934, 28: 'Nur spricht er [i.e., Chambers] sich leider mit keinem Wort aus, wo, wann und in welcher Form sie [i.e., the original story] entstanden sein mag.' Concerning the age of the 'old legend' Ritchie Girvan maintains that 'a common source ... cannot lie very far back,' but he offers no evidence to back up this claim. See Girvan 1935, 58.

34 Chambers 1959, 474.

35 Klaeber 1950, xx.
36 Mackie 1938, 456.
37 Chickering 1977, 254.
38 Chickering 1977, 132–3.

9: The Big Bang Theory

1 Chadwick 1959, 190.
2 See, e.g., Niles 1983, 10–11, Dragland 1977, 606–7, and Clark 1973 and 1990, 30–3.
3 See Clark 1973.
4 Clark 1990, 30–1.
5 See also Arent 1969, 189–90: 'the fact that many of the motifs are reused in the
    ghost-slaying in Kár's barrow, in the Halogaland bear episode, and at Thórhalls-
    stadir, suggests an interchangeability and availability of a common stock of closely
    associated motifs.'
6 Harris 1973, 30–1.
7 Jorgensen 1986, 201–2.
8 See Jorgensen 1973, 55.
9 Jorgensen 1975, 40.
10 Jorgensen 1975, 37 and 40: 'the saga's description of the trek to the cave and the bat-
    tle with the female monster are closer to the Old English epic version than is the
    famous *Grettis saga* or any other single Norse saga.'
11 Jorgensen 1986, 208.
12 Here Jorgensen must mean Grendel's mother.
13 Jorgensen 1975, 37–40.
14 See Jónsson and Vilhjálmsson 1944, vol. 3, 330–3.
15 Jorgensen 1978, 56–7: 'The swimming contests discussed above show that
    Beowulf's swimming exploits brought up by Unferth at Hrothgar's court have
    numerous analogues in Scandinavia. Even though the saga versions show some inde-
    pendence they bear testimony to the great popularity which the tale enjoyed in north-
    ern Europe. By comparing those motifs which are found in what seems to be the
    most conservative version, *Hálfdanar saga*, with those which keep recurring in the
    other sagas, one can arrive at a probable Old Norse archetype for the swimming
    match. By cross-checking with the Old English epic, one can more reasonably say
    which motifs were present in the older Scandinavian version and common to the
    source of *Beowulf* ... Both the Old English and Old Norse variants support a Ger-
    manic original which already had an immediately following acquatic battle
    attached.'
16 Jorgensen 1978, 56.
17 Jorgensen 1978, 52.

18 Jorgensen 1979, 89: 'In the case of the English epic, *Beowulf*, it is clear that the king's gift of the useless weapon was of Scandinavian provenance and similar to the saga versions discussed above, but instead of making King Hrōthgār the donor, the *Beowulf* poet protected Hrōthgār's reputation by having the tainted present given by Unferth.'

19 See Jorgensen 1986.

20 Jorgensen 1975, 38.

21 Jorgensen 1986, 203–4.

22 I am, unfortunately, not aware of what Jorgensen considers to be the sixth genetically related analogue in *Grettis saga*.

23 Jorgensen 1986, 205.

24 Harris 1973, 52.

25 Harris 1973: 52.

10: A Saga Author Shops Around

1 See Jónsson 1936, xvii–xxix.

2 For examples of such repetitions, see Halldórsson 1982, 14.

3 Smith 1881, 66.

4 See Boer 1898, 62.

5 Boer had earlier noted similarities in the descriptions of Glámr and Þórólfr bægifótr in his article. See Boer 1898, 55.

6 See Panzer 1910, 334–5.

7 See Dehmer 1927, 28–9.

8 See Dehmer 1928, 205.

9 See Dehmer 1928, 205–6.

10 See von Unwerth 1911, 168.

11 See Stitt 1992, 141. Here the battle takes place inside the ghost's gravemound.

12 See Jónsson 1936, 96.

13 See von Unwerth 1911, 44–54.

14 In the above paragraph the chapter numbers refer to Guðni Jónsson's 1953 edition of *Íslendinga sögur*, vols. 1–12, and in the case of the three *fornaldarsǫgur* that I mention, *Þorsteins þáttr bæjarmagns*, *Hrómundar saga Gripssonar*, and *Áns saga bogsveigis*, to the edition of Guðni Jónsson and Bjarni Vilhjálmsson 1943–4, Fornaldarsögur Norðurlanda, vols. 1–3.

15 Translated into English by William Morris and Eiríkur Magnússon in 1891, and again by Alan Boucher in 1986.

16 Andersson 1967, 196.

17 See Þórólfsson and Jónsson 1943, lxxxix: 'að líkindum samin eftir gömlum vestfirzkum arfsögnum á fyrri hluta 13. aldar. Að vísu verður nú ekkert með vissu sagt um aldur hennar, nema að hún hefir verið eldri en Sturlubók Landnámu, sem er líklega samin á síðustu æviárum Sturlu lögmanns.' See also Þórólfsson 1923, lviii.

18 See Nordal 1968, 157 and 160: 'Samanburður við Sturlubók sýnir svo mikil frávik
þess, sem hlýtur að hafa staðið í eldri sögunni, að menn hafa einna helzt hallast að
því, að ekki væri um nein rittengsl að ræða milli þessara tveggja gerða. Mjög er þó
varasamt að gera ráð fyrir slíku.'

19 See Þórólfsson 1923, lviii, Þórólfsson and Jónsson 1943, xc, and Nordal 1968, 159–
60.

20 Von Unwerth 1911, 170: 'Die Schilderungen der beiden Kämpfe decken sich also
nahezu vollständig. Die einzelnen Abweichungen sind nicht so bedeutsam, dass man
um ihretwillen die beiden Erzählungen als unabhängig voneinander ansehen könnte.
Literarische Abhängigkeit auf der einen oder der andern Seite muss angenommen
werden.'

21 Von Unwerth 1911, 169–70. Translation mine. Von Unwerth obviously followed
those saga editions that were available at the time, but for the sake of convenience, I
have taken the liberty of 'updating' the examples that he presented by using the text
of the *Íslenzk fornrit* series. According to those editions, the original text of these
passages is as follows:

Hávarðarsaga Ísfirðings, *ÍF* 6, 298–9	*Grettis saga*, *ÍF* 7, 119–20
Óláfr lá í stafnrekkju útar við dyrr …	[Grettir] lagðisk niðr í setit gegnt lokrekkju bónda …
Ljós brann í skálanum …	Ljós brann í skálanum …
Óláfr lagðisk niðr í skyrtu ok brókum …	vildi Grettir eigi fara af klæðum …
hann kastaði á sik feldi einum …	hann hafði rǫggvarfeld yfir sér …
gekk Þormóðr inn í skálann ok lét róa tinglit …	sá Grettir, at þrællinn rétti inn hǫfuðit …
Hann sá at rekkja var skipuð, er ekki var vani á …	Glámr sá, at hrúga nǫkkur lá í setinu …
snýr hann þangat ok þrífr í feldinn …	ok rézk nú innar eptir skálanum ok þreif í feldinn stundar fast …
þeir skipta feldinum með sér …	kippðu nú í sundr feldinum í millum sín …
Ok er Þormóðr finnr, at afl er í þeim, er fyrir er …	[Glámr] undraðisk mjǫk, hverr svá fast mundi togask við hann …
Þormóðr hljóp undir hendr honum …	hljóp Grettir undir hendr honum …
tókst þar inn harðasti atgangr …	Áttu þeir þá allharða sókn …
flest gekk ok upp, þat sem fyrir varð …	allt brotnaði, þat sem fyrir varð …
Þormóðr sótti þá í ákafa, ok þar kømr at lykðum, at þeir horfa út …	Glámr fœrðisk í aukana ok kneppði hann at sér, er þeir kómu í anddyrit …

22 Von Unwerth 1911, 171: 'aus dieser [i.e., *Hávarðar saga Ísfirðings*] hat sie der Verfasser der Grett. in seine grosse Gespenstergeschichte aufgenommen.'

23 See, e.g., Andersson 1967, 193.

24 There is no mention of it in Chambers's entries in his bibliography for the year 1911. See Chambers 1959, 576.

25 The term 'author' is a loaded word in saga studies, and I want to emphasize that in using it as I do – i.e., for convenience – I am not trying to imply anything about the actual composition of *Grettis saga*.

26 Translation mine. The original reads: 'Grettir var síðan á Sandhaugum um vetrinn ok dulðisk þó fyrir alþýðu manna.' Jónsson 1936, 218.

27 In his article 'Objects and Oral Tradition in Medieval Iceland,' Richard Perkins describes a number of interesting cases of a similar kind that are to be found within the context of the saga tradition. See Perkins 1989, 239–66.

28 See Boer 1898, 62.

29 Sagas with which the author of *Grettis saga* is known to have been familiar are marked with an asterisk.

30 The chapter numbers given throughout the following discussion refer to Guðni Jónsson's 1953 edition of *Íslendinga sögur*, vols. 1–12; for *fornaldarsǫgur* to the edition of Guðni Jónsson and Bjarni Vilhjálmsson 1943–4, *Fornaldarsǫgur Norðurlanda*, vols. 1–3; for *konungasǫgur* to the edition of Páll Eggert Ólason 1946–8, *Heimskringla Snorra Sturlusonar – Konungasögur*, vols. 1–3; and for *riddarasǫgur* to the edition of Bjarni Vilhjálmsson 1982, *Riddarasögur*, vols. 1–6.

31 Heinz Dehmer, who investigated the Sandhaugar episode as a potential ghost story, concluded that the loss of an arm by the troll-woman had no counterpart in the stories that he examined as possible parallels. See Dehmer 1927, 54.

32 See Boer 1898, 62–3. Boer thought that the first fight in the Sandhaugar episode was merely a variant of the Glámr story, whereas the second fight showed a direct contact – in some form – with *Beowulf*. For a full discussion of his position, see Boer 1923, 107–8.

33 See Jónsson 1936, xlix, and 58n. 4.

34 See Panzer 1910, 317.

35 Chambers 1959, 66 and 380: 'in Zealand, one of the faithless companions is called *Stenhuggeren* (the Stone-hewer), in Schleswig *Steenklöwer*, in Hanover *Steinspieler*, whilst in Iceland he has the same name *Stein*. which he has in the *Grettis Saga*.'

36 Translation mine. The original (see Jónsson and Vilhjálmsson 1944, 239) reads: 'Þá leiddust Faxa höggin, ok stökk hann fyrir borð ok í kaf, svá at í iljar honum var at sjá.' Grettir's dive into the waterfall is described with these words: 'síðan hljóp hann [i.e., Grettir] af bjarginu ok niðr í forsinn. Sá prestr í iljar honum ...' Jónsson 1936, 215.

37 W.P. Lehmann, who first called attention to this chapter of *Njáls saga*, is quite mistaken when he claims that 'Gunnarr cuts [this wooden weapon] with his sword.'

Lehmann 1967, 227. In reality Gunnarr's opponent, Hallgrímr, intends to stab him, but his weapon gets stuck in a piece of wood. Gunnarr hits him on the hand with his sword; the *atgeirr* comes loose, and Gunnarr kills Hallgrímr with his own weapon.

38 See Panzer 1910, 317: 'der Priester *Steinn,* der nachher das Seil hält, ist eben eigentlich der Wandergenosse des Märchenhelden ...'

39 In *Hálfdanar saga Brönufóstra* the hero notices that the trolls are cooking human flesh and horse meat together in a cauldron. He also discovers living prisoners.

40 In *Bósa saga ok Herrauðs* the hero's opponents are not trolls, but a witch and a vulture in her service.

11: Conclusion

1 Quoted from Helgason 1958, 113: 'Svo gengur það til í heiminum, að sumir hjálpa erroribus á gang, og aðrir leitast síðan við að útryðja aptur þeim sömu erroribus. Hafa svo hverirtveggju nokkuð að iðja.'

2 Doyle 1928, 79.

3 See, e.g., Klaeber 1950, xiv; Lawrence 1928, 171; and Chambers 1959, 47.

4 See also Klaeber 1950, xiv n. 1: 'it may be remarked in general that the folk-tale element is not necessarily to be considered the germ pure and simple of the Beowulfian legend. Priority may be claimed for the heroic "historical" features.'

5 Klaeber 1922, cxviii.

6 Lawrence 1928, 259.

7 Lawrence 1928, 165.

8 See, e.g., Niles 1983, 6: 'The basic plot of the poem may be the heroic equivalent of an internationally known wondertale.' Or Liberman 1986, 363: 'Once a motif got into the artistic web of the *Beowulf* poet, it was turned around and around.' See also a Proppian reconstruction of the 'old legend' in Halldórsson 1982, 18–22.

9 Barnes 1970, 432.

10 Rosenberg 1975, 205 and 207.

11 See Ólsen 1937–9, 292–3.

12 See Jónsson 1936, 213n. 1; and Kristjánsson 1978, 292–3.

13 J. Michael Stitt, for instance, has argued along this line. See Stitt 1992, 207–8.

14 Chambers 1959, 484.

15 Translation mine. See Jónsson 1936, 46: 'mart er ǫðru líkt.'

16 Malone 1958, 308.

Bibliography

Icelandic names are listed under the patronymic.

Aarne, Antti, and Stith Thompson. 1961. *The Types of the Folktale: A Classification and Bibliography*. FF Communications No. 184. Helsinki: Suomalainen Tiedeakatemia.

Andersson, Theodore M. 1967. *The Icelandic Family Saga: An Analytic Reading*. Cambridge, Mass.: Harvard University Press.

– 1997. 'Sources and Analogues.' In Robert E. Bjork and John D. Niles (eds.), *A Beowulf Handbook*. Lincoln: University of Nebraska Press. 125–48.

Arent, A. Margaret. 1969. 'The Heroic Pattern: Old Germanic Helmets, *Beowulf* and *Grettis saga*.' In Edgar C. Polomé (ed.), *Old Norse Literature and Mythology: A Symposium*. Austin: University of Texas Press. 130–99.

Barnes, Daniel R. 1970. 'Folktale Morphology and the Study of *Beowulf*.' *Speculum* 45: 416–34.

Benson, Larry D. 1970. 'The Originality of *Beowulf*.' In Morton W. Bloomfield (ed.), *The Interpretation of Narrative: Theory and Practice*. Harvard English Studies, 1. Cambridge, Mass.: Harvard University Press. 1–43.

Boer, R.C. 1898. 'Zur Grettissaga.' *Zeitschrift für deutsche Philologie*, 30: 1–71.

– (Ed.). 1900. *Grettis saga Ásmundarsonar*. Altnordische Saga-Bibliothek, Heft 8. Halle: Max Niemeyer.

– 1912. *Die Altenglische Heldendichtung*. Erster Band: *Beowulf*. Germanische Handbibliothek, 11. Halle: Verlag der Buchhandlung des Waisenhauses.

– 1923. 'Review of Chambers 1921.' *English Studies*, 5: 105–18.

Boucher, Alan. Trans. 1986. *The Saga of Havard the Halt together with the Saga of Hen-Thorir*. Iceland Review Saga Series. Reykjavík: Iceland Review.

Brady, Caroline. 1979. '"Weapons" in *Beowulf*: An Analysis of the Nominal Compounds and an Evaluation of the Poet's Use of Them.' *Anglo-Saxon England*, 8: 79–141.

162 Bibliography

Brandl, Alois. 1901–9. 'Englische Literatur.' In Hermann Paul (ed.), *Grundriss der germanischen Philologie*. 2nd ed. Vol. 2, pt. 1. Strassburg: Karl J. Trübner, 1901–9. 941–1134.

Brodeur, Arthur G. 1959. *The Art of Beowulf*. Berkeley, Los Angeles: University of California Press.

Brooke, Stopford A. 1905. *The History of Early English Literature: Being the History of English Poetry from its Beginnings to the Accession of King Ælfred*. New York: Macmillan.

Bugge, Sophus. 1887. 'Studien über das Beowulfepos.' *Beiträge zur Geschichte der deutschen Sprache und Literatur*, 12: 1–112.

Carens, Marilyn M. 1976. 'Handscóh and Grendel: The Motif of the Hand in Béowulf.' In Donna G. Fricke and Douglas C. Fricke (eds.), *Aeolian Harps: Essays in Literature in Honor of Maurice Browning Cramer*. Ohio, Bowling Green: Bowling Green University Press. 41–55.

Carney, James. 1955. *Studies in Irish History and Literature*. Dublin: Dublin Institute for Advanced Studies.

Chadwick, H. Munro. 1912. *The Heroic Age*. Cambridge: Cambridge University Press.

Chadwick, H. Munro, and N. Kershaw Chadwick. 1932. *The Growth of Literature*. Vol. 2, *The Ancient Literatures of Europe*. Cambridge: Cambridge University Press.

Chadwick, Nora K. 1959. 'The Monsters and Beowulf.' In Peter Clemoes (ed.), *The Anglo-Saxons, Studies in Some Aspects of Their History and Culture Presented to Bruce Dickens*. London: Bowes & Bowes. 171–203.

Chambers, R.W. 1921. *Beowulf: An Introduction to the Study of the Poem with a Discussion of the Stories of Offa and Finn*. Cambridge: Cambridge University Press.

– 1929. 'Beowulf's Fight with Grendel, and its Scandinavian Parallels.' *English Studies* 11: 81–100.

– 1959. *Beowulf: An Introduction to the Study of the Poem*. 3rd ed. with a supplement by C.L. Wrenn. Cambridge: Cambridge University Press.

Chickering, Howell D., Jr. 1977. *Beowulf: A Dual-Language Edition*. New York: Doubleday.

Clark, George. 1973. '*Beowulf* and *Njálssaga*.' In Peter Foote, Hermann Pálsson, and Desmond Slay (eds.), *Proceedings of the First International Saga Conference, University of Edinburgh, 1971*. London: Viking Society for Northern Research. 66–87.

– 1990. *Beowulf*. Boston: Twayne Publishers.

Collins, Rowland R. 1983. 'Blickling Homily XVI and the Dating of *Beowulf*.' In Wolf-Dietrich Bald and Horst Weinstock (eds.), *Medieval Studies Conference Aachen 1983*. Bamberger Beiträge zur Englischen Sprachwissenschaft, Heraugegeben von Prof. Dr. Wolfgang Viereck, Band 15. Frankfurt am Main: Verlag Peter Lang. 61–9.

Danielli, Mary. 1945. 'Initiation Ceremonial from Norse Literature.' *Folk-Lore*, 56: 229–45.

Davidson, H.R. Ellis. 1962. *The Sword in Anglo-Saxon England: Its Archaeology and Literature.* Oxford: Clarendon Press.

Dehmer, Heinz. 1927. *Primitives Erzählungsgut in den Íslendinga-Sögur.* Von deutscher Poeterey. Forschungen und Darstellungen aus dem Gesamtgebiete der deutschen Philologie 2. Leipzig: Verlagsbuchhandlung von J.J. Weber.

– 1928. 'Die Grendelkämpfe Beowulfs im Lichte moderner Märchenforschung.' *Germanisch-Romanische Monatsschrift*, 16: 202–18.

Deutschbein, Max. 1909. 'Die sagenhistorischen und literarischen Grundlagen des Beowulfepos.' *Germanisch-Romanische Monatsschrift*, 1: 103–19.

Doyle, Arthur Conan. 1928. *Sherlock Holmes: The Complete Short Stories.* London: John Murray.

Dragland, S.L. 1977. 'Monster-Man in *Beowulf*.' *Neophilologus*, 61: 606–18.

Earle, John. 1884. *Anglo-Saxon Literature.* London: Society for Promoting Christian Knowledge.

– (Trans.). 1892. *The Deeds of Beowulf: An English Epic of the Eighth Century Done into Modern Prose.* Oxford: Clarendon Press.

Einarsson, Stefán. 1933. *Saga Eiríks Magnússonar.* Reykjavík: Ísafoldarprentsmiðja.

– 1938. 'Review of Guðni Jónsson's edition of *Grettis saga*.' *JEGP*, 37: 289–91.

– 1956. 'Bjólfur and Grendill in Iceland.' *Modern Language Notes*, 71: 79–82.

– 1961. *Íslensk bókmenntasaga 874–1960.* Reykjavík: Snæbjörn Jónsson.

Eliason, Norman E. 1963. 'The Þyle and Scop in *Beowulf*.' *Speculum*, 38: 267–84.

Evison, Vera I. 1963. 'Review of Davidson's *The Sword in Anglo-Saxon England*' *Medium Ævum*, 32: 136–40.

Falk, Hjalmar. 1914. *Altnordische Waffenkunde.* Videnskapselskapets Skrifter. II. Hist.-Filos. Klasse. 1914. No. 6. Kristiania: In Kommission bei Jacob Dybwad.

Fjalldal, Magnús. 1993. 'How Valid Is the Anglo-Scandinavian Language Passage in *Gunnlaugs Saga* as Historical Evidence?' *Neophilologus*, 77: 601–9.

Fontenrose, Joseph. 1959. *Python: A Study of Delphic Myth and Its Origins.* Berkeley: University of California Press.

Fox, Denton, and Hermann Pálsson. (Trans.). 1974. *Grettir's Saga.* Toronto: University of Toronto Press.

Frank, R. 1986. '"Mere" and "Sund": Two Sea-Changes in *Beowulf*' In P.R. Brown, G.R. Crampton and F.C. Robinson (eds.), *Modes of Interpretation in Old English Literature: Essays in Honour of Stanley B. Greenfield.* Toronto: University of Toronto Press. 153–72.

Fry, Donald K. 1969. *Beowulf and the Fight at Finnsburh: A Bibliography.* Charlottesville: The University Press of Virginia.

Garmonsway, G.N, Jacqueline Simpson, and Hilda Ellis Davidson. 1968. *Beowulf and Its Analogues.* London: J.M. Dent & Sons.

Garnett, James.1880. 'Review of *Anglia*, volume 3, 1879–1880.' *American Journal of Philology*, 1 (1880): 491–7.

Genzmer, Felix. 1950. 'Die skandinavischen Quellen des Beowulfs.' *Arkiv för nordisk filologi*, 65: 17–62.

Gering, Hugo. 1880. 'Der *Beówulf* und die islaendische *Grettissaga*.' *Anglia*, 3: 74–87.

Girvan, Ritchie. 1935. *Beowulf and the Seventh Century*. London: Methuen.

Goldsmith, Margaret E. 1970. *The Mode and Meaning of 'Beowulf.'* London: Athlone Press.

Gordon, E.V. 1927. *An Introduction to Old Norse*. Oxford: Clarendon Press.

Halldórsson, Óskar. 1982. 'Tröllasaga Bárðdæla og Grettluhöfundur.' *Skírnir*, 156: 5–36.

Halvorsen, Eyvind Fjeld. 1974. 'Troll.' In Finn Hødnebø (ed.), *Kulturhistorisk Leksikon for nordisk middelalter*, vol. 18. Oslo: Gyldendal Norsk Forlag. 655–7.

Halvorsen, Eyvind Fjeld, and Anna Birgitta Rooth. 1962. 'Jotner.' In Finn Hødnebø (ed.), *Kulturhistorisk Leksikon for nordisk middelalter*. Vol. 7. Oslo: Gyldendal Norsk Forlag. 693–700.

Harris, Richard L. 1973. 'The Deaths of Grettir and Grendel: A New Parallel.' *Scripta Islandica*, 24: 25–53.

Hasenfratz, Robert J. 1993. *Beowulf Scholarship: An Annotated Bibliography, 1979–1990*. New York: Garland Publishing.

Hastrup, Kirsten. 1990. *Island of Anthropology: Studies in Past and Present Iceland*. The Viking Collection: Studies in Northern Civilization. Vol. 5. Odense: Odense University Press.

Hatto, A.T. 1957. 'Snake-words and Boar-helms in *Beowulf*.' *English Studies*, 38: 145–60.

Helgason, Jón. 1958. *Handritaspjall*. Reykjavík: Mál og menning.

Heusler, Andreas. 1911–13. 'Beowulf.' In Johannes Hoops (ed.), *Reallexikon der germanischen Altertumskunde*. 245–8.

– 1924. 'Review of "Beowulf och Bjarke" by C.W. von Sydow.' *Anzeiger für deutsches Altertum und deutsche Litteratur*, 43: 52–4.

Hübener, Gustav. 1927–8. 'Beowulf und nordische Dämonenaustreibung.' *English Studies*, 62: 293–327.

Hughes, Geoffrey. 1977. 'Beowulf, Unferth and Hrunting: An Interpretation.' *English Studies*, 58: 385–95.

Hulbert, James R. 1929. 'A Note on the Psychology of the *Beowulf* Poet.' In Kemp Malone and Martin B. Ruud (eds.), *Studies in English Philology: A Miscellany in Honor of Frederick Klaeber*. Minneapolis: University of Minnesota Press. 189–95.

Hume, Kathryn. 1975. 'The Thematic Design of Grettis Saga.' *JEGP*, 73: 469–86.

– 1980. 'From Saga to Romance: The Use of Monsters in Old Norse Literature.' *Studies in Philology*, 77: 1–25.

Irving, Edward B. 1968. *A Reading of Beowulf*. New Haven: Yale University Press.

Jack, George (ed.). 1994. *Beowulf: A Student Edition*. Oxford: Clarendon Press.

Janzén, Assar. 1947. *Nordisk Kultur VII Personnamn*. Stockholm: Albert Bonniers Forlag.

Jones, Gwyn. 1972. *Kings, Beasts, and Heroes*. London: Oxford University Press.

Jónsson, Finnur.1923. *Den oldnorske og oldislandske Litteraturs Historie*. Vol. 2. 2nd ed. Copenhagen: G.E.C. Gads Forlag.

Jónsson, Guðni (ed.). 1936. *Grettis saga Ásmundarsonar*. *Íslenzk fornrit*, 7. Reykjavík: Hið íslenzka fornritafélag.

– (Ed.). 1953. *Íslendinga sögur*. 12 vols. Reykjavík: Íslendingasagnaútgáfan.

– (Ed.). 1954. *Edda Snorra Sturlusonar, Nafnaþulur og Skáldskapartal*. Reykjavík: Íslendingasagnaútgáfan.

Jónsson, Guðni, and Bjarni Vilhjálmsson (eds). 1943–4. *Fornaldarsögur Norðurlanda*. 3 vols. Reykjavík: Bókaútgáfan Forni.

Jorgensen, Peter A. 1973. 'Grendel, Grettir, and Two Skaldic Stanzas.' *Scripta Islandica*, 24: 54–61.

– 1975. 'The Two-Troll Variant of the Bear's Son Folktale in *Hálfdanar saga Brönufóstra* and *Gríms saga loðinkinna*.' *Arv*, 31: 35–43.

– 1978. 'Beowulf's Swimming Contest with Breca: Old Norse Parallels.' *Folklore*, 89: 52–9.

– 1979. 'The Gift of the Useless Weapon in *Beowulf* and the Icelandic Sagas.' *Arkiv för nordisk filologi*, 94: 82–90.

– 1986. 'Additional Icelandic Analogues to *Beowulf*.' In Rudolf Simek et al. (eds.), *Sagnaskemmtun: Studies in Honour of Hermann Pálsson on His 65th birthday, 26th May, 1986*. Vienna: Hermann Böhlaus. 201–8.

Kennedy, Charles W. (trans.). 1940. *Beowulf: The Oldest English Epic*. New York: Oxford University Press.

Kiessling, Nicolas K. 1968. 'Grendel: A New Aspect.' *Modern Philology*, 65: 191–201.

Klaeber, Fr. (ed.). 1922. *Beowulf and the Fight at Finnsburg*. 1st ed. Boston: D.C. Heath.

– 1950. *Beowulf and the Fight at Finnsburg*. 3rd ed. Boston: D.C. Heath.

Kögel, R. 1892. 'Beowulf.' *Zeitschrift für deutsches Altertum*, 37: 268–76.

Kristjánsson, Jónas. 1978. 'Bókmenntasaga.' In Sigurður Líndal (ed.), *Saga Íslands*. Vol. 3. Reykjavík: Hið íslenzka bókmenntafélag, Sögufélagið. 261–350.

Kuhn, Sherman M. 1984. '*Beowulf* and the Life of Beowulf: A Study in Epic Structure.' In his *Studies in the Language and Poetics of Anglo-Saxon*. Ann Arbor: Karoma Publishers. 243–64.

Laborde, E.D. 1923. 'Grendel's Glove and His Immunity from Weapons.' *The Modern Language Review*, 18 : 202–4.

Laistner, Ludwig. 1889. *Die Rätsel der Sphinx. Grundzüge einer Mythengeschichte*. Vol. 2. Berlin: W. Hertz.

Lawrence, William Witherle. 1912. 'The Haunted Mere in *Beowulf*.' *PMLA*, 27: 208–45.

– 1928. *Beowulf and Epic Tradition*. Cambridge, Mass.: Harvard University Press.

– 1929. '*Beowulf* and the *Saga of Samson the Fair*.' In Kemp Malone and Martin B.

Ruud (eds.), *Studies in English Philology: A Miscellany in Honor of Frederick Klaeber.* Minneapolis: University of Minnesota Press. 172–81.

- 1939. 'Grendel's Lair.' *JEGP,* 38: 477–80.

Laxness, Halldór Kiljan. 1949. 'Lítil samantekt um útilegumenn.' *Tímarit Máls og menningar,* 2: 86–130.

Leach, Henry, G. 1921. *Angevin Britain and Scandinavia.* Harvard Studies in Comparative Literature. Vol. 6. Cambridge, Mass.: Harvard University Press.

Lehmann, Edv. 1901. 'Fandens oldemor.' *Dania,* 8: 179–94.

Lehmann, W.P. 1967. 'Atertanum Fah.' In Walter W. Arndt et al. (eds.), *Studies in Historical Linguistics in Honor of George Sherman Lane.* University of North Carolina Studies in Germanic Languages and Literatures, no. 58. Chapel Hill: University of North Carolina Press. 221–31.

Liberman, Anatoly. 1986. 'Beowulf-Grettir.' In Bela Brogyanyi and Thomas Krömmelbein (eds.), *Germanic Dialects: Linguistic and Philological Investigations.* Amsterdam and Philadelphia: John Benjamins Publishing Company. 353–401.

Lie, Hallvard. 1939. 'Noen metodologiske overveielser i anl. av et bind av *Íslenzk Fornrit.' Maal og Minne.* 97–138.

Liestöl, Knut. 1930. 'Beowulf and Epic Tradition.' *The American-Scandinavian Review,* 6: 370–3.

Mackie, W.S. 1938. 'The Demons' Home in *Beowulf.' JEGP,* 37: 455–61.

Magnússon, Ásgeir Blöndal. 1989. *Íslensk orðsifjabók.* Reykjavík: Orðabók Háskólans.

Malone, Kemp. 1932. 'Review of *Beowulf: An Introduction to the Study of the Poem with a Discussion of the Stories of Offa and Finn* by R.W. Chambers.' *English Studies,* 14: 190–3.

- 1944. 'On the Etymology of *runt' Language,* 20: 87–8.

- 1946. 'Hrungnir.' *Arkiv för nordisk filologi,* 284–5. Reprinted in Stefán Einarsson and Norman E. Eliason (eds.), *Studies in Heroic Legend and in Current Speech,* Copenhagen: Rosenkilde and Bagger, 1959. 202–3.

- 1958. 'Grendel and His Abode.' In A.G. Hatcher and K.L. Selig (eds.), *Studia Philologica et Litteraria in Honorem L. Spitzer.* Bern: Francke Verlag. 297–308.

Malone, Kemp, and Martin B. Ruud. 1929. *Studies in English Philology: A Miscellany in Honor of Frederick Klaeber.* Minneapolis: University of Minnesota Press.

Mastrelli, Carlo Alberto. 1985–6. 'Motivi indraici nel *Beowulf* e nella *Grettis Saga* (ags. *hæftmēce* e a.isl. *heptisax*).' *AIUON, filologia germanica,* 28–9: 405–20.

McConchie, R.W. 1982. 'Grettir Ásmundarson's Fight with Kárr the Old: A Neglected *Beowulf* Analogue.' *English Studies,* 63: 481–6.

Mitchell, Stephen A. 1991. *Heroic Sagas and Ballads.* Ithica: Cornell University Press.

Mogk, Eugen. 1919. 'Altgermanische Spukgeschichten. Zugleich ein Beitrag zur Erklärung der Grendelepisode in *Beowulf.' Neue Jahrbücher für das klassische Altertum, Geschichte und deutsche Literatur und für Pädagogik,* 22: 103–17.

Morris, William, and Eiríkur Magnússon (trans.). 1891. *The Story of Howard the Halt. The Story of the Banded Men. The Story of Hen Thorir. Done into English out of the Icelandic. The Saga Library.* Vol. 1. London: B. Quaritch.

Mossé, Fernand (ed.). 1933. *La Saga de Grettir.* Paris: Éditions Montaigne, Aubier.

Motz, Lotte. 1982. 'Giants in Folklore and Mythology: A New Approach.' *Folklore*, 93: 70–84.

Murphy, Gerard (ed.). 1953. *Duanaire Finn. The Book of the Lays of Fionn.* Part 3. Irish Texts Society, 43. Dublin: The Educational Company of Ireland.

Niles, John D. 1983. *Beowulf: The Poem and Its Tradition.* Cambridge, Mass. Harvard University Press.

Nordal, Sigurður. 1968. *Um íslenzkar fornsögur.* Trans. Árni Björnsson. Reykjavík: Mál og menning.

Ólason, Páll Eggert (ed.). 1946–8. *Heimskringla Snorra Sturlusonar: Konungasögur.* Vols. 1–3. Reykjavík: Menntamálaráð og Þjóðvinafélag.

Ólason, Vésteinn, et al. (eds.). 1993. *Íslensk bókmenntasaga, 2.* Reykjavík: Mál og menning.

Olrik, Axel. 1903. *Danmarks Heldedigtning: En Oldtidsstudie.* Copenhagen: Universitetsboghandler G.E.C. Gad.

Ólsen, Björn M. 1937–9. *Um Íslendingasögur: kaflar úr háskólafyrirlestrum.* In *Safn til sögu Íslands og íslenzkra bókmennta að fornu og nýju.* Vol. 6. Reykjavík: Hið íslenzka bókmenntafélag.

Orchard, Andy. 1995. *Pride and Prodigies: Studies in the Monsters of the Beowulf Manuscript.* Cambridge: D.S. Brewer.

Pálsson, Hermann. 1980. 'Glámsýni í Grettlu.' In Jónas Kristjánsson (ed.). *Gripla*, 4. Reykjavík: Stofnun Árna Magnússonar. 95–101.

Panzer, Friedrich. 1910. *Studien zur germanischen Sagengeschichte.* Vol. 1. *Beowulf.* Munich: C.H. Beck'sche Verlagsbuchhandlung.

Parks, Ward. 1993. 'Prey Tell: How Heroes Perceive Monsters in *Beowulf.*' *JEGP*, 92: 1–16.

Perkins, Richard. 1989. 'Objects and Oral Tradition in Medieval Iceland.' In Rory McTurk and Andrew Wawn (eds.), *Úr Dölum til Dala: Guðbrandur Vigfússon Centenary Essays.* Leeds Texts and Monographs. New Series 11. Leeds: Leeds Studies in English. 239–66.

Pizarro, Joaquín M. 1976–7. 'Transformations of the Bear's Son Tale in the Sagas of the Hrafnistumenn.' *Arv*, 32–3: 263–81.

Powell, F. York. 1900. 'Review of Boer's Edition of *Grettis saga.*' *Folklore*, 11: 406–14.

– 1901. 'Béowulf and Watanabe-No-Tsuna.' In *An English Miscellany Presented to Dr. Furnivall in Honour of his Seventy-Fifth Birthday.* Oxford: Clarendon Press. 395–6.

Propp, Vladimir. 1968. *Morphology of the Folktale.* Trans. Laurence Scott. Ed. Louis A. Wagner. Austin: University of Texas Press.

Puhvel, Martin. 1979. *Beowulf and Celtic Tradition*. Waterloo, Ontario: Wilfrid Laurier University Press.

Ranisch, W. 1902. 'Review of Boer's edition of *Grettis saga*.' *Anzeiger für deutsches Altertum und deutsche Litteratur*, 28: 216–35.

Robinson, Fred C. 1974. 'Elements of the Marvellous in the Characterization of Beowulf.' In Robert B. Burlin and Edward B. Irving (eds.), *Old English Studies in Honour of John C. Pope*. Toronto: University of Toronto Press. 119–37.

– 1994. 'Did Grendel's Mother Sit on Beowulf?' In Malcolm Godden, Douglas Gray, and Terry Hoad (eds.) *From Anglo-Saxon to Early Middle English: Studies Presented to E.G. Stanley*. Oxford: Clarendon Press. 1–7.

Rooth, Erik G.T. 1917. 'Der name Grendel in der Beowulfsage.' *Beiblatt zur Anglia*, 28: 335–40.

Rosenberg, Bruce A. 1975. 'Folktale Morphology and the Structure of *Beowulf*: A Counterproposal.' *Journal of the Folklore Institute* [Indiana University], 11: 199–209.

– 1991. *Folklore and Literature: Rival Siblings*. Knoxville: University of Tennessee Press.

Rosier, James L. 1962. 'Design for Treachery: The Unferth Intrigue.' *PMLA*, 77: 1–8.

– 1963. 'The Uses of Association: Hands and Feasts in *Beowulf*.' *PMLA*, 78: 8–14.

Russell, Jeffrey B. 1984. *Lucifer: The Devil in the Middle Ages*. Ithaca: Cornell University Press.

Sarrazin, Gregor. 1910. 'Neue Beowulf-Studien, 7. *Fyrgenstrēam*.' *Englische Studien*, 42: 1–37.

Schlauch, Margaret. 1934. *Romance in Iceland*. Princeton: Princton University Press.

– 1956. *English Medieval Literature and Its Social Foundation*. Warsaw: Państwowe Wydawnictwo Naukowe.

Schneider, Hermann. 1934. *Germanische Heldensage*. Vol. 2, pt. 2. In *Grundriss der germanischen Philologie*, 10/3. Ed. begun by Hermann Paul. Berlin and Leipzig: Walter de Gruyter.

– 1952. *Edda, Skalden, Saga: Festschrift zum 70. Geburtstag von Felix Genzmer*. Heidelberg: Carl Winter Universitätsverlag.

Schück, Henrik. 1909. *Studier i Beowulfsagan*. In *Uppsala Universitets Årsskrift*, 1909, Program M.M. Uppsala: Almqvist & Wiksells Boktryckeri.

Sedgefield, Walter J. (ed.). 1935. *Beowulf*. 3rd edition. Manchester: Manchester University Press.

Shetelig, Haakon, and Hjalmar Falk. 1937. *Scandinavian Archaeology*. Trans. E.V. Gordon. Oxford: Clarendon Press.

Shippey, T.A. 1978. *Beowulf*. London: Edward Arnold.

Short, Douglas D. 1980. *Beowulf Scholarship: An Annotated Bibliography*. New York: Garland Publishing.

Sigfússon, Björn. 1960. 'Grettis saga Ásmundarsonar.' In Finn Hødnebø (ed.), *Kulturhistorisk Leksikon for nordisk middelalter*, vol. 5. Oslo: Gyldendal Norsk Forlag. 461–2.

Smith, C.S. 1881. 'Beówulf Gretti.' *The New Englander*, 4: 49–67.

Stedman, Douglas. 1913. 'Some Points of Resemblance Between *Beowulf* and the *Grettla* (or *Grettis Saga*).' *Saga Book of the Viking Society*, 8 (Part 1): 6–28.

Stitt, J. Michael. 1992. *Beowulf and the Bear's Son: Epic, Saga, and Fairytale in Northern Germanic Tradition*. New York: Garland Publishing.

Sveinsson, Einar Ól. (ed.). 1934. *Laxdœla saga. Íslenzk fornrit*, 5. Reykjavík: Hið íslenzka fornritafélag.

Sveinsson, Einar Ól., and Matthías Þórðarson (eds.). 1935. *Eyrbyggja saga, Grænlendingasögur. Íslenzk fornrit*, 4. Reykjavík: Hið íslenzka fornritafélag.

Sydow, Carl W. von. 1923. 'Beowulf och Bjarke.' *Studier i nordisk filologi* 14:3. In *Skrifter utgivna av svenska litteratursällskapet i Finland*, 170. 1–46.

Taylor, A.R. 1952. 'Two Notes on *Beowulf*.' *Leeds Studies in English and Kindred Languages*, 7 and 8: 5–17.

Turville-Petre, Joan. 1974–7. '*Beowulf* and *Grettis saga*: An Excursion.' *Saga Book of the Viking Society*, 19: 347–57.

Unwerth, Wolf von. 1911. *Untersuchungen über Totenkult und Ódinnverehrung bei Nordgermanen und Lappen mit Excursen zur altnordischen Literaturgeschichte*. Germanistische Abhandlungen, 37. Heft. Breslau: Verlag von M. & H. Marcus.

Vigfusson, Gudbrand (ed.). 1878. *Sturlunga Saga Including the Islendinga Saga of Lawman Sturla Thordsson and Other Works*. Vol. 1. Oxford: Clarendon Press.

Vigfusson, Gudbrand, and F. York Powell (eds.). 1879. *An Icelandic Prose Reader with Notes, Grammar and Glossary*. Oxford: Clarendon Press.

– 1883. *Corpus Poeticum Boreale: The Poetry of the Old Northern Tongue*. Vol. 2. Oxford: Clarendon Press.

Vilhjálmsson, Bjarni (ed.). 1982. *Riddarasögur*. 6 vols. Reykjavík: Íslendingasagnaútgáfan, Haukadalsútgáfan.

Wachsler, Arthur, A. 1985. 'Grettir's Fight with a Bear: Another Neglected Analogue of *Beowulf* in the *Grettis Sage Asmundarsonar*.' *English Studies*, 66: 381–90.

Wardale, E.E. 1965. *Chapters on Old English Literature*. New York: Russell & Russell.

Whitbread, L. 1949. 'The Hand of Æschere: A Note on *Beowulf* 1343.' *Review of English Studies*, 25: 339–42.

Whitman, F.H. 1977. 'Corrosive Blood in *Beowulf*.' *Neophilologus*, 61: 276.

– 1977. 'The Kingly Nature of Beowulf.' *Neophilologus*, 61: 277–86.

Wilson, David. 1971. *The Anglo-Saxons*. Harmondsworth, Middlesex: Penguin.

Wrenn, C.L. (ed.). 1953. *Beowulf: With the Finnesburg Fragment*. London: George G. Harrap.

Wright, Charles D. 1993. *The Irish Tradition in Old English Literature*. Cambridge Studies in Anglo-Saxon England, no. 6. Cambridge: Cambridge University Press.

Þórólfsson, Björn K. (ed.) 1923. *Hávarðar saga Ísfirðings*. Copenhagen: J. Jørgensen.

Þórólfsson, Björn K., and Guðni Jónsson (eds.) 1943. *Vestfirðinga sǫgur. Íslenzk fornrit*, 6. Reykjavík: Hið íslenzka fornritafélag.

Index

Icelandic names (except Grettir's) are listed under the patronymic.

analogous episodes in *Beowulf. See*
Beowulf's fight with Grendel and
Beowulf's fight with Grendel's mother
analogous episodes in *Grettis saga. See*
Grettir's death in Drangey (Grettir as a
'monster'); Grettir's fight with Glámr;
Grettir's fight with Kárr the Old;
Grettir's fight with the brown bear;
Sandhaugar episode
'analogues': as evidence of a genetic rela-
tionship, vii, 135n. 3; use of the word,
135–6n. 1
Andersson, Theodore M.: criticism of
Panzer, 95; on problems in *Hávarðar
saga Ísfirðings*, 123
Arent, A. Margaret: criticism of Vigfús-
son, 65; on Grettir's fight with the
brown bear, 12–13; on the narrow
footpath, 67
AT 301. *See* Panzer's 'Bear's Son'
Thesis

Barnes, Daniel R.: on the genre of
Beowulf, 132. *See also* Rosenberg,
Bruce A.

'Bear's Son' Tale. *See* Panzer's 'Bear's
Son' Thesis
Benson, Larry D.: on the first fight of the
'old legend,' 40; reconstruction of the
'old legend,' 103–4; on the relationship between *Beowulf* and *Grettis
saga*, vii. *See also* Theory of Common
Origin
Beowulf: compared to Grettir, 17–21. *See
also* Beowulf's fight with Grendel and
Beowulf's fight with Grendel's mother
Beowulf and Its Analogues: on the relationship between the Sandhaugar
trolls, 29
Beowulf's fight with Grendel: compared
to Grettir's fight with Glámr, 42–4;
description of, 37–9
Beowulf's fight with Grendel's mother:
46–8. *See also* landscape of the mere
in *Beowulf*
Big Bang Theory: criticism of, 113–16;
definition of, 108; examples of critical
methods, 109–15; on Beowulf–Grettir
studies, 110–11; on the relationship
between *Beowulf* and *Grettis saga*, 110

Boer, R.C.: criticism of Panzer, 94; defence of the English Hypothesis, 82; on the composition of the Sandhaugar episode, 120–1, 127; on Grettir's fight with Kárr the Old and the Sandhaugar episode, 128

borrowings from Icelandic texts other than *Hávarðar saga Ísfirðings* in *Grettis saga*: in the saga as a whole, 119; in the Sandhaugar episode, ix, 135n. 6

Brady, Caroline: on *bill* and *mece* in *Beowulf*, 59

Brodeur, Arthur: on sex roles in the 'old legend,' 99

Bugge, Sophus: on the origin of the 'old legend,' 81, 150 n. 3. *See also* English Hypothesis

Carney, James: criticism of the Theory of Common Origin, 101; on Glámr and Cain, 25; on Grettir and Cain, 26–7

Chadwick, H. Munro and N. Kershaw: on the development of the 'old legend,' 98

Chadwick, Nora K.: contribution to the Big Bang Theory, 108–10; critical reaction to 'The Monsters and Beowulf,' 109–10; on the etymology of Grettir's name, 33; interpretation of the Sandhaugar episode, 49, 109; proposes Grettir as a monster, 33; on the term *draugr*, 109. *See also* Big Bang Theory

Chambers, R. W.: criticism of the English Hypothesis, 85–7; criticism of Panzer, 91–2; defence of the Theory of Common Origin, 96–7; on desertion in *Beowulf* and *Grettis saga*, 52–3; on the development of the 'old legend,' 97, 154n. 6; embraces the 'waterfall theory,' 69; on the genre of the 'old legend,' 131; on *hæftmece* being misplaced, 61; on inconsistencies in *Beowulf*, 47; reconstruction of the 'old legend,' 100–1; on sex roles in the 'old legend,' 99. *See also* Theory of Common Origin

Clark, George: on Nora Chadwick's theory, 109–10. *See also* Big Bang Theory

Davidson, H.R. Ellis: on the *heptisax* and the sword owned by Grendel's mother, 62–3; on Hrunting as a weapon, 60; on the misplacement of swords at Sandhaugar, 54–5

Dehmer, Heinz: on the cloak in Grettir's fight with Glámr, 43; on the genre of the Sandhaugar episode, 121; on Glámr, 121

Earle, John: on the development of the 'old legend,' 98

Eliason, Norman E.: on the name of Hrunting, 60

English Hypothesis, the: Beowulf story in Iceland, 84–5; Boer's version of, 82; criticism of, 85–7; criticism of its Irish version, 84; definition of, 81; Irish version of, 82–3; other versions of, 82

Evison, Vera I.: criticism of Davidson, 63

fyrgenstream. *See* landscape of the mere in *Beowulf*

Garnett, James: criticism of Vigfússon, 6

Genzmer, Felix: reconstruction of the 'old legend,' 102–3. *See also* Theory of Common Origin

giant at Sandhaugar: description of, 29;

description of his cave, 75–6; fire and light in his cave, 77–8; location of his cave, 74. *See also* Sandhaugar episode

giant sword owned by Grendel's mother: hilt of, 62–3; type of sword, 61–2. *See also* Beowulf's fight with Grendel's mother

Glámr: compared to Grendel, 26–7; as an eclectically fashioned ghost, 121; frightening eyes of, 26, 44; nature and powers of, 25–6; origin and meaning of his name, 24–5; relationship to the curse of Cain, 25–6; special position of, 8; as a traditional ghost, 121

Goldsmith, Margaret E.: on the eyes of Grendel and Glámr, 44

Grendel: etymology of his name, 23–4, 34; frightening eyes of, 44, 143n. 28; physical attributes and behaviour of, 24; special position of, 8

Grendel and his mother: 'aristocratic' nature of, 22–3; description of their cave, 76; lights in their cave, 76–7; location of their cave, 74–5; origin of, 22; strangeness of, 23

Grettir Ásmundarson: compared to Beowulf, 17–21; etymology of his name, 33–4; Glámr's curse, 26–7. *See also* Grettir's death in Drangey (Grettir as a 'monster'); Grettir's fight with the brown bear; Grettir's fight with Glámr; Grettir's fight with Kárr the Old; Sandhaugar episode

Grettir's death in Drangey (Grettir as a 'monster'): accepted as a *Beowulf* analogue, 16; criticism of as an analogue, 15–16, 34–6, 45–6; proposed as an analogue, 14–15; summary of, 13–14

Grettir's fight with the brown bear: accepted as a *Beowulf* analogue, 13;

brown bear as a 'monster,' 32; criticism of as an analogue, 12, 31–3, 45–6; proposed as an analogue, 11–13; summary of, 11

Grettir's fight with Glámr: accepted as a *Beowulf* analogue, 9; compared to Beowulf's fight with Grendel, 42–4; compared to the ghost fight in *Hávarðar saga Ísfirðings*, 123–4, 158n. 21; criticism of as an analogue, 9, 41–4; eclectic composition of, 124–5; literary traits in, 122; primary status of, 99, 120; proposed as a *Beowulf* analogue, 8; summary of, 7, 41; thought to be largely borrowed, 124

Grettir's fight with Kárr the Old: accepted as a *Beowulf* analogue, 13; criticism of as an analogue, 10, 30, 48–9; proposed as an analogue, 10–11; resemblance to the Sandhaugar episode, 128; summary of, 10; traditional pattern in, 49

hæftmece (Hrunting): as a weapon, 59; association with *heptisax*, 64–5; incomplete correspondence to *heptisax*, 65; linguistic relationship to *heptisax*, 64; put in a wrong context, 61, 63; special importance of, 4, 54; translation of, 107. *See also* *heptisax*

Halldórsson, Óskar: on reconstructing the 'old legend,' 104–5; on the origin of the Sandhaugar episode, 133

Harris, Richard L.: on the Irish-English Hypothesis, 82–3; methodology of as a critic, 115–16; proposes Grettir's death in Drangey as an analogue, 14–15; on the relationship between *Beowulf* and *Grettis saga*, 110. *See also* Big Bang Theory

Hávarðar saga Ísfirðings: its composition, 123; its ghost story compared to
Grettir's fight with Glámr, 123–4,
158n. 21
heptisax: association with *hæftmece*, 64–
5; commented on in *Grettis saga*, 56;
as a familiar weapon, 58; as an impossible weapon, 58; incomplete correspondence to *hæftmece*, 65; linguistic
relationship to *hæftmece*, 64; misunderstood by the saga author, 57–8; as
the name of a sword, 102–3; origin and
meaning of, 55; purpose obscured in
the saga, 63; special importance of, 4,
54. See also *hæftmece*
Hrunting (*hæftmece*): etymology of, 59–
60; references to in *Beowulf*, 60;
viewed differently as a weapon, 60; in
wrong hands, 59

Japanese analogue to *Beowulf*: viii
Jónsson, Guðni: on the genre of the
Sandhaugar episode, 133
Jorgensen, Peter A.: on Beowulf–Grettir
studies, 110–11; emendation of stanza,
61, 51; on *heptisax*, 57–8; methodology
of as a critic, 51, 114; on the narrow
footpath, 67; on the 'old legend' in Icelandic sagas, 111–15; on parallels with
Beowulf, 112–13; on the Sandhaugar
trolls, 29. See also Big Bang Theory

Kársnautr (Grettir's short-sword): compared to *heptisax*, 55; given to Grettir,
10; its hilt, 63–4
Klaeber, Fr.: on Beowulf's fight with
Grendel's mother, 47; criticism of Panzer, 94; on the development of the 'old
legend,' 98; embraces the 'waterfall
theory,' 69; on the genre of the 'old

legend,' 131–2; on Grettir's fight with
Kárr the Old, 10; on the origin of the
'old legend,' 105–6; on the reconstruc-
tion of the 'old legend,' 102. *See also*
Theory of Common Origin
Kristjánsson, Jónas: on the genre of the
Sandhaugar episode, 133

landscape of the mere in *Beowulf*: dismissal of sea terms in, 72; dismissal of
sea terms criticized, 73; *fyrgenstream*,
68–9: inconsistent features in, 68, 72;
inconsistent features rejected, 73;
Lawrence's 'waterfall theory,' 68–9;
the narrow footpath, 67–8; 'waterfall
theory' rejected, 69–71, 84
landscape described in *Grettis saga*:
Lawrence's view of, 71, 147–8nn. 15,
17; narrow footpath in, 67–8
Lawrence, W.W.: criticism of the English
Hypothesis, 86; on the development of
the 'old legend,' 97–8; embraces Panzer's thesis, 93; on the genre of the
'old legend,' 131–2; on the landscape
of the mere, 72; on landscape in the
Sandhaugar episode, 71, 147–8nn. 15,
17; on the origin of the Grendels, 22;
on the realism of the Sandhaugar episode, 96; on sea terms in the mere
scene, 72; 'waterfall theory' of,
68–9
Lehmann, W.P.: on Hrunting as a
weapon, 60
Liberman, Anatoly: criticism of Harris,
15–16; criticism of the Irish-English
Hypothesis, 84; criticism of Jorgensen,
51; on the etymologies of Grettir and
Grendel, 34; reconstruction of the 'old
legend,' 104. *See also* Theory of Common Origin

McConchie, R.W.: proposes Grettir's fight with Kárr the Old as an analogue, 11, 30. *See also* Taylor, A.R., proposes Grettir's fight with Kárr the Old as an analogue

Mackie, W.S.: criticism of Lawrence, 69–70, 73; criticism of the Theory of Common Origin, 106

Magnússon, Árni: views on scholarship, 130

Malone, Kemp: criticism of Lawrence, 70–1, 73; on the etymology of Hrunting, 59–60

Mastrelli, Carlo Alberto: on the origin of *hæft-* and *hepti-*, 65

Mogk, Eugen: on the development of the 'old legend,' 98

Ólason, Vésteinn: on the origin of the Sandhaugar episode, 133

'old legend.' *See* Vigfússon, Guðbrandur; Theory of Common Origin

Ólsen, Björn M.: on the genre of the Sandhaugar episode, 133

Panzer's 'Bear's Son' Thesis: accepted by critics, 93; criticism of, 91–5; definition of, 88, 152n. 2; folktale compared to *Beowulf*, 89–90; folktale compared to *Grettis saga*, 90–1; on Glámr as a character, 121; on the genre of the 'old legend,' 131; summary of the Bear's Son Tale, 88–9

Puhvel, Martin: criticism of Chambers, 61; on the Irish-English Hypothesis, 83

Rosenberg, Bruce A.: criticism of Barnes, 132–3

Sandhaugar episode: characteristics of, 126; criticism of as an analogue, 28–30, 126–9; differs from *Beowulf*, 6–7, 136 n. 13; eclectic composition of, ix, 120–1, 126–9; genre of, 121, 131; Grettir's fight with the giant, 50–3; Grettir's fight with the troll-woman, 39–40; inconsistencies in, 71–2; origin of, 126–7; its primary status, 121; proposed as an analogue, 4; realism of, 96; resembles *Beowulf*, 5–6; resembles Grettir's fight with Kárr the Old, 128; summary of, 3–4; traditional saga motifs in, 127–9; as a version of the 'old legend,' 28, 126. *See also* landscape described in *Grettis saga*: Lawrence's view of the Sandhaugar episode

Schneider, Hermann: criticism of the Theory of Common Origin, 105

Schück, Henrik: criticism of the English Hypothesis, 85, 151n. 23; on the development of the 'old legend,' 98; on *hæftmece* and *heptisax*, 65

Sedgefield, Walter J.: on Panzer's 'Bear's Son' Thesis, 93

Shetelig, Haakon and Hjalmar Falk: on *heptisax* as a familiar weapon, 58; on the etymology of Hrunting, 60

Smith, C.S.: on *fyrgenstream*, 68; on the relationship between *Beowulf* and *Grettis saga*, vii; on Grettir's fight with Glámr, 99, 120

Stitt, J. Michael: on the Bear's Son folktale in Scandinavia, 94–5; on blood on the water as a literary motif, 52; criticism of the English Hypothesis, 86

sword on the wall in the giant's cave at Sandhaugar: its misplacement, 54–5

Sydow, Carl W. von: criticism of Lawrence, 84; criticism of Panzer,

93–4, 153nn. 32–3; criticism of the
Theory of Common Origin, 84; on
landscape and oral tradition, 67; views
on the English Hypothesis, 83–4,
151n. 14

Taylor, A.R.: contribution to the Big
Bang Theory, 108; on *heptisax* and
hæftmece as misplaced weapons, 63;
on the hilt of *Kársnautr*, 63; proposes
Grettir's fight with the brown bear as
an analogue, 11–12; proposes Grettir's fight with Kárr the Old as an analogue, 10. *See also* Big Bang Theory
theories attempting to link *Beowulf* and
Grettis saga. *See* Big Bang Theory;
English Hypothesis; Panzer's 'Bear's
Son' Thesis; Theory of Common Origin
Theory of Common Origin: criticism of,
84, 104–7; definition of, 96; development of the 'old legend,' 97–8; origin
of the 'old legend,' 81, 105–6; reconstructions of the 'old legend,' 100–4;
sex roles in the 'old legend,' 99; its
usefulness as a criterion, 106
troll woman at Sandhaugar: description
of, 29
Turville-Petre, Joan: criticism of the

English Hypothesis, 86; on *heptisax* as
an impossible weapon, 58;

Unwerth, Wolf von: on the composition
of the Sandhaugar episode, ix, 135n. 6;
on Grettir's fight with Glámr, 121–4;
on *Hávarðar saga Ísfirðings*, 123–4,
158n. 21

Vigfússon, Guðbrandur: on *Beowulf* and
Grettis saga, 4; on the importance of
hæftmece-heptisax, 4, 54; on the origin
of the 'old legend,' 81
Vigfússon, Guðbrandur, and F. York Powell: on Glámr's curse and Beowulf, 8

Wachsler, Arthur, A.: proposes Grettir's
fight with the brown bear as an analogue: 30–1; view of the brown bear,
32. *See also* Taylor, A.R.: proposes
Grettir's fight with the brown bear as
an analogue
weapons in *Beowulf*. *See* giant sword
owned by Grendel's mother; *hæftmece*;
Hrunting
weapons in *Grettis saga*. *See heptisax*;
Kársnautr (Grettir's short-sword);
sword on the wall in the giant's cave at
Sandhaugar